The U.S. Supreme Court and the Legitimization of Surveillance

INTERNATIONAL RELATIONS IN ASIA, AFRICA AND THE AMERICAS

The series International Relations in Asia, Africa and the Americas is edited by the Centre for International Studies and Development of the Jagiellonian University in Kraków.

Edited by Andrzej Mania & Marcin Grabowski

Vol. 21

Paweł Laidler

The U.S. Supreme Court and the Legitimization of Surveillance

PETER LANG

Berlin - Bruxelles - Chennai - Lausanne - New York - Oxford

Bibliographic Information published by the Deutsche Nationalbibliothek
The Deutsche Nationalbibliothek lists this publication in the Deutsche Nationalbibliografie; detailed bibliographic data is available in the internet at http://dnb.d-nb.de.

Library of Congress Cataloging-in-Publication Data
A CIP catalog record for this book has been applied for at the Library of Congress.

The publication is a result of research conducted in the project "Trust and Transparency in an Age of Surveillance. American, German and Polish perspectives" (Beethoven-2), funded by Polish National Science Center UMO-2016/23/G/HS5/01864.

The cover image courtesy of Paweł Laidler.

ISSN 2511-588X
ISBN 978-3-631-86391-6 (Print)
E-ISBN 978-3-631-92872-1 (E-Book)
E-ISBN 978-3-631-92895-0 (E-PUB)
DOI 10.3726/b22487

Published by Peter Lang GmbH, Berlin, Deutschland

info@peterlang.com - www.peterlang.com

This publication has been peer reviewed.
www.peterlang.com

Contents

Introduction: Surveillance as Governance

The Culture of Government Surveillance

In his superb book *The Culture of Surveillance: Watching as a Way of Life* David Lyon portrays 21st century society as fully embedded in the processes of surveillance, both as a surveilling entity and a subject under surveillance. The overwhelming culture of surveillance, as Lyon notes, is deeply connected with social, economic, and political processes, with private and public entities and institutions engaged in imposing surveillance measures[1]. In many other studies devoted to the phenomenon of surveillance, scholars focus on the power relations between the surveilling and the surveilled, and the consequences of these relations for the operation of state and society from the political and economic perspectives.[2] Numerous researchers, experts, and activists have been stressing the negative consequences of broad and often uncontrolled government surveillance, referring to the necessity of protecting the constitutional rights of the people in democratic societies[3]. However, there are also scholars and analysts who justify the

1 David Lyon, *Culture of Surveillance: Watching as a Way of Life*, Polity, Oxford 2018, pp. 17–18.

2 See: Matthias Risse, *Political Theory of the Digital Age*, Cambridge University Press, New York 2023; Shoshana Zuboff, *The Age of Surveillance Capitalism: The Fight for a Human Future at the New Frontier of Power*, Public Affairs, New York 2019; pp. 107–120. Kirstie Ball, Laureen Snider (eds.), *The Surveillance-Industrial Complex: A Political Economy of Surveillance*, Routledge, London 2013; David Lyon, *Surveillance, Power, and Everyday Life* in: *Emerging Digital Spaces in Contemporary Society: Properties of Technology*, Phillip Kalantzis-Cope, Karim Gherab-Martin, (eds.), Palgrave Macmillan, London 2010.

3 See: Timothy J. Edgar, *Beyond Snowden, Privacy, Mass Surveillance, and the Struggle to Reform the NSA*, Brookings Institution Press, Washington DC 2017; William W. Keller, *Democracy Betrayed. The Rise of the Surveillance Security State*, Counterpoint, Berkeley 2017; Julia Angwin, *Dragnet Nation: A Quest for Privacy, Security, and Freedom in a World of Relentless Surveillance*, Henry Holt and Company, New York 2014; Susan N. Herman, *Taking Liberties. The War on Terror and the Erosion of American Democracy*, Oxford University Press, New York 2011; Anthony D. Romero, Dina Temple-Raston, *In Defense of Our America: The Fight for Civil Liberties in the Age of Terror*, William

scope of surveillance measures imposed by state authorities, arguing for the importance of providing a greater degree of security to contemporary societies, despite the challenges it brings to the constitutional protection of individual rights.[4] All this leads to the conclusion, in a contemporary world functioning in the shadow of overwhelming polarization, that these contradictory arguments should be balanced in such a way as to satisfy the proponents of both approaches. There are two key challenges stemming from this conclusion: first, who should evaluate the values and arguments involved, and, second, whether the result of such a balancing will satisfy both a government and its citizenry.

Although recent research in surveillance studies pertains mainly to post-9/11 period or post-Snowden era, when we focus on the analysis of the sources, conduct and consequences of the digitalization of surveillance it seems obvious that the practices of watching and spying were laid down as foundations of the functioning of countries and societies centuries earlier, when the technology was far simpler. From the beginning of mankind people have been spying on each other, and governments have been prone to collecting information about their allies and enemies in international relations, as well as on their own citizens. Ancient rulers used spies to collect information about imminent threats and dangers, or to learn about the weaknesses of the lands they wanted to conquer. Similarly, medieval kings based their knowledge on the secret work of agents, collecting information which could be used to strengthen their domestic powers and international position. In the following centuries, in times of enhanced collaboration among countries, when stable diplomatic missions became a demanded

---

Morrow, New York 2007; Bruce Akerman, *Before the Next Attack: Preserving Civil Liberties in an Age of Terrorism*, Yale University Press, New Haven 2006.

4 See: Michael V. Hayden, *The Assault on Intelligence. American National Security in an Age of Lies*, Penguin Press, New York 2018; Loch K. Johnson, *Spy Watching: Intelligence Accountability in the United States*, Oxford University Press, New York 2018; Stephen G. Calabresi, John R. Yoo, *The Unitary Executive: Presidential Power from Washington to Bush*, Yale University Press, New Haven 2012; Eric E. Posner, Adrian Vermeule, *Terror in the Balance: Security, Liberty, and the Courts*, Oxford University Press, New York 2006; Clayton Northouse, (ed.), *Protecting What Matters: Technology, Security, and Liberty Since 9/11*, Brookings Institution Press, Washington D.C. 2006.

feature of bilateral relations, many governments decided to use these units as a source of spying and watching how allies (or enemies) operated.[5]

In the 19th century, with the advent of the telegraph and the telephone, the scope of government surveillance measures imposed within industrialized societies increased significantly, leading to the often uncontrolled wiretapping of criminal suspects by law enforcement agencies or the surveillance of political opponents by the authorities.[6] There is no doubt, however, that the fastest technological growth resulting in the introduction of enhanced surveillance procedures has occurred since the second half of the 20th century. According to Gary T. Marx, that period saw

> "a significant increase in the use of technology for the discovery of personal information. Examples include video and audio surveillance, heat, light, motion, sound and olfactory sensors, night vision goggles, electronic tagging, biometric access devices, drug testing, DNA analysis, computer monitoring including e-mail and web usage and the use of computer techniques such as expert systems, matching and profiling, data mining, mapping, network analysis and simulation."[7]

However, it is in the 21st century that the scope of surveillance measures and the extent to which people are watching and are being watched seems most significant in influencing the functioning of countries and societies. Such a situation has been enhanced, on the one hand, by the development of technology, leading to the use of advanced information-collecting techniques and systems of surveillance resulting in the production of the 'Big Data' now used by governments and corporations to monitor, categorize, and evaluate citizens, and, on the other, by the overwhelming need of contemporary societies and governments to have access to said information. Contemporary surveillance is properly called dataveillance[8] due to the enormous amount

---

5 See: Maurits A. Ebben, Louis Sicking (eds.), *Beyond Ambassadors: Consuls, Missionaries, and Spies in Premodern Diplomacy*, Brill, Leiden 2020.

6 See: Andreas Marklund, Laura Skouvig (eds), *Histories of Surveillance from Antiquity to the Digital Era: The Eyes and Ears of Power*, Routledge, New York 2021.

7 Gary T. Marx, "What's New About the New Surveillance? Classifying for Change and Continuity", *Surveillance & Society*, 1(1), 2002, p. 9.

8 See: David Lyon, "Surveillance, Snowden, and Big Data: Capacities, Consequences, Critique", *Big Data & Society*, 1(2), 2014; Jose van Dijck, „Datafication, Dataism and Dataveillance: Big Data between Scientific Paradigm and Ideology". *Surveillance & Society*, 1(2), 2014.

of data collected by the executive or independent agencies equipped with powers to gather, process, and analyze various types of information regarding people suspected of presenting a threat to domestic or national security. Collecting information is also characteristic of members of societies playing various roles, such as parents, employers, the leaders and administrators of educational institutions, business managers, journalists, or the heads of other organizations. No matter the social position and function, everybody is a member of a society that has been plunged into the stream of surveillance culture.

Apart from the very broad impact that the culture of watching and being watched has had on contemporary societies and economies, it seems obvious that without the significant role of governments in that process the development of national surveillance frameworks would not have been so rapid and effective as can be observed nowadays. Surveillance, as a tool of law enforcement agencies and intelligence institutions, has become a natural element of the process of governing, regardless of political system, form of government, or geographical and geopolitical location. The need to provide safety and security to the citizens of a country has forced state leaders to reach for the best available and effective tools for the conduct of domestic and foreign policies. Therefore, surveillance has become an indispensable means of power, and, at the same time, an attractive measure imposed by authorities willing to pursue their goals and policies in an efficient and effective way. This enhancement of the ability of governments to surveil their citizens has raised concerns about potential violations of constitutional rights, including the due process of law, the right to privacy, freedom of expression, and several other individual freedoms possibly limited by restrictions imposed by the practice of broad interception.[9] This has led to tensions between two contradictory approaches to constitutional interpretation – on the one hand as presented by authorities convinced of the necessity to protect their country and its citizens from interior and exterior danger, and on the other a critical approach shared by the majority of those in communities represented by institutions and organizations arguing for the stronger protection of the fundamental rights of individuals, such as

9 See: Anthony D. Romero, Dina Temple-Raston, *In Defense…*, op. cit.

the right to privacy, freedom of speech, and procedural rights.[10] These tensions have dominated political rhetoric, especially in times of real or potential threats to state security and the safety of the people, defining the language of public debates, legislative processes, and judicial disputes. The politics of surveillance has become an important element of the policies of all governments in the world; however, it was the U.S. government which, due to its growing role in international relations, accompanied by the development of enhanced technology, became the leader in 20th century in using surveillance measures to pursue the goals of the state, as well as the political interests of those who govern.

Governmental spying led to the development of surveillance measures in the United States from the beginning of the 20th century, with the establishment of the Bureau of Investigation (later the Federal Bureau of Investigation, the FBI), and especially in the late 1940s and early 1950s, when the emergence of the Cold War, which redefined and determined the foreign and domestic policies of the country for almost 45 years. The creation of the Central Intelligence Agency (CIA) and the National Security Agency (NSA) marked the beginning of the new era of spying focused on foreign intelligence, but domestically the Red Scare and anti-communist sentiments of the 1950s expanded the scope of the surveillance of American citizens and equipped the federal executive branch with almost uncontrolled power.[11] This was the first time the practice of mass surveillance occurred as a consequence of the use of signals intelligence and broad espionage measures applied by a government expanding its eavesdropping power. As Ivan Greenberg observes, the "political intelligence system was created not only as a government's response to insecurities, radicalism, nativism, conspiracy theories, but rather the centralization of power in the federal government"[12]. It soon transpired that the use of political surveillance was an effective way to control the society, as well as to spy on political rivals,

10 See: Susan N. Herman, *Taking Liberties...*, op. cit.

11 See: Athan G. Theoharis, *Spying on Americans: Political Surveillance from Hoover to Huston Plan*, Temple University Press, Philadelphia 1978.

12 Ivan Greenberg, *Surveillance in America: Critical Analysis of the F.B.I., 1920 to the Present*, Lexington Books, Lanham 2012, p. 7.

including organizations and individuals sharing ideologies inconsistent with the interests of the rulers.

The above-mentioned system turned out to function in an overwhelming culture of secrecy which had been evolving since the beginning of American statehood. Appealing to the necessity to limit the access of unauthorized actors to the communications and activities of the government, the executive tried to prevent other branches from controlling its surveillance powers. This policy led to numerous abuses and scandals involving law enforcement and intelligence agencies overusing their competences and creating a secret world of controversial and potentially illegal surveillance.[13] The role of the free press and engagement of whistleblowers raised public awareness of the possible abuse of power within the executive branch, leading to the first comprehensive congressional investigations into the secret world within which it operated. As the result of the work of two congressional committees functioning in the mid-1970s, multi-page reports were created proving massive usurpations of power and constitutional violations on the part of the FBI, CIA and NSA.[14] Secret surveillance became synonymous with governmental abuse and one of the main sources of the growing distrust among the population towards the authorities. As a reaction to the critical approach of American citizens towards the law enforcement and intelligence agencies, the authorities decided to implement new laws and policies aiming at assuring greater transparency and control over the system of surveillance.[15] Time showed, however, that with the growing role of digital technology leading to massive Internet-based surveillance, the government has been equipped with very effective means of eavesdropping

---

13 See: John Prados, *The Family Jewels. The CIA, Secrecy, and Presidential Power*, University of Texas Press, Austin 2014; Athan G. Theoharis, *Abuse of Power: How Cold War Surveillance and Secrecy Policy Shaped the Response to 9/11*. Temple University Press, Philadelphia 2011; Christian Parenti, *The Soft Cage: Surveillance in America. From Slavery to the War on Terror*, Basic Books, New York 2003.

14 See: Peter M. Shane, *Madison's Nightmare. How Executive Power Threatens American Democracy*, Chicago University Press, Chicago 2009.

15 See: Michael J. Glennon, *National Security and Double Government*. Oxford University Press, New York 2015; Athan G. Theoharis, *Abuse of Power…*, op. cit.

and gathering information. Old-new dangers for civil rights abuses turned out to be crucial concerns of politicians and the public alike, especially after the outbreak of so-called Snowden Affair in 2013.

The release of hundreds of thousands of classified documents by a whistleblower working as an NSA contractor revealed the challenges concerning the scope and character of the surveillance measures that had been imposed by the agency. The public was informed about secret interception programs which expanded the powers of the executive branch and showed a lack or ineffectiveness of their oversight and control by the legislative and judicial branches. Although the leaked documents referred mostly to the intelligence-gathering activities of the NSA, they presented potential violations of the constitutional rights of U.S. citizens, who had been subject to almost unlimited surveillance legitimized by the government's War on Terror. People realized that they could be subject to surveillance measures effected both by the government and private entities which were able to collect enormous amount of data using access to online sources.[16] Consequently, the Snowden Affair amplified the political and public debate over the scope of executive surveillance powers, as well as the need to apply controlling measures which would assure greater transparency in the government's activities.[17]

As a result of the events and processes described in the foregoing, in 2024 the United States may be considered a surveillance state, or a secret surveillance state, or a national security surveillance state, having established a huge intelligence and law enforcement network designed to collect an unlimited amount of information and data about individuals, social groups, institutions, and political organizations and their leaders. The government claims that the main purpose of the practice of broad interception is connected with the need to protect domestic and national security, to

---

16 See: Glenn Greenwald, *No Place to Hide: Edward Snowden, the NSA, and the U.S. Surveillance State*, Henry Holt & Company, New York 2014.

17 See: Heidi Kitrosser, *Reclaiming Accountability. Transparency, Executive Power, and the U.S. Constitution*, University of Chicago Press, Chicago 2015; Edward Goldfarb (ed.), *After Snowden: Privacy, Secrecy, and Security in the Information Age*, Thomas Dunne Books, New York 2015; Timothy J. Edgar, *Beyond Snowden…*, op. cit.

prevent or investigate crimes, and, generally, to effectively pursue the policy of providing safety to the country and its citizens. However, at the same time the programs of massive surveillance in question go far beyond their initial purposes, raising concerns over the scope of the rights and freedoms of individuals. This gives researchers an attractive topic to analyze, but as citizens we feel more worried about the consequences of this overwhelming culture of surveillance. To paraphrase David Lyon, this involves not only watching as a way of life but also surveillance as governance.

The Scope of the Research

The analysis of the history of government surveillance in the United States demands a dual approach to the issue, as two types of surveillance policy have been put in place by the government: the domestic and the foreign. The first of these is comprised mainly of the investigative measures applied by law enforcement agencies in criminal procedures against suspects and defendants, but also, as history shows, of eavesdropping on political opponents and selected social groups, aimed at maintaining power and control. Foreign surveillance, at least theoretically, refers to all the measures imposed on non-U.S. citizens by intelligence agencies with regard to foreign operations or activities which threaten national security. The surveillance of foreigners may lead, however, to initiatives which indirectly, or sometimes even directly, affect U.S. citizens, raising concerns over its scope and character. In both cases, surveillance should be understood as the development and imposition of tools which help the authorities to gather information and data that allow the government to pursue goals which could be broadly defined as keeping the country and its citizens secure, on the one hand, and assuring that their rights and freedoms are not violated on the other.

Surveillance is about power, therefore the knowledge the government gains from collecting data on citizens or foreigners allows for more effective policy, strengthening, at the same time, the competences of the surveilling institutions. Although 'the government' refers to all subjects involved in the process of governing, the reality of the politics of surveillance indicates that the biggest beneficiary of the expansion of power is the executive, often at the expense of the two other branches, the legislative and judicial.

Regardless of the relationships between the three branches it is the government, broadly understood, that imposes surveillance measures, thus strengthening its powers over people who are forced to experience a limited protection of their constitutional rights. All of this leads to the conclusion that such processes may occur effectively only if the government finds a proper interest it should protect, being able, temporarily or permanently, to restrict the individual freedoms guaranteed by the supreme law of the land. Therefore, the secret of the successful imposition of surveillance measures lies not only in their effective implementation by the government in its policies, but, most importantly, in the proper legitimization of the politics of surveillance on the part of the authorities which can justify infringements of the rights of the people. That is why my research will focus mainly on the issue of the legitimacy and justification of government surveillance policies in the United States in the 20th and 21st centuries, as I believe this is the key to understanding the direction of travel of American policies in said period, as well as a chance to understand the sources and outcomes of institutional and political relations within the government.

Before presenting the methodology and the main research questions, it seems crucial to observe that the topic of surveillance has been extensively analyzed in recent scholarly literature. In the aftermath of the Snowden affair, research was conducted regarding surveillance imposed by the U.S. government in general, or by one of its three branches, with a focus on the concrete institutions or agencies responsible for conducting or controlling surveillance procedures, such as the FBI, CIA, or NSA. Despite the fact that the majority of the studies have concerned the relationship between vital values of American democracy which were in conflict, such as freedom versus security, security versus privacy, the right to know versus privacy, or transparency versus secrecy[18], all these conflicts had one thing

18 See: Charles N. Davis, David Cuillier (eds.), *Transparency 2.0. Digital Data and Privacy in a Wired World*, Peter Lang, New York 2014; Daniel J. Solove, *Nothing to Hide. The False Tradeoff between Privacy and Security*, Yale University Press, New Haven 2011; Kevin D. Haggerty, Minas Samatas (eds.), *Surveillance and Democracy*, Routledge, New York 2010; Daniel Farber (ed.), *Security v. Liberty: Conflicts Between Civil Liberties and National Security in American History*, Russell Sage Foundation, New York 2008; Darren W. Davis, Brian D. Silver, "Civil Liberties v. Security: Public Opinion in the Context of

in common: they were the product of institutional factors determined by the scope of powers of the U.S. government. Some scholars focused mainly on the institutional analysis of U.S. surveillance policies, but most of the research has pertained to the historical and contemporary analysis of government agencies equipped with the power to conduct domestic or foreign surveillance[19]. It comes as no surprise that the most discussed institution has been the NSA[20], but research has also been carried out regarding the surveillance policies of the CIA[21], as well as the FBI.[22] Even such limited analysis of the surveillance policies of concrete governmental institutions had at least one thing in common: a broader reference to the role of presidential administrations, or the executive branch in general, in building, preserving, and defending a complex system of secret surveillance aimed at providing safety and security to the United States and its citizens.

Considering this significant scholarly interest in the post-Snowden surveillance reality, one can also find research concerning the relationship between the executive, legislative and judiciary with respect to the U.S. politics of surveillance; however, the analysis of the character of the principle of the separation of powers and the scope of the checks and balances system has rarely been the main research goal. For various experts on the American

---

the Terrorist Attacks on America", *American Journal of Political Science* 48(1), 2003, pp. 28–46; Eric E. Posner, Adrian Vermeule, *Terror in the Balance…*, op. cit.

19 See: Heidi Kitrosser, *Reclaiming Accountability…*, op. cit.; Michael J. Glennon, *National Security…*, op. cit.; Athan G. Theoharis, *Abuse of Power…*, op. cit.

20 See: Chris Edelson, *Power Without Constraint. The Post-9/11 Presidency and National Security*. The University of Wisconsin Press, Madison 2016; James Bamford, *Body of Secrets: Anatomy of the Ultra Secret National Security Agency*, Anchor, New York 2002; Timothy J. Edgar, *Beyond Snowden…*, op. cit.

21 See: Huw Dylan, David Gioe, Michael S. Goodman, *The C.I.A. and the Pursuit of Security: History, Documents, and Contexts*, Edinburgh University Press, Edinburgh 2020; John Prados, *The Family Jewels…*, op. cit.

22 See: David S. Price, *The American Surveillance State: How the U.S. Spies on Dissent*, Pluto Press, London 2022; Andrew G. McCabe, *The Threat: How the FBI Protects America in the Age of Terror and Trump*, St. Martin's Press, New York 2019; Douglas M. Charles, *J. Edgar Hoover and the Anti-Interventionists: FBI Political Surveillance and the Rise of the Domestic Security State 1939–1945*, Ohio State University Press, Columbus 2007; Ivan Greenberg, *Surveillance in America…*, op. cit.

political system and the Constitution, it was obvious that the system revealed by Snowden uncovered a secret web of programs and activities of the federal executive which were illegal and remained uncontrolled by Congress and the courts, thus affecting the separation of powers doctrine.[23] Some researchers placed the responsibility for the existence of such a secretive surveillance state on certain presidential administrations[24], some tried to find the explanation for temporary violations of the rights and freedoms of individuals in the state of emergency stemming from the threat of terrorism[25], while others explained that presidents (and governmental agencies) acted in accordance with the Constitution.[26] For many, it was the Fourth Amendment – its text and meaning – which played the role of the main constitutional reference point in the analysis and interpretation of the proper scope of government surveillance powers and the right to privacy of American citizens.[27]

The analysis of post-Snowden research on U.S. government surveillance provides a few general findings concerning its scope and character. First, the vast majority of scholars have focused on foreign rather than domestic surveillance, although some research findings led to the analysis of government surveillance in a broader context. Second, the most often applied research methods were institutionalism, providing for the analysis of certain

---

23 See: Heidi Kitrosser, *Reclaiming Accountability…*, op. cit. Athan G. Theoharis, *Abuse of Power…*, op. cit.

24 See: Mary Graham, *Presidents' Secrets. The Use and Abuse of Hidden Power*, Yale University Press, New Haven 2017; Chris Edelson, *Power Without Constraint…*, op. cit.; Jack Goldsmith, *Power and Constraint: The Accountable Presidency after 9/11*, W.W. Norton and Company, New York 2012.

25 See: David Cole, *Terrorism and the Constitution: Sacrificing Civil Liberties in the Name of National Security*, Norton & Norton Company, New York 2006; Anthony D. Romero, Dina Temple-Raston, *In Defense…*, op. cit.; Michael J. Glennon, *National Security…*, op. cit.

26 See: Michael V. Hayden, *The Assault…*, op. cit.; Loch K. Johnson, *Spy Watching…*, op. cit.; Stephen G. Calabresi, John R. Yoo, *The Unitary Executive…*, op. cit.

27 See: Michael J.Z. Manheimer, *The Fourth Amendment: Original Understandings and Modern Policing*, University of Michigan Press, Ann Arbor 2023; Christopher Slobogin, *Privacy at Risk: The New Government Surveillance and the Fourth Amendment*, University of Chicago Press, Chicago 2008.

governmental institutions responsible for imposing surveillance policies, and other actors politically involved in the process, and constitutionalism, focusing on of the meaning and scope of constitutional values and provisions regarding government surveillance. In that context, it was important to determine the proper constitutional protection of the rights of individuals vis-à-vis the powers of the authorities which increased due to the imposition of surveillance measures. Third, the analysis of the surveillance powers of the executive led to scholarly debates on the tensions between secrecy and transparency, or security and freedom, which – in a broader perspective – raised concerns about the state of American democracy and the rule of law. Taking that into consideration, and not neglecting the up-to-date research on government surveillance in the United States, I would like to apply both institutional and constitutional analyses to the issue, focusing on the Supreme Court's adjudication regarding domestic and foreign surveillance. However, the proposed analysis will not simply refer to the outcomes of SCOTUS judgments in surveillance cases, but rather examine the arguments used by the justices in majority, concurring, and dissenting opinions from the perspective of the potential legitimization of government policies in this sphere.

Regardless of whether they adopt a negative or positive approach towards the scope of government surveillance in the United States, hardly any researcher has focused on constitutional justifications of surveillance policies stemming from the early Supreme Court decisions, which, for obvious reasons, did not concern national surveillance powers. During their analysis of the development of national security surveillance since the 1940s, scholars have most often focused on SCOTUS adjudication from the Cold War era concerning the powers of government in implementing national security policies, and, more recently, on the early 21st century precedents determining the constitutionality of the post-9/11 policies of the Bush administration[28]. Others, searching for the constitutional foundations of surveillance policies, have invoked concrete parts of the documents which – directly or indirectly – related to the powers of government, or quoted the statements of the Founding Fathers about the role of national

28 See: Athan G. Theoharis, *Abuse of Power...*, op. cit.

government vis-à-vis state jurisdictions[29]. No study, however, has tried to explain the scope of government surveillance with reference to one of the concepts presented by Chief Justice John Marshall in the 1819 Supreme Court decision in *McCulloch v. Maryland* – the "legitimate end" approach.

One may ask why government surveillance should be analyzed from the perspective of an old SCOTUS precedent which, even indirectly, does not relate either to domestic or foreign surveillance policy. Obviously, the main topic of *McCulloch* concerns the functioning of the central bank and political and economic relations between the federal government and the states in the early times of the Republic, with no direct references made to the problems faced by the 20th or 21st century administrations pursuing their surveillance policies. However, the meaning of the rationale in *McCulloch* should not be read only from its traditional understanding – as a basis for determining the scope of federal-state relations – but rather from a broader perspective, as one of the fundamental concepts in American constitutionalism and one of the most influential means of constitutional interpretation used in U.S. history.

The main legal problem in the dispute concerned the constitutional status of the Bank of the United States (BUS), a central monetary institution established in the early years of American statehood which, after the expiry of its charter, was re-established in 1816 in an effort to strengthen an economy weakened by the war with Great Britain. The state of Maryland, on the territory of which the Bank had one of its branches, decided to tax the financial operations of the federal institution, thus leading to a conflict of competences which had to be solved by the judicial branch. Three years later, Chief Justice John Marshall announced the decision of the Court which, on the one hand, affirmed the constitutionality of the BUS, and, on the other, declared the unconstitutionality of the state tax imposed on it[30]. Apart from important constitutional aspects of the case, such as determining the legal status of states as non-sovereign entities, strengthening the national identity of Americans by providing a "federalist" interpretation of the preamble, and introducing the doctrine of implied powers of the

---

29 See: Jack Goldsmith, *Power and Constraint...*, op. cit.

30 *McCulloch v. Maryland* 17 U.S. 316 (1819).

federal government, Marshall offered a very broad interpretation of the Constitution, focusing not only on its "letter" but also on its "spirit". By confirming that the national government did not have unlimited powers, the Chief Justice presented the Supreme Court's approach to legitimate end, which set the extent to which the government could operate without violating the supreme law of the land:

> "Let the end be legitimate, let it be within the scope of the constitution, and all means which are appropriate, which are plainly adapted to that end, which are not prohibited, but consist with the letter and spirit of the constitution, are constitutional."[31]

Although the above-quoted part of the Court's decision did not become the core element of the precedent set by the justices, it clearly presented Marshall's approach towards the (future) scope of government powers. According to the legitimate end approach, which in *McCulloch* was applied to the powers of Congress to create a national bank despite the absence of such a direct provision in the enumeration clause of Article One, the government could adopt certain measures or apply concrete means in its operation, provided they were constitutional. In this perspective, not only the exact words of the Constitution but also the purposes of specific policies, and the means used to implement them, could be constitutionally legitimized. Importantly, however, the determination of the appropriateness and constitutionality of these means and policies belonged to the judicial branch, which was responsible for the judicial review of the acts of other branches of government. In other words, all policies of the government could be constitutionally justified, even if they there was no direct reference to them in the text of the document, provided that the purposes of these policies and the means imposed to implement them were legitimized by the judicial branch.

The legitimate end approach was not a one-off and isolated attitude towards constitutional interpretation in the Court's history and has been applied several times by subsequent justices in cases which raised concerns about the character of government powers, as well as the scope of the rights and freedoms of individuals, thus strengthening the liberal interpretation

31 *Ibid.* at 421.

of the Constitution, which has dominated U.S. constitutionalism in recent decades. It would be an exaggeration to state that the legitimate end approach has dominated the constitutional adjudication of the Court, but it has definitely left its mark on American constitutionalism by promoting a functionalist approach towards the reading and understanding of the provisions and values of the Constitution.

Therefore, the main purpose of the study is to present the politics of surveillance developed by the U.S. government in 20th and 21st centuries from the perspective of the legitimate end approach presented in the *McCulloch* reasoning. By reviewing Marshall's approach towards constitutional interpretation in the context of both domestic and foreign surveillance I aim to demonstrate how significantly this approach has been applied in recent decades by both conservative and liberal justices in their interpretation of the Constitution with regard to surveillance disputes. I believe that, despite the liberal constitutional interpretation offered in *McCulloch,* and having been predominantly neglected by conservatives, there has been an unwritten consensus between subjects involved in shaping, conducting, and interpreting the scope of government surveillance to broaden the constitutional powers of the branches involved in the politics of surveillance, especially when security has been endangered. Using different argumentation and sometimes contradictory rhetoric, SCOTUS justices have referred, often unconsciously, to the legitimate end approach, thus promoting the need to uphold broad surveillance programs imposed by the U.S. government in various times of emergency in American history.

In order to reach research conclusions, it is necessary to analyze the Court's adjudication in cases regarding the scope of government surveillance powers in the context of the Fourth Amendment's Search and Seizure clause, as well as the Warrant Clause. By expanding the meaning of the Fourth Amendment for the operation of law enforcement agencies, justices have built the background for a proper understanding of the executive's surveillance powers, and the impact of the character of surveillance measures on their constitutionality. From the 1920s until today the SCOTUS has adjudicated in hundreds of disputes raising constitutional questions about the scope of domestic surveillance, and it seems crucial to determine the most decisive judgments in that context, analyzing the way the justices applied the legitimate end approach in their opinions. On the other hand, although there have been fewer cases concerning foreign intelligence surveillance, SCOTUS decisions in such disputes seem especially significant from the perspective of the *McCulloch* reasoning. The research findings may bring contradictory conclusions with regard to the approach of justices towards the scope of domestic and foreign surveillance, despite referring to the same source in the U.S. Constitution: the reasonableness of search and seizure, and the conditions of obtaining warrants, both derived from the judiciary's interpretation of the Fourth Amendment's.

In the study I also argue that the approach offered by the Supreme Court in its constitutional interpretation of the surveillance powers of the government has led to the imposition of measures aimed at almost unlimited control of the society. The collection, analysis, and use of bulk metadata by government agencies has become a natural element of their everyday functioning and is difficult to limit due to the political consensus of the three branches of federal government in jointly protecting national security matters. The legitimization of these processes is strengthened by the government using the rhetoric of security, or national security, and referring to extraordinary times, or a state of emergency, examples of which can be observed almost continuously since the 1940s. One of the purposes of the analysis is to show how such rhetoric has determined the operation and policies of governments, as well as accounting for the attitude of the justices towards the process of determining the scope of the rights and freedoms of individuals in domestic and foreign surveillance case-law.

At the same time, I want to assess what impact the implementation of the legitimate end approach has had on the separation of powers doctrine and checks and balances system, which are fundamental features of American constitutionalism. It is especially important to determine how SCOTUS judgments in surveillance disputes have affected the operation of the executive, legislative and judicial branches of the government, and whether it has enhanced collaboration or rivalry among them. Despite the undisputed position of the Supreme Court in the process of constitutional adjudication, in the national security area the main initiative belongs to Congress and presidential administrations, supported by executive or independent agencies; therefore, the study may reveal how the legitimate end approach has influenced the functioning of all three branches in 21st century America. This seems especially crucial from the perspective of the control and oversight of the surveillance policies of the U.S. government conducted by stable or ad hoc congressional committees, and special tribunals devoted to procedural checks on the foreign intelligence surveillance, such as the Foreign Intelligence Surveillance Court (FISC), as well as the Supreme Court having the final word in the process of determining the constitutional character of the separation of powers and system of checks and balances.

By applying the legitimate end approach to 20th and 21st century domestic and foreign surveillance case-law I argue that the meaning and impact of *McCulloch* is still significant, especially in the area of surveillance justified by national security arguments. The rationale of Marshall's approach towards constitutional interpretation is not only broadly applied by politicians and judges in national security surveillance, but it also limits the possibility of pursuing the effective control and oversight of government's activities, weakening the possibility of achieving greater transparency in the government surveillance policies. In my study, I go a step further and claim that the legitimate end approach does a lot more than just justify the current direction of national security surveillance: it makes the quest for transparency of government surveillance programs (almost) impossible to achieve, explaining why in transparency is something of an illusion.

Acknowledgments

The idea for the book came to my mind during the process of conducting research as a principal investigator in the TATAS (*Trust and Transparency in an Age of Surveillance. American, German, and Polish perspectives*) project, funded by the Polish and German National Science Centers, within the international Beethoven program. I had an opportunity to cooperate with Professor Lora Anne Viola from the JFK Institute for North American Studies of the Free University in Berlin, who was the principal investigator on the German side; I am grateful for her sharing her knowledge and experience, as well as the open-mindedness and collaborative approach which enabled us to achieve promising research results in the project. We co-edited a book published by Routledge on the relationships between trust, transparency, and surveillance in the post-Snowden world, collecting interesting and original articles prepared by international scholars representing European and North American universities. The volume offers a contemporary and interdisciplinary approach to the tensions between trust and transparency in the surveillance society, surveillance culture, and surveillance state[32]. During fruitful research seminars and consultation meetings we were able to discuss the phenomenon of surveillance in global and regional context, with a special focus on the character of government surveillance powers, as well as the scope of the rights of individuals in confrontation with the technologically enhanced surveillance machinery. I would like to thank the whole TATAS team[33] for showing me their individual research perspectives and for all substantive remarks about my study. Special thanks go to Professor David Lyon for his constructive criticism mixed with unique expertise in surveillance studies, and for numerous articles and books on various challenges of the surveillance states and societies which have framed the thinking of many researchers fascinated with the phenomenon of surveillance.

The book could not have been completed without research visits to the John F. Kennedy Institute for North American Studies at the Free University in Berlin and the San Diego State University Library in California. I would like to thank, once again, Professor Viola for her support in Berlin and Professor Janusz Supernak from SDSU for his help during my research visit to the U.S. I thank all the scholars and researchers I had an opportunity to meet and talk to during the process of preparing the book, including experts from international and Polish universities, and, especially, colleagues at the Institute of American Studies and Polish Diaspora and the Faculty of International and Political Studies of the Jagiellonian University in Krakow who believed in the final success of the book. Special thanks should go to Professor Magdalena Musiał-Karg for her intellectually inspiring book review and all the remarks which allowed me to limit the biases and weaknesses of my research, as well as to Professor Garry Robson for, as

32 See: Lora Anne Viola, Paweł Laidler (eds.), *Trust and Transparency in an Age of Surveillance*, Routledge, London 2022.

33 In an alphabetical order: Kirstie Ball, Fredrika Bjorklund, Shaul Duke, Sara degli Esposti, Paweł Frankowski, Dominika Furtak, David Arroyo Guardeno, Katherina Hadjimatheu, Matthew Hall, Markus Kienscherf, Mateusz Kolaszyński, Paweł Laidler, Eric Lastic, David Lyon, Andre Meister, Abel Reiberg, Ola Svenonious, Miguelangel Verde Garrido, Lora Anne Viola, Killian Vieth, and Thorsten Wetzling.

usual, perfect proofreading and all the necessary suggestions for making the book more reader-friendly. I would like to thank Professor Marcin Grabowski for arranging the possibility to publish the book in the series edited by him, as well as Ms. Małgorzata Jasek and Ms. Agnieszka Steczko for their administrative support.

Last but not least, I want to thank my Family – Monika, Maciek and Patryk – for their understanding in this hard, and often lengthy process of achieving scientific goals at the expense of the time we could have spent together.

Chapter One *McCulloch v. Maryland* and the Legitimate End Approach

The SCOTUS in the Governmental System

To understand the importance of any approach or mode of constitutional interpretation offered by the U.S. Supreme Court it is important to acknowledge its unique position in the American system of government. The SCOTUS was the only federal judicial institution established in the Constitution of 1787 to serve as the highest judicial instance in the country, mostly as an appellate court, deciding cases brought from lower federal and state courts. Since the beginning of American statehood, the Court has existed as one of the three branches of federal government in a system driven by two important doctrines and principles: the separation of powers and the system of checks and balances. However, the SCOTUS' position among the other branches was then quite weak due to the lack of effective tools of control which it could imposed on the executive or the legislative, except for the power to solve disputes between government institutions, which seemed hardly possible to exercise without having an impact on the meaning and scope of the Constitution – the main source of power of the federal government. Therefore, the first Supreme Courts did not acknowledge any serious challenges in their operation, and the justices served more often in appellate courts rather than adjudicating in disputes raising issues of a fundamental character.[34]

Everything changed at the beginning of the 19th century, with the appointment of John Marshall to the post of Chief Justice of the Court by President John Adams. Marshall, who was an active politician and a strong supporter of the Federalists' approach towards the governance of the new

34 More about the beginnings of the Court's functioning see: Paweł Laidler, *Sąd Najwyższy Stanów Zjednoczonych Ameryki: od prawa do polityki*, Wydawnictwo Uniwersytetu Jagiellońskiego, Kraków 2011; Christopher Collier, *Decision in Philadelphia: The Constitutional Convention of 1787*, Ballentine Books, New York 2007; Christopher Tomlins (ed.), *The United States Supreme Court: The Pursuit of Justice*, Houghton Mifflin Company, Boston 2005.

country, had the opportunity as the chief justice to introduce his vision of constitutional interpretation, thus modifying the position of the SCOTUS in the governmental system. In 1803, the Court, under Marshall's leadership, established the power of judicial review derived from the analysis of Articles Three and Six of the Constitution, based on which the judges were able to solve disputes of constitutional stature and determine the final meaning of the supreme law of the land. The Chief Justice used the conflict between the Adams' appointee to federal judgeship, William Marbury, and James Madison, Marshall's successor in the position of secretary of state, to announce the power of the courts to declare the constitutionality of the acts of the other branches of government, arguing that it was "the province and duty of the judicial department to say what the law" was.[35] The *Marbury* precedent became the most significant Court decision in history, defining the SCOTUS as the final interpreter of constitutional clauses, values and principles, thereby strengthening its position in relation to Congress and the federal executive, as well as state and local governments. Although judicial review has not been applied in each of the Court's cases since 1803, the statistics prove the effective use of their power by the justices who, as of 2024, invalidated in part or in whole almost 200 acts of Congress and around 1,000 acts of state legislatures.[36]

The specific status of the Court's adjudication stemmed not only from its special position within the judicial branch, and the possibility to exercise the power of judicial review, but also from the general lawmaking ability of the judges in the common law system. That feature was taken over from the British legal reality and implemented in the colonies and, later, in the United States, becoming one of the crucial elements of the Anglo-American common law, having an impact on the character of functioning of both state and federal courts. The English common law theory was based on precedents, defined as rules and principles created in concrete

35 *Marbury v. Madison* 5 U.S. 137 (1803).

36 *Acts of Congress Held Unconstitutional in Whole or in Part by the Supreme Court of the United States*, available at: https://law.justia.com/constitution/us/acts-of-congress-held-unconstitutional.html; *State Laws Held Unconstitutional*, available at: https://law.justia.com/constitution/us/state-laws-held-unconstitutional.html .

cases and applied by the judges, in a binding or non-binding manner, to the circumstances of future disputes. It was supported by the doctrine of stare decisis, imposing the duty on judges to apply once-established precedents in all future cases, based on the similarity of circumstances of disputes.[37] These theories were introduced in the British colonies in North America and were used by the Founding Fathers as the essence of the operation of the judicial branch, thus making the SCOTUS the creator of the most binding precedents among all judicial institutions. Consequently, after gaining the power of judicial review, the Court became not only the most powerful institution within the judicial branch, but an institution with the potential to determine the functioning of other branches of government. As a result, U.S. constitutional history is full of binding SCOTUS precedents which modified the scope of the powers of federal and state institutions.

Numerous studies have shown the evolving role of the SCOTUS and its growing position within the American system of government. The active use of judicial review and the ability to interpret the constitution has made the Court an important legal and political actor, with its precedents determining the scope of powers of the president and Congress, the relations between the federal and state governments, and the meaning of the constitutional rights and freedoms of the people.[38] The analysis of SCOTUS adjudication provides several examples of how the justices modified the meaning of constitutional clauses regarding the powers of the executive, especially the president, such as their appointment and removal powers, position as commander-in-chief, foreign policy competences, and the scope of doctrines determining the constitutional position of the chief executive.[39] Similarly,

37 See: Douglas E. Edlin, *Common Law Theory*, Cambridge University Press, New York 2010.

38 See: Paweł Laidler, *The Supreme Court of the United States: Legitimate Law maker and Constitutional Interpreter* in: *Constitutional Law and Precedent: International Perspectives on Case-Based Reasoning*, Monika Florczak-Wątor (ed.), Routledge, London 2022, pp. 9–31; Lawrence A. Baum, *The Supreme Court*, Congressional Quarterly Press, Washington D.C. 2021; Paweł Laidler, *Sąd Najwyższy…*, op. cit.; Christopher Tomlins (ed.), *The United States…*, op. cit.

39 See: Peter M. Shane, *Democracy's Chief Executive. Interpreting the Constitution and Defining the Future of Presidency*. University of California Press, Durham 2022; Michael J.C. Taylor, *The Constitution and the American Presidency.*

there have been decisions declaring the unconstitutionality in part or in whole of important congressional legislation concerning such issues as federal-state relations, the Commerce Clause, the delegation of powers to other branches of government, national security legislation, and acts concerning various rights of individuals.[40]

On the other hand, a significant number of the Court's decisions have affected the scope of constitutional guarantees introduced in the Bill of Rights, such as freedom of speech, religion, assembly, and association, the right to bear arms, the right to privacy, and certain procedural rights, including due process of law, as well as the Fourteenth Amendment's equal protection of law. Especially significantly, the interpretation of the Due Process Clause leading to the so-called incorporation of Bill of Rights to the states, initiated in the 1920s, has enabled the justices to determine which constitutional rights and freedoms had a fundamental character, "implicit in the concept of ordered liberty", expanding their protection to state governments.[41] The Supreme Court has also been involved in supporting the federal government's position in both foreign and domestic policies, becoming an important element in the tripartite form of the government puzzle, often determining the direction of the country's politics. Still, there were periods during which the justices limited the powers of the federal government at the expense of the state jurisdictions, although such an approach was usually the result of ideological voting in the Court reflected

---

Peter Lang, New York 2021; Kimberley Fletcher, *The Collision of Political and Legal Time: Foreign Affairs and the Court's Transformation of Executive Authority*, Temple University Press, Philadelphia 2018; Louis Fisher, *Supreme Court Expansion of Presidential Power: Unconstitutional Leanings*, University Press of Kansas, Lawrence 2017; Richard J. Ellis (ed.), *Judging Executive Power. Sixteen Supreme Court Cases that Have Shaped the American Presidency*, Rowman & Littlefield, Lanham 2009.

40 See: Mark Tushnet, *In the Balance: Law and Politics in the Roberts Court*, W.W. Norton and Company, New York 2013; Michael A. Bailey, Forrest Maltzman, *The Constrained Court: Law, Politics, and the Decisions Justices Make*, Princeton University Press, Princeton 2011; Neal Devins, Keith E. Whittington (ed.), *Congress and the Constitution*, Duke University Press, Durham 2005; Richard Pacelle, *The Role of the Supreme Court in American Politics: The Least Dangerous Branch?* Taylor and Francis, New York 2001.

41 See: *Palko v. Connecticut* 302 U.S. 319 (1937).

by the majority of conservative votes.[42] Therefore, the SCOTUS has played both positive and negative law-making roles, as a counter-majoritarian institution broadening the rights of the people and imposing broader control of the government's powers, or as the national policymaker, expanding the competences of national and state authorities, thereby limiting the constitutional guarantees of U.S. citizens.[43] In that context, one of the most challenging roles the justices had to play was balancing conflicting norms and values, and weighing arguments supporting the protection of these norms and values.

Serving as a constitutional court, the SCOTUS strengthened its position within the governmental system, especially when judicial activism turned out to be a dominating approach among the justices, with judicial restraint occurring less frequently over time. As a consequence, the Court became involved in active judicial review, deciding not only on legal issues but often being plunged into the middle of political relations. Activism led to the appearance of two significant processes affecting the operation and constitutional position of the SCOTUS: the politicization of justice and the judicialization of politics.[44] The first process could be observed in the growing interest of political actors in the direction of Court's precedents

---

42 See: Lawrence A. Baum, *The Supreme Court...*, op. cit; Richard Pacelle, *The Transformation of the Supreme Court's Agenda: From the New Deal to the Reagan Administration*, Routledge, New York 2019; Christopher P. Banks (ed.), *Controversies in American Federalism and Public Policy*, Routledge, New York 2018; Susan L. Bloch, Vicky Jackson, *Federalism. A Reference Guide to the United States Constitution*. ABC-Clio, Santa Barbara 2013; Christopher P. Banks, John C. Blakeman, *The U.S. Supreme Court and New Federalism: From the Rehnquist to the Roberts Court*, Rowman & Littlefield, Boston 2012.

43 Compare the approaches presented in: Alexander M. Bickel, *The Least Dangerous Branch: The Supreme Court at the Bar of Politics*, Bobbs-Merrill, New York 1962; Robert Dahl, "Decision-Making in a Democracy: The Supreme Court as a National Policy-Maker", *Journal of Public Law*, 6, 1957.

44 More on both concepts see: Ron Hirschl *Towards Juristocracy: The Origins and Consequences of the New Constitutionalism*, Harvard University Press, Cambridge 2004; Martin M. Shapiro, Alec Stone Sweet, *On Law, Politics, and Judicialization*, Oxford University Press, New York 2002; Alec Stone Sweet, "Judicialization and the Construction of Governance", *Comparative Political Studies* 32(2), 1999, pp. 147–184.

on fundamental issues, such as the powers of the government and of the people. That interest was reflected mainly in the appointment of justices by presidents with the advice and consent of senators, making the procedure partisan and ideologically driven. As a result, the majority of SCOTUS appointments in the 20th and 21st centuries have been made along party lines, with Republicans supporting the choice of conservative justices and Democrats liberal ones.[45] The process of the judicialization of politics, on the other hand, could be seen in the growing involvement of judicial actors in political decision-making, despite self-imposed constraints by the justices, including the political question doctrine or judicial restraint.[46] The dual role the Court played – as the highest judicial instance solving legal disputes, and as a constitutional interpreter having the potential to modify the meaning of the supreme law of the land – made the institution politically attractive and politically involved. In such a way, the SCOTUS has become the most politicized judicial actor in the world.

Analysis of the Supreme Court's adjudication allows for the identification of various interpretative approaches used by its justices throughout history, some of which were connected with their ideology. The vast majority of Court members have belonged to either the liberal or conservative wing, with only a few which could be labelled as centrists. Several studies have shown the impact of justices' ideology on the Court's adjudications, especially in disputes concerning federal-state relations, or the scope of rights and freedoms of individuals.[47] Regardless of their ideology, many justices have produced their own way of legally interpretating the Constitution, including the reference to the rule of law, the value of precedent, invoking legal theory and history, and, sometimes, adherence to the stare decisis doctrine or deciding a case on the basis of first impression. Among the most popular modes of constitutional interpretation, promoted especially by conservative justices, there is originalism, which refers to the original intent

45 See: Henry J. Abraham, *Justices, Presidents, and Senators: A History of the U.S. Supreme Court Appointments from Washington to Bush II*, Rowman & Littlefield, Boston 2007.

46 See: Paweł Laidler, *The Supreme Court...*, op. cit.

47 See: Jeffrey A. Segal, Harold J. Spaeth, Sara C. Benesh, *The Supreme Court in American Legal System*, Cambridge University Press, New York 2005.

of the authors of the document, or its textual analysis of the words and their meaning, and the more liberal approach called living constitutionalism, focusing on the changing social, political, and economic reality, which is taken into consideration by justices in their process of redefining the meaning of certain constitutional clauses and provisions.[48] The latter attitude became a legacy of the Court under the chief justiceship of John Marshall, who was responsible for not only establishing judicial review, but also introducing the functionalist approach to constitutional interpretation and offering the legitimate end approach, both of which were the result of *McCulloch v. Maryland.*

McCulloch v. Maryland: Dispute and Decision

Although the case was decided by the Supreme Court in 1819, the source of the conflict dates from the beginning of American statehood. The early Republic was healing its wounds following the Revolutionary War and the unsuccessful experiment of the Articles of Confederation, which led to an economic crisis and the weakness of the central government, when the constitution was ratified, and the Federalist government was established.[49] The leading politicians had contradictory attitudes towards the possible means of strengthening the economy and providing general welfare to American society. One of the key conflicts concerned the process of establishing the government institutions which were to be responsible for carrying out economic reforms and assuring the proper development of the country, and the most controversial of these institutions was a national bank. The proponents of the creation of a central financial institution, among whom was the Secretary of the Treasury, believed that it would serve as a guaranteed way of strengthening the finances of the young country, and as an institution reaffirming the position of the federal government in relation to the states. There was, however, strong opposition against

48 See: Robert W. Bennett, Lawrence B. Solum, *Constitutional Originalism. A Debate*, Cornell University Press, Ithaca 2011; Saul Brenner, Joseph W. Whitmeyer, *Strategy on the U.S. Supreme Court*, New York: Cambridge University Press 2009; Thomas G. Hansford, James F. Spriggs, *The Politics of Precedent on the U.S. Supreme Court*, Princeton University Press, Princeton 2008.

49 See: Christopher Collier, *Decision in Philadelphia…*, op. cit.

establishing such an institution, led by Secretary of State Thomas Jefferson, who invoked the principle of limited government according to which the federal authorities did not have the power to create a national bank, as it was not directly listed among the enumerated powers of Congress in Article One of the Constitution. After receiving support from President George Washington, the bill was introduced to Congress, which, following a tense political debate, passed the new legislation and granted a twenty-year charter for the Bank of the United States (BUS).[50]

In 1811 the charter expired and Congress, led by supporters of Jefferson, did not vote to renew it, and therefore the Bank terminated its operation. The antifederalist arguments which twenty years earlier were in the minority, this time dominated the debates in the House of Representatives and Senate, during which the institution was called a threat to the functioning of the states. However, the succeeding years brought new circumstances which forced the leaders of the country to revise their approach towards the central bank. After fighting an unsuccessful war with Great Britain, 1812–1814, President James Madison – earlier a staunch opponent of the idea of a national bank – initiated a debate over re-establishing the institution as a necessary instrument in helping the government to recover from the economic crisis caused by the war. In 1816, Congress approved the new charter for the bank and it began operating as the Second Bank of the United States.[51]

The effectiveness and efficiency of its functioning was to be achieved by establishing several branches of the BUS at the state level, and one of such branches started to operate in Maryland, raising concerns about the future existence of state and local banks. The state legislature, under the influence of local bankers and anti-federalist politicians, decided to introduce legislation which, among other things, imposed a state tax on the financial operations of the Bank. Before the law could be properly executed, James McCulloch, the officer representing the federal institution, refused to follow the provisions of Maryland's legislation and filed a suit

50 See: David J. Cowen, *The Origins and Economic Impact of the First Bank of the United States, 1791–1797*, Garland Publishing, New York 2000.

51 See: Edward S. Kaplan, *The Bank of the United States and the American Economy*, Greenwood Press, Westport 1999.

challenging the constitutionality of the state tax. After the lower federal courts – Baltimore County Court and the Maryland Court of Appeals – ruled in favor of the state, the case was brought on appeal to the Supreme Court, the role of which was to determine whether McCulloch could refuse to pay the tax imposed by the state on a federal institution.

McCulloch v. Maryland was not the first important decision of the Supreme Court led by John Marshall since the fundamental precedent of 1803 recognizing the power of judicial review. The justices determined a few important constitutional issues before 1819, such as the scope of the right to property[52], or the supremacy of the SCOTUS over state courts[53], but, next to *Marbury v. Madison,* the 1819 precedent was to become the most vital constitutional legacy of the Marshall Court in history. The Chief Justice, who presented the Court's ruling, used the dispute to raise some fundamental questions concerning the operation of the federal government and the scope of the rights of states, as well as the issue of sovereignty and national identity. He introduced two questions which became the main legal issues determined by the Court: whether Congress had a right to create a national bank, and whether the legislation imposing a state tax on financial operations of a federal bank was constitutional.

Before directly answering the first question about the legality of the BUS, Marshall announced the special character of the case, which stemmed from his understanding of the supreme law of the land:

> "The constitution of our country, in its most interesting and vital parts, is to be considered; the conflicting powers of the government of the Union and of its members, as marked in the constitution, are to be discussed; and an opinion given, which may essentially influence the great operations of the government."[54]

In the same paragraph, Marshall reaffirmed the judicial review principle set out in the *Marbury* precedent, announcing that "[o]n the Supreme Court of the United States has the constitution of our country devolved this important duty,"[55] claiming that there was only one authority which could determine in a responsible way the scope of government powers and

52 *Fletcher v. Peck* 10 U.S. 87 (1810).
53 *Martin v. Hunter's Lessee* 14 U.S. 304 (1816).
54 17 U.S. 316 (1819) at 400.
55 *Ibid.*

the meaning of the Constitution. Such an introduction clearly explained that the dispute was, on the one hand, a continuation of the process of broadening the powers of the federal judiciary, and, on the other, a debate over the meaning and scope of the federal Constitution.

The Chief Justice decided to explain the real position of states in the American system of government determined by the constitutional document. Reviewing the text of the Preamble, he stressed the importance of the invocation of the document reflected in the famous words: "We the People of the United States", which was designed to ensure that the government was created by the individuals constituting the American nation and society. A specific reading of that part of the document allowed him to underline the importance of the unification which was achieved by the Founding Fathers during the Philadelphia convention of 1787. For Marshall, and for the rest of the Court, the word "united" became crucial in understanding the process of establishing a federal form of government, as a solution to the ineffective idea of the confederation existing on American soil in the early 1780s. Such an approach not only emphasized the importance of popular sovereignty in U.S. constitutionalism but, at the same time, the lack of states' sovereignty, for which Maryland and other states strongly argued. As Marshall stated:

> "The government of the Union, is, emphatically, and truly, a government of the people. In form and in substance it emanates from them. The powers are granted by them, and are to be exercised directly on them, and for their benefit.[56]"

The principle of popular sovereignty was echoed by the reference to the rest of the Preamble, where the Founding Fathers set out the goals and purposes of the Constitution, reflecting upon the direction in which the new country and government should go. In Marshall's opinion, the Philadelphia Convention decided to transfer the whole power to the People, and the Preamble with its concrete goals of providing "a more perfect union", "justice", "domestic tranquility", "liberty", and "posterity" was the best proof of the necessity of such a transfer. Interestingly, that part of the SCOTUS opinion was the only significant interpretation of the Preamble in the history of its adjudication.

---

56 *Ibid.* at 404, 405.

In the following part of the opinion, the Court acknowledged that congressional powers were enumerated, referring to Section 8 of Article One, which included eighteen clauses listing the concrete competences of the federal legislative body. Not surprisingly, there was no reference to a bank or any other central financial institution which could be established by Congress, but Marshall observed that it would be impossible to include a detailed enumeration of all the powers of the government and that not everything was directly expressed in the Constitution, because the document was intended to have a general character:

> "A constitution, to contain an accurate detail of all the subdivisions of which its great powers will admit, and of all the means by which they may be carried into execution, would partake of the prolixity of a legal code, and could scarcely be embraced by the human mind. It would probably be never understood by the public. Its nature, therefore, requires, that only its great outlines should be marked, its important objects designated, and the minor ingredients which compose those objects be deduced from the nature of the objects themselves.[57]"

Confirming his broad approach towards the constitutional interpretation of the powers of Congress, the Chief Justice listed several competences of national legislature which pertained to financial issues, such as laying and collecting taxes, borrowing money, and regulating commerce, as well as to its war powers, including the declaration and conduct of a war, and the raising and supporting of armies. He stressed that, among other goals, the role of the government was to effectively pursue the policies of "the sword and the purse", by using the most efficient and available tools or instruments, which he called the "means", and which could be chosen by the policy makers:

> "The government which has a right to do an act, and has imposed on it the duty of performing that act, must, according to the dictates of the reason, be allowed to select the means; and those who contend that it may not select any appropriate means, that one particular mode of effecting the object is excepted, take upon themselves the burden of establishing that exception.[58]"

Despite directly granting Congress the right to select the means of the execution of its powers of the sword and the purse from his reasoning,

57 *Ibid.* at 407.
58 *Ibid.* at 409, 410.

Marshall decided to confirm this approach by referring once again to the Constitution, where he found an exact justification for such an interpretation. He quoted the last part of the enumeration of Section 8, Article One, called the Necessary and Proper Clause, which, in the opinion of the Court, complemented the scope of the powers exercised by Congress, it being able to make

> "All laws which shall be necessary and proper for carrying into execution the foregoing powers, and all other powers vested by this constitution, in the government of the United States, or in any department thereof.[59]"

For the state of Maryland, which represented many other states concerned with the growing powers of the federal government, the existence of the Necessary and Proper Clause appropriately emphasized by the Supreme Court meant a drastic limitation of state powers, despite the existence of the Tenth Amendment. The most important part of the Bill of Rights for the state governments lost its meaning, which, during the process of constitutional ratification, was invoked several times by state legislatures afraid of the national government's accumulation of power. The establishment of the Tenth Amendment, introducing the principle of states' rights, was to provide assurance that certain powers which were not enumerated in the main body of the Constitution belonged to the states.

In *McCulloch*, the SCOTUS not only limited the scope of that Amendment, but it also broadened the powers of the federal government to an extent never expected by the Founding Fathers, who defended states' rights during the Convention. John Marshall was aware of these fears and concerns, which is why he proposed a limitation on the powers of national government, invoking the principle of limited government and introducing the legitimate end approach in constitutional interpretation:

> "We admit, as all must admit, that the powers of the government are limited, and that its limits are not to be transcended. But we think the sound construction of the constitution must allow to the national legislature that discretion, with respect to the means by which the powers it confers are to be carried into execution, which will enable that body to perform the high duties assigned to it, in the manner most beneficial to the people. Let the end be legitimate, let it be within the scope of the constitution, and all means which are appropriate, which are

59 *Ibid.* at 411, 412.

plainly adapted to that end, which are not prohibited, but consist with the letter and spirit of the constitution, are constitutional.[60]"

According to the Chief Justice, not only the means justified the possibility of the government to operate, but, generally, the purposes which the government wanted to achieve by initiating concrete activity. The "end" which in Marshall's approach could be understood as the "purpose", "aim" or the "objective", could legitimize the actions and operations of the state, provided it was consistent with the Constitution. In other words, the actions and operations were constitutional if the end/purpose/aim for which they were initiated was also constitutional. Such an approach was clearly affirmed in another part of the opinion, where Marshall related the issue to the creation of a bank (defined here as a corporation): "The power of creating a corporation is never used for its own sake, but for the purpose of effecting something else.[61]" On the other hand, the Chief Justice noted that the purpose should not serve as the only reason for certain activity and that it should lead to the achievement of some other important goals: "It is never the end for which other powers are exercised, but a means by which other objects are accomplished.[62]" From the perspective of the adjudicated case, this meant that Congress created a bank not for the purpose of its existence, but to pursue financial policies and provide economic growth in times of crisis.

Before analyzing other aspects of the legitimate end theory, it is necessary to present the rest of the SCOTUS ruling with regard to the power of taxation. After confirming the right of Congress to establish a national bank, Marshall moved to the second question which concerned the imposition of state tax on the financial operations of the federal bank. This time, the Chief Justice proposed a 'test' as an effective way of solving the problem of conflicting federal-state powers, which is known as the 'test of the constitution':

"This great principle is, that the constitution and the laws made in pursuance thereof are supreme; that they control the constitution and laws of the respective States, and cannot be controlled by them. From this, which maybe almost termed

60 *Ibid.* at 421.
61 *Ibid.* at 411.
62 *Ibid.*

> an axiom, other propositions are deduced as corollaries, on the truth or error of which, and on their application to this case, the cause has been supposed to depend. These are, 1st. that the power to create implies a power to preserve. 2nd. That a power to destroy, if wielded by a different hand, is hostile to, and incompatible with these powers to create and to preserve. 3d. That were this repugnancy exists, that authority which is supreme must control, not yield to that over which it is supreme.[63]"

By referring to the supremacy clause of the constitution, the Court applied the circumstances of the case to the general principles it introduced, declaring that, if Congress could establish a national bank, the institution could function legally ("power to create implies a power to preserve"), unless some other source of power, such as a state government, tried to limit its operation ("power to destroy, if wielded by a different hand, is hostile to, and incompatible with these powers to create and preserve"). In such a situation, the supreme authority "must control", therefore the tax imposed by the state was unconstitutional as it limited the functioning of the legally established BUS. Although the last part of the opinion seemed quite easy to predict, considering the character of the supremacy clause, it complemented the whole judgment, which expanded the powers of the federal government at the expense of states and confirmed the unique position of the SCOTUS as the final interpreter of the Constitution and controller of the legality of the actions undertaken by both federal and state institutions.

The *McCulloch* Legacy

It would be a truism to state that the Court's opinion of 1819 had a significant impact on the future of American constitutionalism, despite the controversies it raised in the era in which it was announced. As a continuation of the rationale from *Marbury*, which was never overruled by a single piece of legislation, including a constitutional amendment, *McCulloch* became the key to understanding the status of state governments in the union, as well as a legitimization of the expansion of the powers of national government. The direct effect of the precedent, establishing a ban on states' taxation of federal institutions, and explaining the scope of the Necessary and Proper Clause, was never officially rejected by subsequent

63 *Ibid.* at 426.

Courts and justices, which seems obvious considering the arguments raised by the Chief Justice in his analysis of the Constitution and the character of the federal form of government. A few years later Marshall himself used the reasoning from the case in other important rulings, expanding them into new areas of constitutional adjudication such as the Commerce Clause in *Gibbons v. Ogden*. By interpreting the powers of Congress in economic affairs, the Chief Justice confirmed the constitutional right of the federal legislature to regulate interstate commerce, referring several times to the legitimate end approach and the necessity of employing proper means in conducting the country's economic policy.[64]

There is no surprise in observing that the *McCulloch* precedent had an impact on judicial opinions in cases concerning the scope of federal-state relations, controversies relating to taxation issues, and, especially, the Commerce Clause disputes[65]. Interestingly, justices cited the rationale of the 1819 ruling in majority opinions, but also as dissenters, and sometimes the reference to *McCulloch* led to a limitation of federal powers, as in *Hammer v. Dagenhart*, where the interpretation of the Enumeration Clause led to the striking down of a federal law regulating child labor[66]. One of the most direct applications of the judgment came in 1941 in *United States v. Darby*, in which the justices used Marshall's interpretation of the Necessary and Proper Clause to strengthen the powers of national government and declare the constitutionality of the Fair Labor Standards Act:

> "The power of Congress over interstate commerce extends to those intrastate activities which so affect interstate commerce or the exercise of the power of Congress over it as to make their regulation an appropriate means to the attainment of a legitimate end -- the exercise of the granted power of Congress to regulate interstate commerce."[67]

Apart from the Commerce Clause cases, disputes pertaining to the power of taxation also invoked the *McCulloch* holding, directly citing the most significant parts of the 1819 ruling, as in the famous precedent on the

64 22 U.S. 1 (1824).
65 See: *Champion v. Ames* 188 U.S. 321 (1903); *United States v. Darby* 312 U.S. 118 (1941); *United States v. Lopez* 514 U.S. 549 (1995).
66 247 U.S. 251 (1918).
67 312 U.S. 100 (1941), at 118.

constitutionality of Obamacare[68]. There is also a vast array of SCOTUS decisions which do not directly refer to *McCulloch* but present a similar approach towards a broader interpretation of the Constitution and the process of finding legitimate end in expanding the scope of the rights of the people. The analysis of *Brown v. Board of Education* (which determined that racial segregation in public schooling was unconstitutional), *Roe v. Wade* (which declared the existence of a constitutional right to abortion), or *Obergefell v. Hodges* (which established a constitutional right to same-sex marriages) reveals the *McCulloch*-type attitude of justices who shaped majority opinions in these very important but controversial constitutional disputes[69]. In a broader context, one may admit that not only precedents related to the expansion of government powers could be viewed from the perspective of the *McCulloch* rationale, but also many of the rulings which have applied the expanding interpretation of the Constitution. Importantly, the justices did not have to quote the *McCulloch* rationale directly to support Marshall's understanding of how to read and understand the Constitution.

Marshall's interpretation of the Preamble has also become the fundament of the idea of popular sovereignty, and his numerous references to the values of the rule of law were often quoted in cases which raised concerns as to the scope of American democracy. It is crucial to understand that before *McCulloch* there was no SCOTUS opinion which directly focused on the character of the rule of law – a principle which was also not addressed in the text of the Constitution until the appearance of the Fourteenth Amendment, introducing the Equal Protection of Law Clause. It would be an exaggeration to claim that without Marshall's view on the rule of law reflected in his 1819 opinion, the United States would have been less democratic, but his reference to the "government of laws, not of men", accompanied by the earlier statements presented in *Marbury* invoking "government of the people", have constituted the foundation of the constitutional approach towards the character of early American democracy, or – in Madison's words – Republic. Therefore, although the rule of law was finally directly introduced in the Constitution, some of the Supreme Court decisions which

68 *National Federation of Independent Business v. Sebelius* 567 U.S. 519 (2012).
69 347 U.S. 483 (1954); 410 U.S. 113 (1973); 576 U.S. 644 (2015).

interpreted the character of U.S. democracy in the context of the powers of government or the rights of the people were made in the spirit of Marshall's approach towards a "government of laws, not of men".

Additionally, the judgment is treated as the source of the functionalist approach to constitutional interpretation, stressing the importance of the purposes and roles of certain institutions in the governmental system. The main references made by the proponents of functionalism are the purposes which guide the government's operation of concrete institutions equipped with powers granted by the Constitution. However, the process of constitutional interpretation does not focus only on the text of a particular provision or clause, but also discerns the sense of the government's activities as regards the functions performed by its institutions.[70] As Marshall argued, "the letter and spirit of the Constitution" are equally significant in the process of determining the scope of governmental powers, thus introducing the broader interpretation of constitutional norms and values. His attitude towards the implied powers of the federal government and the analysis of the Necessary and Proper Clause serves as the best example of how he understood the possible expansion of government powers in the mode of the functionalist approach towards the reading of the Constitution.

The 20th and 21st century SCOTUS adjudications clearly show the impact of the *McCulloch* rationale, especially in cases concerning the economic powers of the federal government, as in the New Deal era and in the period of the welfare state legislation, including a series of Commerce Clause disputes.[71] Accordingly, functionalism was promoted by justices who supported the expansion of the powers of the executive, especially in the area of foreign relations, were the Constitution was unclear as to the scope of presidential prerogatives affecting these. There were also disputes which raised concerns about the character of the separation of powers principle, in which functionalism clashed with a contrary mode of interpretation – formalism – whose proponents defended the "letter" of the Constitution against its "spirit", such as in *Morrison v. Olson* (on the constitutionality of

70 Nat Stern, "Separation of Powers, Executive Authority, and Suspension of Disbelief", *Houston Law Review* 54, 2016, pp. 130–131.

71 *United States v. Darby* 312 U.S. 100 (1941); *Wickard v. Filburn* 317 U.S. 111 (1942).

independent counsel), *Clinton v. City of New York* (concerning presidential powers under the Line Item Veto Act) and *Zivotofsky v. Kerry* (the scope of the presidential power to recognize foreign states).[72]

Despite the visible impact of the *McCulloch* precedent on future SCOTUS adjudication, there was a lot of criticism of the direct effects of the decision, as well as Marshall's reasoning about the possible expansion of the meaning of the Constitution. Criticism came, predictably, from some state governments and politicians, who treated the 1819 precedent as an attempt to limit state powers and as a personification of some fears of the dominant power of national government shared by the delegates during the Philadelphia Convention. In several states there were debates commenting on the short- and long-range impact of the SCOTUS judgment, especially criticizing the limitation the decision put on the principle of states' sovereignty, and suggesting the creation of a new federal court, consisting of state chief judges responsible for adjudicating in federal-state disputes[73]. Republican politicians attacked Marshall for abandoning legal arguments in favor of political ones and representing the economic interests of the bank rather than the general interest of American society[74]. Journalists wrote articles and essays in which they undermined the right of the federal judiciary to expand the meaning of the Constitution in a way that directly affected states' rights. Even James Madison, who became a proponent of the Second Bank of the United States, felt that the Court used the case to pursue a general and abstract doctrine, dangerously expanding the Constitution without, practically, any limits[75]. For proponents of the antifederalist approach, the precedent of 1819 became the biggest threat to states' sovereignty, limiting the scope of the Tenth Amendment, assumed by them to be an inviolable border around states' rights.

---

72 487 U.S. 654 (1988); 524 U.S. 417 (1998); 576 U.S. 1 (2015).

73 R. Kent Newmyer, "John Marshall, *McCulloch v. Maryland*, and the Southern States' Rights Tradition", *John Marshall Law Review* 33, 2000, pp. 875–876.

74 Thomas C. Shevory (ed.), *John Marshall's Law: Interpretation, Ideology, and Interest*, Greenwood Press, Westport 1994, p. 55.

75 Richard E. Ellis, *Aggressive Nationalism: McCulloch v. Maryland and the Foundation of Federal Authority in the Young Republic*, Oxford University Press, New Yok 2007, p. 102.

One of the staunchest opponents of the consequences the *McCulloch* judgment brought to American political reality was President Andrew Jackson, who in the 1830s criticized some aspects of the operation of the BUS despite its positive impact on the U.S. economy. Jackson not only dismissed the idea of a central financial institution, which he defined as "privately controlled" and "profit-making", but he also pressed on his attorney general, Roger Taney, to prepare a legal opinion which would undermine Marshall's reasoning presented in *McCulloch*.[76] For the President, a strong and active judiciary, enjoying almost unlimited competences and having an impact on the meaning of the Constitution, was a threat to the proper operation of the state and a danger which could limit presidential powers. Taney's opinion convinced Jackson to veto the bill rechartering the Bank in the middle of presidential campaign of 1832, and his clear victory strengthened Jackson's opposition towards the Bank, leading to further confrontation with Marshall's Court over the scope of national powers[77].

Apart from politicians of the 1820s and 1830s, contemporary scholars and researchers have raised a number of concerns about the way in which the Marshall reached his conclusions in *McCulloch* and who undermine the idea of liberal constitutionalism offered by him. Mark Tushnet argues that Marshall, while using references to the rule of law to justify the establishment of the national bank, in fact had an attitude towards constitutional interpretation that proved to be more political, and thus arbitrary[78]. According to Tushnet, the chief justice used the dispute to purse his own perspective on the interpretation of the law, which Tushnet labelled "nationalist constitutional views."[79] Similarly, Keith Whittington, who called the 1819 precedent a "sweeping nationalist vision", blames the Marshall Court for creating the basis for the vast expansion of the powers of the SCOTUS, especially by conducting an activist judicial review, which

76 See: Charles W. Smith, jr. *Roger B. Taney: Jacksonian Jurist*, University of North Carolina Press, Durham 2018.

77 See: Jerry W. Markham, *From Christopher Columbus to the Robber Barons: A Financial History of the United States 1492–1900*, Routledge, New York 2002.

78 See: Mark Tushnet, "The Dillemas of Liberal Constitutionalism", *Ohio State Law Review* 42, 1981, pp. 411–426.

79 See: Mark Tushnet (ed.), *I Dissent: Great Opposing Opinions in Landmark Supreme Court Cases*, Beacon Press, New York 2008.

led to the Court gaining supremacy among three branches of government.[80] This chimes with the approach presented by Nelson Lund who, despite noticing a significant impact of *McCulloch* on American democracy, criticizes Marshall for taking unnecessary and improper means and ignoring other possible ways of solving the dispute over the constitutionality of the BUS.[81]

David S. Schwartz, one of the authors critical of contemporary constitutional law scholars' praise of the legacy of *McCulloch v. Maryland*, argues that Marshall was not a visionary and did not develop any new constitutional idea, and that his decision would not have a significant impact on today's understanding of the Constitution if lawyers and judges had not defined it as a great case:

> "They found material in it that was useful to their constitutional arguments, and they had come to believe that John Marshall was an iconic figure whose words carried great weight. *McCulloch* has thus been given a central role in a modern-day foundation myth for constitutional law.[82]"

Despite strong opposition to *McCulloch v. Maryland*, among both the politicians responsible for the implementation of the judgment in the 1820s and 1830s and critics of the broad constitutional interpretation offered by Marshall, there is one aspect of the Court's opinion which became crucial in understanding the federal governments' attitude towards certain policies implemented in 20th and 21st centuries, which has already been mentioned and which I call the "legitimate end" approach. Regardless of Marshall's vision or lack of such, this part of the ruling has played an important role in American constitutional history and has been used in different circumstances to justify concrete policies of the government. Therefore,

---

80 Keith E. Whittington, *Political Foundations of Judicial Supremacy: The Presidency, the Supreme Court, and Constitutional Leadership in History*, Princeton University Press, Princeton 2007, p. 111.

81 See: Nelson Lund, *The Destructive Legacy of McCulloch v. Maryland* in: *McCulloch v. Maryland at 200: Debating John Marshall's Jurisprudence*, Gary Schmitt, Rebecca Burgess (eds.), American Enterprise Institute Press, Washington D.C. 2020.

82 David S. Schwartz, *The Spirit of the Constitution: John Marshall and the 200-Year Odyssey of McCulloch v. Maryland*, Oxford University Press, New York 2019, pp. 3–4.

before applying the legitimate end approach to government surveillance case-law, it is worth analyzing its significance for American constitutional law and politics.

It seems obvious that the main role of any judge is to balance or weigh the evidence and arguments presented by the parties of a dispute. In civil and criminal cases judges apply different evidentiary standards, but they perform similar work, which is the determination of the facts of the case, analysis of the applicable law, and deciding which party shall prevail. In constitutional cases, the role of judges or justices is theoretically similar, although the issues presented before the courts often refer to the broader context of governmental power and/or the rights of the people. Apart from analyzing the facts of the dispute, the courts interpret the Constitution in order to explain the scope of its values and provisions with regard to the issues raised in the case. They play similar roles in balancing or weighing legal arguments raised by the parties, but their main point of reference is the Constitution, and therefore they may apply different standards depending on their approach to constitutional interpretation. This process is especially crucial for the state of American democracy when SCOTUS justices are exercising judicial review of the acts of the legislative and executive branches which affect their powers, as well as rights and freedoms enjoyed by the people. The crucial question raised in such disputes concerns the interest which should be protected by the judiciary, which is obliged to act independently of any political pressures. It all comes down, then, to the process of balancing the constitutional argumentation and legitimizing the expansion or limitation of power.

As one of the three branches in the separation of powers system, the Supreme Court plays an important role in preserving the powers of the government, and many disputes in history focused on the scope of governmental powers in relation to the constitutional protection of the rights of individuals. One of the sources of decisions in such cases is the legitimate interest of the government, or, in other words, the legitimate state interest which may be considered by the justices in the process of justifying the legality of concrete governmental actions possibly resulting in an expansion of the power of certain branches or governmental institutions. Such an expansion may occur at the expense of the powers of the people; therefore, it follows that the Court has to present strong argumentation in support of the legitimate interest of the government. There are different levels of scrutiny applied by the justices, depending on the character of the case and their preferred interpretive approach among the available options: the rational basis test, intermediate scrutiny, and strict scrutiny. The first approach applies the lowest scrutiny standard, justifying governmental action by showing any legitimate interest which the authorities may have. The second approach refers to disputes in which the government must prove that it has an important interest in imposing concrete regulations which may limit the scope of individual rights. Finally, the strict scrutiny standard justifies governmental intrusion into the sphere of rights and freedoms only when it shows a so-called compelling interest which is argued to be indispensable to the proper operation of the system.[83]

As history shows, the level of scrutiny applied has depended on the type of issues raised in the disputes which reached the Supreme Court, on the justices' approach towards the mode of constitutional interpretation, and their ideological stance. The first important reference to judicial scrutiny was presented in the footnote of one of the SCOTUS Commerce Clause decisions by Justice Harlan Fiske Stone. By applying the rational basis test to the circumstances of the dispute, in the famous Footnote 4 to the *United States v. Carolene Products Co.*, Stone acknowledged a stricter standard of review in cases concerning laws which could violate the Constitution, and, especially, impose discrimination against minorities:

> "There may be narrower scope for operation of the presumption of constitutionality when legislation appears on its face to be within a specific prohibition of the Constitution, such as those of the first ten Amendments, which are deemed equally specific when held to be embraced within the Fourteenth."[84]

As a result, the strict scrutiny standard has become a leading approach of the SCOTUS in most cases concerning the infringement of fundamental constitutional rights of the people, which did not mean, however, that in any dispute in which the government's operations or legislation were challenged

83 See: Louis Fisher, Katy J. Harriger, *American Constitutional Law*, Carolina Academic Press, Durham 2019; Richard H. Fallon, jr., *Law and Legitimacy in the Supreme Court*. The Belknap Press of Harvard University Press, Cambridge 2018; Saul Brenner, Joseph W. Whitmeyer, *Strategy...*, op. cit.

84 *United States v. Carolene Products Co.* 304 U.S. 144 (1938), *Footnote 4*.

on the basis of violation of fundamental rights the Court would always rule against the government. A good example of this is the application of the strict scrutiny standard in *Korematsu v. United States*, where the justices acknowledged a compelling state interest in establishing internment camps for Japanese Americans, despite it being a violation of their constitutional rights.[85]

In that context the legitimate end approach introduced by the Marshall Court in *McCulloch v. Maryland* led to at least three consequences for the future constitutional interpretation applied by the judiciary with regard to the operation of the government. First, it allows the courts to declare actions of the government constitutional when the ends/purposes of these actions are within the limits of the Constitution. Second, it suggests that the government may choose the means by which it will conduct its policies, unless these means are appropriately adapted to the ends/purposes of governmental actions. And third, the legitimate end approach allows the justices to interpret the Constitution with regard to its "letter and spirit", stressing that the functions the government performs are crucial to the final understanding of the scope of its powers. Such a reading of the part of *McCulloch* opinion analyzed here shows how much leeway Marshall left to subsequent justices for the interpretation of the constitutional powers of the government, despite his clear argumentation supporting the idea of "limited government". For him, limitations were obvious, as they were reflected in the Constitution; however, in view of the fact that courts could exercise active judicial review in the future, the document could be interpreted even more broadly than Marshall himself could have predicted. In that perspective, it is not only the *Marbury* holding, but also the *McCulloch* rationale which plays significant role in the legitimization of the expansion of government powers, which is visible in 20th and 21st century SCOTUS adjudication.

There are examples of direct references to the *McCulloch* legacy, such as in *Lochner v. New York*, where the Court had to determine the constitutionality of a New York law imposing limits on the number of working hours required in the employment of a baker. The justices declared

85 323 U.S. 214 (1944).

the unconstitutionality of the state legislation as it violated the due process and right of contract of Lochner, but the majority opinion made a clear reference to the spirit of legitimate end, weighing against one another two competing values:

> "It is a question of which of two powers or rights shall prevail -- the power of the State to legislate or the right of the individual to liberty of person and freedom of contract. The mere assertion that the subject relates though but in a remote degree to the public health does not necessarily render the enactment valid. The act must have a more direct relation, as a means to an end, and the end itself must be appropriate and legitimate, before an act can be held to be valid which interferes with the general right of an individual to be free in his person and in his power to contract in relation to his own labor."[86]

A different and more recent example is *National Federation of Independent Business v. Sebelius*, better known as the Obamacare case, in which the Court in a majority opinion written by Chief Justice John Roberts, Jr. referred a few times to *McCulloch*, placing Marshall's interpretation of the Constitution at the very center of the rationale of this controversial ruling. One of the references directly quoted the legitimate end approach, which the chief justice defined as a principle introduced in order "to give Congress great latitude in exercising its powers".[87]

Although the 1819 precedent has not been cited directly by subsequent Courts as often as *Marbury*, it – paraphrasing John Marshall's words – is not only the letter but the spirit of SCOTUS decisions that affects their adjudications in constitutional disputes. Opinions in cases in which the justices applied different standards of scrutiny had their source in the legitimate end approach. In this way every expansion of the powers of government permitted by the Court could be legitimized by the spirit of Marshall's attitude towards constitutional interpretation. Without overestimating the role of *McCulloch* in SCOTUS history, the legitimate end approach seems crucial in adjudication concerning the scope of government actions aimed at strengthening security, both domestic and national. Having that in mind, it seems important to analyze justices' argumentation concerning domestic and foreign government surveillance,

86 198 U.S. 45 (1905) at 57.
87 567 U.S. 519 (2012).

in order to understand the letter and spirit of U.S. constitutional law. It may be especially important to discern whether and how the Supreme Court legitimized governmental use of the modern surveillance tools and techniques which have affected the scope of individuals' right to privacy, and other constitutional guarantees, and what consequences it has had for the tension between security and freedom.

Chapter Two The Fourth Amendment and Domestic Surveillance

The Fourth Amendment: Text and Meaning

The Fourth Amendment, as a part of the Bill of Rights adopted in 1791, was a result of the Founding Fathers' concern over potential governmental intrusion into the private affairs of citizens. The Fourth, along with the Fifth, Sixth, and Eighth Amendments, is devoted to the conduct of the criminal justice system in imposing certain limits on the activities of law enforcement officers and agencies; in other words, its role is to set the boundaries within which the investigative powers of the government can be used. Compared to other parts of the Bill of Rights concerning the rights of suspects and defendants being subject to criminal investigations, the Fourth Amendment seems very specific is determining the necessary means that law enforcement operatives may use in the implementation of their investigative powers. While the Fifth Amendment lists several rights of subjects of criminal procedure, and the Sixth focuses on two fundamental guarantees of a fair criminal trial, the Fourth refers to a concrete procedure, introducing two clauses which define the character and scope of searches and seizures in a criminal investigation being conducted by the police:

> "The right of the people to be secure in their persons, houses, papers, and effects, against unreasonable searches and seizures, shall not be violated, and no Warrants shall issue, but upon probable cause, supported by Oath or affirmation, and particularly describing the place to be searched, and the persons or things to be seized."

Before analyzing the language of the clauses, it seems important to acknowledge that the Amendment contains references to both "the people" and "persons". As Akhil Reed Amar claims, the character of the provision, which introduces "houses", and the individualistic focus of "the people to be secure in their persons", leaves no doubt as to the real intent of the Amendment: the protection of people as private persons rather than people in the public square. Explaining the existence of "the people" at the beginning of the Amendment, Amar believes that, similarly to other parts of the Bill of Rights, the authors of the document wanted to protect popular rights via institutions that would embody "the people" themselves.[88] Supporting such an interpretation, I would suggest that both categories - "the people" and "persons" - play a crucial role in determining the character of the Fourth Amendment, which aims at the protection of the individual rights of persons, as well as providing security to the people.

The first part of the Amendment, the Search and Seizure Clause, imposes a ban on unreasonable activities of the government which fall into the category of searches and seizures, although there is no direct definition of what constitutes a proper search and an effective seizure. The only condition which is expressed refers to the reasonableness of the search and seizure, which has to be ensured by the subjects equipped with the competences required to carry out such a procedure. An important element of the Amendment is its opening language, which determines the main purpose (or end) for which the document has become an integral part of U.S. constitutionalism. The rights of the people are limited to security issues which define the subject and area of protection, such as persons, houses, papers, and effects. There is no doubt that for the Founding Fathers there were two values which the Amendment had to protect: security and privacy. Such an interpretation may be derived from the fact that at the beginning of American statehood both values were invoked as fundamental to the functioning of the country.[89] Importantly, however, the right to privacy, despite the broad language of the Search and Seizure Clause, which referred to personal and property rights, was limited to the notion of privacy understood as freedom from encroachments of the government into the physical space occupied by a U.S. citizen in private.

The second part of the Amendment, known as the Warrant Clause, establishes conditions for the government to obtain a document, in the form of a court order necessary for the conduct of an effective search and seizure. These conditions were a consequence of historical experience from the colonial period, when the British searched premises of the colonists using general warrants which did not contain any references to specific locations, allowing them to conduct unlimited searches and seizures.[90] In

---

88 Akhil Reed Amar, *America's Constitution. A Biography*, Random House, New York 2005, pp. 326–327.

89 Daniel Farber (ed.), *Security v. Liberty...*, op. cit.

90 Daniel J. Solove, *Nothing to Hide...*, op. cit., p. 4.

order to prevent such illegal operations of the part of the authorities, the clause assumes the necessary cooperation between various branches of government: Congress, which cannot implement legislation violating the Amendment's purposes; the executive branch, which has to act within the limits set out in the Warrant Clause; and the judiciary, responsible for issuing documents legalizing a search and seizure conducted by the government.

The language of these clauses clearly proves that the purpose of its authors was to address it to law enforcement officers by establishing some prohibitions in their investigative operations, which could be limited by the scope of the rights of the people. Contrary to other procedural prohibitions set out in the Bill of Rights, which provide certain rights to the subjects of criminal investigations, such as the right to trial by jury, the right to counsel and protection against self-incrimination, the provisions of the Fourth Amendment guarantee that the government will not overuse its competences while gathering the evidence necessary to determine the conduct and outcome of criminal events. In other words, the Search and Seizure Clause may be understood as a confirmation of the delegation of investigative power to the government, based on the assumption that the actions undertaken by law enforcement must occur according to a fair and just procedure partly introduced in the Warrant Clause.

The Fourth Amendment belongs to the part of the Constitution in which the tensions between freedom and security are reflected. On the one hand, its language confirms the possibility of the government's intrusion into the private affairs of its citizens, but on the other it assures its readers that these actions will not be unlimited and will not negatively affect the rights and freedoms enjoyed by these citizens. Furthermore, the word "security" is used with reference to the people, not the law enforcement agency responsible for the effective collection of the evidence necessary to complete a successful investigation. As Linda R. Monk points out, the character of the Fourth Amendment may be derived, as has already been noted, from the colonial era, when the invasive power of the British government was reflected in numerous intrusions into the homes of Americans, resulting in warrantless arrests.[91] This proves that, for the Founding Fathers, it was crucial to ensure that every individual would feel safe and secure in their private spaces and

91 Linda R. Monk, *The Words We Live By: The Annotated Guide to the Constitution*, Hyperion, New York 2003, p. 157.

would not be subject of illegal means of obtaining evidence for the sake of fulfilling the purposes of a pending investigation. In such a way, two types of security were confronted: the security and protection of individuals from the actions of government, and the broader security of the society from the dangers of potential criminals. The role of the Amendment was to ensure that both types of security were provided, and that the authorities were able to conduct an effective investigation without violating the constitutional rights of the persons concerned.

One of the key concepts presented in the spirit of the Amendment is the danger of arbitrariness of the authorities in the choice of people or places to be subjected to searches and seizures. As a consequence, the investigative procedures used by the government should be reasonable and should identify probable cause, legitimizing the actions of law enforcement officers in relation to both the people being subjected to a search and the places in which such searches were conducted. The text of the Amendment introduces legal documents, called warrants, which may be obtained in a special procedure determining the scope of the search, namely its addressees and locations. According to the Constitution, in order to proceed the government has to obtain a warrant by proving probable cause that a crime has been committed, making credible the subject and scope of the search. However, the language of the Amendment does not exclude the possibility of conducting a search or seizure without a warrant, as, according to its wording, the main purpose of the Fourth Amendment with regards to warrants is to determine the conditions necessary for law enforcement to obtain these documents.

Despite detailed reference to the investigative procedure of law enforcement, similarly to other parts of the Constitution, the real meaning of the Fourth Amendment had to be determined via the process of constitutional interpretation imposed by the judiciary. Especially in the 20th and 21st centuries, the Supreme Court has used its power of judicial review to define and redefine the meaning of the Search and Seizure Clause, as well as the Warrant Clause, providing judicial perspective on the extent to which the government may act without violating the right to privacy of American citizens. As a result, in numerous decisions justices have expanded or limited the understanding of such phrases as reasonable and unreasonable search and seizure, probable cause, search with and without a warrant, and security of persons and places. By reviewing the meaning of particular phrases and clauses of the Amendment, the role of SCOTUS has been to provide a balance between the protection of the rights of individuals and the effectiveness of law enforcement procedures aimed at strengthening the security of the society. These tensions between freedom and security have been present in the Court's jurisprudence regarding the scope and meaning of the Fourth Amendment in the context of both the domestic and foreign activities of the government.

The SCOTUS and the Fourth Amendment

The purpose of this chapter is to discuss the Court's adjudication in disputes concerning domestic surveillance; however, as an important introduction to the topic of the analysis of the fundamental Fourth Amendment SCOTUS precedents is necessary if we are to understand the basis and direction of the justices' interpretations.

Before entering the 20th century, to examine Supreme Court case-law referring to the character and scope of searches and seizures imposed by the federal and state governments, it seems vital to analyze the 1886 SCOTUS decision in *Boyd v. United States*, as it presented the attitude of the justices involved as to what constituted a search, as well as the meaning of privacy with regard to documents. Based on an 1874 statute, the law enforcement authorities could use information about the content of private documents during a trial without presenting the actual documents in court. If defendants did not confront the accusations made against them by presenting the documents before the judge, the assumptions made by the prosecution could be approved as evidence against them. In a dispute over the alleged violations of customs laws on the part of E.A. Boyd, he was forced to present to the investigating officers in his case the invoices confirming the payment of customs fees, but he refused to show these documents in the court. After being found guilty in lower courts Boyd appealed to the Supreme Court, arguing that his Fourth Amendment rights had been violated.

Analyzing for the first time the meaning of the Search and Seizure Clause, the justices produced a unanimous decision (with two concurring opinions) declaring that the presentation of someone's private documents in a trial constitutes a search and seizure under the provisions of the Constitution. According to the justices, even the absence of the physical presence of federal officers in Boyd's home or office did not change the fact that the documents used against him in the litigation were his private property and therefore protected by the Fourth Amendment. By referring to the English, colonial, and early American history of the government's role in conducting searches and seizures, the author of the Court's opinion, Justice William P. Bradley, confirmed the necessary limitations on the actions of law enforcement agencies set out in the Amendment's provisions:

> "The principles laid down in this opinion affect the very essence of constitutional liberty and security. They reach farther than the concrete form of the case then before the court, with its adventitious circumstances; they apply to all invasions on the part of the government and its employees of the sanctity of a man's home and the privacies of life. It is not the breaking of his doors and the rummaging of his drawers that constitutes the essence of the offence, but it is the invasion of his indefeasible right of personal security, personal liberty, and private property..."[92]

As Boyd was forced to produce the invoices to the officers, he claimed that the later use of these documents in a court against him also constituted a violation of the protection against self-incrimination contained in the Fifth Amendment. Approving of such an interpretation, Justice Bradley argued in his concurring opinion that the principles protecting American citizens, introduced in both the Fourth and Fifth Amendments, were similarly significant in U.S. constitutional law:

> "We have already noticed the intimate relation between the two amendments. They throw great light on each other. For the "unreasonable searches and seizures" condemned in the Fourth Amendment are almost always made for the purpose of compelling a man to give evidence against himself, which, in criminal cases, is condemned in the Fifth Amendment, and compelling a man "in a criminal case to be a witness against himself," which is condemned in the Fifth Amendment, throws light on the question as to what is an "unreasonable search and seizure" within the meaning of the Fourth Amendment. And we have been unable to perceive that the seizure of a man's private books and papers to be used in evidence against him is substantially different from compelling him to be a witness against himself. We think it is within the clear intent and meaning of those terms."[93]

---

92 116 U.S. 616 (1886) at 630.
93 *Ibid.* at 633.

In this Justice Bradley not only explained the sources and character of the Amendment's provisions, but he also initiated an interpretation which led to the future understanding of the admissibility and inadmissibility of evidence in the proceedings of courts.

One of the most important aspects of the Court's interpretation of the Search and Seizure Clause was the determination of the reasonableness of government procedures regarding the conduct of a search as an element of a pending investigation. The issue was addressed in the early 20th century dispute *Weeks v. United States*, which concerned the actions undertaken by federal officers against a man suspected of illegally distributing lottery tickets via mail. Following the warrantless arrest of Fremont Weeks, agents searched his premises and seized his private letters and documents, which were later used in court as evidence of his guilt. Weeks appealed to the Supreme Court, claiming that his Fourth Amendment rights had been violated by law enforcement officers who did not obtain the search warrant necessary to enter his house and collect evidence against him. In a unanimous decision authored by William R. Day, the justices supported the argumentation presented in support of the defendant, whose constitutional rights were encroached upon by the governments' imposition of an unreasonable search and seizure of his private property. The lack of a warrant was the crucial determinant of the Court's approach, resulting in the creation of the so-called exclusionary rule, which set a limit to illegal searches conducted by the government authorities. According to the rule, all evidence that was collected without a warrant by federal officers during an investigative procedure was unconstitutional and could not be used in a judicial criminal proceeding:

> "If letters and private documents can thus be seized and held and used in evidence against a citizen accused of an offense, the protection of the 4th Amendment, declaring his right to be secure against such searches and seizures, is of no value, and, so far as those thus placed are concerned, might as well be stricken from the Constitution... The United States marshal could only have invaded the house of the accused when armed with a warrant issued as required by the Constitution, upon sworn information, and describing with reasonable particularity the thing for which the search was to be made. Instead, he acted without sanction of law, doubtless prompted by the desire to bring further proof to the aid of the

> government, and under color of his office undertook to make a seizure of private papers in direct violation of the constitutional prohibition against such action."[94]

Weeks, based on the Court's interpretation of the Fourth Amendment as presented in *Boyd*, was the first significant SCOTUS ruling to limit the scope of government search and seizure powers. It was addressed, however, only to the federal government, therefore the exclusionary rule was not yet fundamental enough in the eyes of the justices for it to be applicable also in the state jurisdictions. Such a situation occurred in the early 1960s, as a result of the Court's decision in *Mapp v. Ohio*, but already in 1949, in *Wolf v. Colorado*, the SCOTUS had an opportunity to expand the scope of the Amendment's reach.

The issue concerned illegal abortions being performed by Julius Wolf in Colorado. During the investigation, state law enforcement officers entered Wolf's clinic without a warrant and collected documentation which was used in a trial against the physician. By referring to the *Weeks* precedent and invoking the exclusionary rule, the defendant claimed that the evidence could not be admissible in his case, but the state courts rejected his argumentation and convicted the physician. The Supreme Court decided the case on appeal, addressing the question of the scope of Fourth Amendment's exclusionary rule. In a majority opinion written by Justice Felix Frankfurter, the SCOTUS confirmed the findings and conclusions of the *Weeks* decision but refused to expand the Amendment's binding character, referring to other similar cases in which justices were reluctant to use the Fourteenth Amendment as a tool with which to impose criminal procedure amendments on the states:

> "Unlike the specific requirements and restrictions placed by the Bill of Rights (Amendments I to VIII) upon the administration of criminal justice by federal authority, the Fourteenth Amendment did not subject criminal justice in the States to specific limitations. The notion that the "due process of law" guaranteed by the Fourteenth Amendment is shorthand for the first eight amendments of the Constitution, and thereby incorporates them, has been rejected by this Court again and again, after impressive consideration."[95]

Frankfurter argued that Wolf's due process of law was not violated, as the exclusionary rule and other limitations stemming from the Court's earlier

---

94 232 U.S. 383 (1914), at 393.
95 338 U.S. 25 (1949), at 26.

jurisprudence were only applicable to the federal government and could not be applied to state governments. In the conclusion of the opinion the justices suggested that only congressional action may effectively expand the scope of the Fourth Amendment's exclusionary rule:

> "We hold, therefore, that, in a prosecution in a State court for a State crime, the Fourteenth Amendment does not forbid the admission of evidence obtained by an unreasonable search and seizure. And though we have interpreted the Fourth Amendment to forbid the admission of such evidence, a different question would be presented if Congress, under its legislative powers, were to pass a statute purporting to negate the *Weeks* doctrine. We would then be faced with the problem of the respect to be accorded the legislative judgment on an issue as to which, in default of that judgment, we have been forced to depend upon our own. Problems of a converse character, also not before us, would be presented should Congress, under § 5 of the Fourteenth Amendment, undertake to enforce the rights there guaranteed by attempting to make the *Weeks* doctrine binding upon the States."[96]

Despite the Court's suggestion, in the next decade Congress did not implement any legislation which would expand the meaning of the exclusionary rule into the states, and the issue came back to the judicial branch in a dispute concerning a search and seizure operation conducted by Ohio law enforcement in the late 1950s. In the course of an investigation Cleveland police officers entered Dollree Mapp's abode in search of an individual suspected of bombing her ex-husband's house. The policemen showed the house owner a document claiming it was a warrant, and Mapp took it but did not read it and the document was later lost and thus could not be presented in court. Still, officers conducted a search and found, among other things, illegal obscene materials, possession of which was a crime under Ohio law. Mapp was arrested, tried, and convicted of a felony; she appealed to the Supreme Court, which reviewed the case in 1961 and overturned her conviction.

The main theme of the dispute was the determination of the behavior of the policemen who conducted the search and seized Mapp's property in the absence of a binding warrant that could be presented to the court. In a 6-3 decision, the SCOTUS supported the argumentation critical of the law enforcement officers who did not fulfill their constitutional duties. The

---

96 *Ibid.* at 33.

majority opinion invoked the Court's rulings from both *Boyd* and *Weeks*, rejecting, at the same time, the possibility of applying the rationale from *Wolf* in Mapp's case:

> "It therefore plainly appears that the factual considerations supporting the failure of the *Wolf* Court to include the *Weeks* exclusionary rule when it recognized the enforceability of the right to privacy against the States in 1949, while not basically relevant to the constitutional consideration, could not, in any analysis, now be deemed controlling."[97]

By referring to the evolution of the exclusionary rule on the state level, the justices pointed out that this principle was fundamental to the effectiveness of the Fourth Amendment's protections of individuals against the intrusion of the government into their affairs:

> "Since the Fourth Amendment's right of privacy has been declared enforceable against the States through the Due Process Clause of the Fourteenth, it is enforceable against them by the same sanction of exclusion as is used against the Federal Government. Were it otherwise, then, just as without the *Weeks* rule the assurance against unreasonable federal searches and seizures would be "a form of words," valueless and undeserving of mention in a perpetual charter of inestimable human liberties, so too, without that rule, the freedom from state invasions of privacy would be so ephemeral and so neatly severed from its conceptual nexus with the freedom from all brutish means of coercing evidence as not to merit this Court's high regard as a freedom implicit in the concept of ordered liberty."[98]

As a consequence of Court's opinion, the Fourth Amendment's prohibition of the use of unconstitutionally obtained evidence, even if it was valid and reliable, was made binding on all jurisdictions, both federal and state. The decision became a crucial precedent in the process of the incorporation of the Bill of Rights by the states, and a judgment which shaped the contemporary understanding of the scope of the admissibility of evidence in criminal trials, despite the fact that in the following decades there were other precedents which modified the understanding of the Fourth Amendment's Search and Seizure Clause, as well as the Warrant Clause. In particular, during the 1960s there were cases in which the justices redefined the meaning of

---

97 367 U.S. 643 (1961), at 653.
98 *Ibid.* at 655.

probable cause, including the famous *Terry v. Ohio* dispute concerning the police's stop and frisk procedure.

In an almost unanimous decision, the SCOTUS expanded the powers of law enforcement by holding that experienced officers could conduct search and seizure on the people they stopped, based on reasonable suspicion. In weighing two conflicting values, the guarantee of suspects to be subject to reasonable search and seizure procedures, and the right of the government to conduct search and seizure effectively and without threat to the life of law enforcement officers, the justices chose the latter, arguing, however, that all other conditions constituting a legal search and seizure must be met:

> "We merely hold today that, where a police officer observes unusual conduct which leads him reasonably to conclude in light of his experience that criminal activity may be afoot and that the persons with whom he is dealing may be armed and presently dangerous, where, in the course of investigating this behavior, he identifies himself as a policeman and makes reasonable inquiries, and where nothing in the initial stages of the encounter serves to dispel his reasonable fear for his own or others' safety, he is entitled for the protection of himself and others in the area to conduct a carefully limited search of the outer clothing of such persons in an attempt to discover weapons which might be used to assault him."[99]

In the following years the SCOTUS had an opportunity to broaden the catalogue of exceptions in which the government could apply a less strict standard in carrying out search and seizure procedures. It is worth mentioning here exceptions concerning automobiles (stemming from complex and multi-threaded circumstances related to the type of activity and the reasons for stopping and searching a car), border searches (based on legislation referring to the security of borders and the role of U.S. Border Patrol), plain view doctrine (when evidence, for which there is probable cause, is visible to the searcher), or other circumstances legitimizing a quick and warrantless search of people or places aimed at protecting people's lives.[100] Still, the *Mapp* rationale has remained untouched, making the exclusionary rule one of the leading exceptions imposed on the investigative powers of domestic law enforcement units.

---

99 392 U.S. 1 (1968), at 30.

100 See: Phillip A. Hubbart, *Making Sense of Search and Seizure Law: A Fourth Amendment Handbook*, Carolina Academic Press, Durham 2015.

The SCOTUS and Domestic Surveillance: From *Olmstead* to *Katz*

Despite the importance of Court judgments with respect to the scope of the Search and Seizure and the Warrant clauses of the Fourth Amendment, the main purpose of this research is to analyze justices' approach to the surveillance policies of the government in the context of the legitimization of these policies. Taking into consideration the SCOTUS' adjudication in disputes concerning the scope of government powers and the rights of individuals arising from the interpretation of the Amendment, it seems indispensable to focus on precedents which explain the circumstances and conditions in which law enforcement officers could impose surveillance measures without violating the Fourth Amendment rights of suspects and defendants.

Not surprisingly, in time surveillance became one of the most effective tools for collecting evidence in criminal investigations, and the measures imposed by federal agents and state and local police became the subject of analysis of the judicial branch, as it was responsible for determining their constitutionality. With the evolution of the relevant technology and the appearance of new means of interception, such as the wiretapping of telegraph or telephone lines, it became obvious that, for the purposes of law enforcement, the government would use new surveillance measures extensively, justifying this with the need to protect the country and society from the negative consequences of the growing crime rate. The frequency of government surveillance increased proportionally with the growth of criminal activities within the society, as successful investigations were dependent upon the effectiveness of evidence presented by the prosecution during a trial. Consequently, the use of new means of collecting information which, directly or indirectly, led to the acquisition of evidence of a crime having been committed, became the fundamental role of law enforcement institutions. This sometimes resulted in a closer collaboration between the police and telegraph or telephone companies, which were involved in the process of wiretapping despite the lack of judicially approved warrants and legislation prohibiting such practices.[101] At the turn of the 19th and 20th

101 See: David Gray, *The Fourth Amendment in an Age of Surveillance*, Harvard University Press, New York 2017.

centuries the problem became significant in several state jurisdictions, as well as at the federal level, raising concerns about the constitutionality of wiretapping as a technique for collecting evidence, and possible intrusion by the government into the privacy of its citizens.

The first cases pertaining to the issue of surveillance interpreted from the perspective of the Fourth Amendment's prohibition of unreasonable searches and seizures were decided by the SCOTUS in the late 1920s. This period marks a significant moment in U.S. history, with the growing problem of crime, including organized crime, stemming from the challenges of the Prohibition era. In order to prevent such crimes as the illegal production or smuggling of forbidden substances, federal agents used wiretapping devices to listen to telephone conversations, thus obtaining evidence against criminal suspects. Among several disputes reaching lower federal courts there were three which were adjudicated together by the Supreme Court – *Olmstead et. al. v. United States*, *Green et. al. v. United States* and *McInnis v. United States* – unified under the name of *Olmstead*[102]. The lower courts found Olmstead, Green, McInnis, and others guilty of conspiracy and of smuggling, possessing, and selling intoxicating liquors in violation of the National Prohibition Act, based on the evidence obtained from wiretapped phone calls. Importantly, the wiretaps were installed by federal agents without judicial approval. The main issue the Court confronted was the constitutionality of the evidence collected from the wiretapped private telephone conversations.

In a narrow-margin opinion signed by Chief Justice William Howard Taft, the Court affirmed the lower courts' decisions, arguing that the constitutional rights of the defendants had not been violated. On the one hand, Taft rejected the possibility of using the Fifth Amendment's protection against self-incrimination as the basis for reversing the judgment, as Olmstead and others were not forced to conduct conversations over the phone. On the other, the Court focused on the Fourth Amendment's ban on unreasonable searches and seizures as a potential limitation of the powers of federal agents to wiretap the telephone conversations of private persons. By referring to the historical meaning of that provision

102 277 U.S. 438 (1928).

and providing reference to several important SCOTUS precedents, Justice Taft differentiated between telephone wiretaps and other types of physical intrusion into a person's privacy:

> "The well known historical purpose of the Fourth Amendment, directed against general warrants and writs of assistance, was to prevent the use of governmental force to search a man's house, his person, his papers, and his effects, and to prevent their seizure against his will... The amendment itself shows that the search is to be of material things-the person, the house, his papers, or his effects. The description of the warrant necessary to make the proceeding lawful is that it must specify the place to be searched and the person or things to be seized."[103]

Thus, the Court differentiated between telephone wiretaps conducted beyond someone's actual premises and other types of physical intrusion into a person's privacy, including a search of their homes, expanding the powers of federal agents to wiretapping private telephones and using the obtained material (conversations) as evidence in court proceedings. As Taft stressed, in the case of phone wiretapping, "[t]here was no searching. There was no seizure. The evidence was secured by the use of the sense of hearing and that only. There was no entry of the houses or offices of the defendants."[104] In this way the Court introduced the so-called trespass doctrine, which made the constitutionality of the government's surveillance actions dependent upon a physical intrusion into someone's property.

Writing the majority opinion, the Chief Justice referred also to *Carroll v. United States*, in which SCOTUS determined the historical scope of the Fourth Amendment's unreasonable Searches and Seizure Clause and defined the factors limiting the constitutional protection the Amendment provided to private persons:

> "The Fourth Amendment is to be construed in the light of what was deemed an unreasonable search and seizure when it was adopted, and in a manner which will conserve public interests, as well as the interest and rights of individual citizens."[105]

The reference to the public interest seems crucial for the early 20th century understanding of the right to privacy via the interests of the government

103 *Ibid.* at 463.
104 *Ibid.* at 464.
105 *Ibid.* at 465.

in fighting organized crime. The political and social context of the dispute had an impact on the majority of justices, who believed that the public interest overweighed individual rights, despite their acknowledgment of the "interest of liberty" as construed by the Framers of the Constitution. Justices did not reject the possibility of expanding the scope of the Fourth Amendment's protection, but they left the responsibility for such a change to the legislative branch rather than the judiciary:

> "Congress may, of course, protect the secrecy of telephone messages by making them, when intercepted, inadmissible in evidence in federal criminal trials, by direct legislation, and thus depart from the common law of evidence. But the courts may not adopt such a policy by attributing an enlarged and unusual meaning to the Fourth Amendment. The reasonable view is that one who installs in his house a telephone instrument with connecting wires intends to project his voice to those quite outside, and that the wires beyond his house, and messages while passing over them, are not within the protection of the Fourth Amendment. Here those who intercepted the projected voices were not in the house of either party to the conversation."[106]

Although there was no direct reference to the *McCulloch* rationale, by limiting the scope of the Searches and Seizure Clause Taft created an exception based not only on the lack of a physical intrusion into the right to privacy, but also to the general interest of the public, which could be understood as the imperative to capture, try, and punish criminals threatening social order and the proper functioning of the state. In this manner the Court abandoned the traditional interpretation of the Fourth Amendment, which was historically implemented to protect individuals from governmental intrusion, prioritizing the effectiveness of law enforcement over ethical conduct. As Taft wrote: "nice ethical conduct by government officials would make society suffer and give criminals greater immunity than has been known heretofore".[107] Sometime later, the chief justice confirmed his views on the topic in a private correspondence:

> "If they think we are going to be frightened in our effort to stand by the law and give the public a chance to punish criminals, they are mistaken, even though we are condemned for lack of high ideals."[108]

---

106 *Ibid.* at 465, 466.

107 *Ibid.* at 468.

108 Robert C. Post, *The Taft Court: Making Law for a Divided Nation, 1921–1930*, Cambridge University Press, New York 2023.

Apart from the majority decision, four justices dissented, including Justice Oliver Wendell Holmes, who criticized the Court's argumentation, arguing that wiretapping was a "dirty business", as well as Justice Louis D. Brandeis, who praised the importance of privacy and refuted the possibility of the government's violation of law in the name of protecting the public from the negative consequences of crime:

> "The makers of our Constitution undertook to secure conditions favorable to the pursuit of happiness. They recognized the significance of man's spiritual nature, of his feelings and of his intellect. They knew that only a part of the pain, pleasure and satisfactions of life are to be found in material things. They sought to protect Americans in their beliefs, their thoughts, their emotions and their sensations. They conferred, as against the government, the right to be let alone-the most comprehensive of rights and the right most valued by civilized men. To protect, that right, every unjustifiable intrusion by the government upon the privacy of the individual, whatever the means employed, must be deemed a violation of the Fourth Amendment."[109]

As a consequence of the 1928 precedent, wiretapping as a form of domestic surveillance imposed by the government was defined as legal, although as early as in 1934 Congress implemented the Communications Act, which prohibited the use of evidence obtained through wiretapping in federal litigation.[110] A few years later the SCOTUS confirmed the constitutionality of such a ban in *Nardone v. United States*, a dispute concerning a conviction for revenue fraud, claiming that evidence obtained directly from wiretapping was inadmissible in federal criminal trials.[111]

At the state level the laws had been changing in the direction of a gradual limitation of the powers of state authorities to impose surveillance measures, and by the early 1960s about two-thirds of states prohibited wiretapping; however, twenty-seven of them permitted interception of some type, providing for certain exemptions from the general prohibition of illegal surveillance. There were also seven states which allowed electronic eavesdropping based on a court order, New York among them.[112] Until the 1960s, courts did not refer too often to the Fourth Amendment from

109 Brandeis, dissenting, 277 U.S. 438 (1928), at 478.
110 § 605 of *Communications Act*, 48 Stat. 1064 (1934).
111 308 U.S. 338 (1939).
112 See: *Berger v. New York* 338 U.S. 41 (1967), at 47.

the perspective of domestic surveillance, but then in 1967 the SCOTUS adjudicated in two important cases concerning governmental wiretapping: a state dispute – *Berger v. New York*; and a federal case – *Katz v. United States*.

Both disputes serve as examples of the limiting of the powers of law enforcement entities, although they referred to different levels of government intrusion into the rights of individuals. In the first case, New York police officers obtained a wiretap warrant and surveilled a legal attorney named Ralph Berger, who was suspected of corruptive behavior. The warrant was based on a state law which set rules and procedures regarding the duration and manner of evidence collection conducted as a consequence of the use of surveillance measures. As a result of the "bugging" of Berger's telephone, the police collected evidence against him and used it in court during a criminal trial. In an 8-1 opinion authored by Justice Thomas Clark, the Supreme Court held the New York law to be unconstitutional mainly due to the lack of judicial supervision of the eavesdropping procedures:

> "The Fourth Amendment commands that a warrant issue not only upon probable cause supported by oath or affirmation, but also "particularly describing the place to be searched, and the persons or things to be seized." New York's statute lacks this particularization. It merely says that a warrant may issue on reasonable ground to believe that evidence of crime may be obtained by the eavesdrop. It lays down no requirement for particularity in the warrant as to what specific crime has been or is being committed, nor "the place to be searched," or "the persons or things to be seized," as specifically required by the Fourth Amendment. The need for particularity and evidence of reliability in the showing required when judicial authorization of a search is sought is especially great in the case of eavesdropping. By its very nature, eavesdropping involves an intrusion on privacy that is broad in scope."[113]

One of the arguments supporting the Court's rationale referred to the tensions between the use of surveillance measures by the government and the right to privacy of suspects of criminal investigations. Despite acknowledging the government's interest in protecting the safety of the people, Clark stressed, that "[i]n any event, we cannot forgive the requirements of the Fourth Amendment in the name of law enforcement."[114] The majority opinion

---

113 *Ibid.* at 55.
114 *Ibid.* at 62.

quoted the famous concurrence by Chief Justice Earl Warren in *Lopez v. United States*, where the Court upheld the sentencing of a criminal based on evidence obtained thanks to the wiretapping of his conversations with an IRS officer:

> "… the fantastic advances in the field of electronic communication constitute a great danger to the privacy of the individual; … indiscriminate use of such devices in law enforcement raises grave constitutional questions under the Fourth and Fifth Amendments… ."[115]

In this way the scope of surveillance measures imposed by state governments as an element of collecting the evidence necessary for the launching of a criminal investigation was limited by the constitutional requirement that individuals' right to privacy be protected. The SCOTUS did not neglect the vital role of law enforcement in fighting crime, but the justices raised concerns over the methods and techniques used by the police in gathering information. In other words, it was not the aim but the means to which the majority objected, seeing a potential threat to people's privacy in the uncontrolled use of electronic surveillance.

Just a few months later the Court adjudicated in *Katz v. United States*, a federal dispute concerning the use of telephone recordings derived from the electronic surveillance of a telephone booth used by the suspect in a criminal investigation. After collecting preliminary evidence about potential violations of the law on the part of Charles Katz, who was suspected of transmitting gambling information to individuals located in various regions of the country, federal agents decided to attach an eavesdropping device to the phone booth used by him. The surveillance of his conversations produced strong evidence against him, leading to a trial in a district court which found Katz guilty of violating federal law. Importantly, the evidence was gathered without judicial approval; therefore, Katz appealed to the court of appeals which affirmed his sentence, and, as a consequence, the case was brought to the Supreme Court. Katz claimed that federal agents infringed on his Fourth Amendment rights by presenting evidence in court without the necessary warrant.

115 *Ibid.* at 56.

In a 7-1 decision the SCOTUS overturned Katz's conviction, confirming the validity of his argumentation and rejecting the earlier *Olmstead* rationale. According to the justices, Katz had the right to enjoy privacy in the phone booth:

> "The Government's activities in electronically listening to and recording the petitioner's words violated the privacy upon which he justifiably relied while using the telephone booth, and thus constituted a "search and seizure" within the meaning of the Fourth Amendment. The fact that the electronic device employed to achieve that end did not happen to penetrate the wall of the booth can have no constitutional significance."[116]

The Court offered a new approach to the character of searches imposed by the government, rejecting the trespass doctrine and introducing the concept of reasonable expectation of privacy. According to that approach, everyone had a legitimate expectation of privacy once it was recognized as reasonable by the society, or, in practice, once it was determined as reasonable by the judicial branch. In the case of Katz, the use of the phone booth was recognized by the SCOTUS as his enjoying a reasonable expectation of privacy, which meant that the surveillance imposed by federal agents constituted search and seizure as defined by the Fourth Amendment.

The author of the majority decision, Justice Potter Stewart, explained the real scope of the Amendment with regard to individuals' rights, stating famously that it "protects people, not places".[117] Such an approach was a departure from the earlier reasoning established by the *Olmstead* precedent, which made the constitutionality of the government's actions dependent on physical intrusion into a concrete location. Analyzing the procedure conducted by federal officers, the justices underlined the necessity of judicial approval and control of the actions undertaken by law enforcement, even in cases referring to obvious violations of the law:

> "It is apparent that the agents in this case acted with restraint. Yet the inescapable fact is that this restraint was imposed by the agents themselves, not by a judicial officer. They were not required, before commencing the search, to present their estimate of probable cause for detached scrutiny by a neutral magistrate. They were not compelled, during the conduct of the search itself, to observe precise

116 389 U.S. 347 (1967), at 353.
117 *Ibid.* at 351.

> limits established in advance by a specific court order. Nor were they directed, after the search had been completed, to notify the authorizing magistrate in detail of all that had been seized. In the absence of such safeguards, this Court has never sustained a search upon the sole ground that officers reasonably expected to find evidence of a particular crime and voluntarily confined their activities to the least intrusive means consistent with that end."[118]

The only dissenting opinion in *Katz* was written by Justice Hugo Black, who referred to historical argumentation, focusing on the intent of the Founding Fathers and the direct text of the Amendment:

> "The Fourth Amendment was aimed directly at the abhorred practice of breaking in, ransacking and searching homes and other buildings and seizing people's personal belongings without warrants issued by magistrates. The Amendment deserves, and this Court has given it, a liberal construction in order to protect against warrantless searches of buildings and seizures of tangible personal effects. But, until today, this Court has refused to say that eavesdropping comes within the ambit of Fourth Amendment restrictions... The Fourth Amendment protects privacy only to the extent that it prohibits unreasonable searches and seizures of "persons, houses, papers, and effects." No general right is created by the Amendment so as to give this Court the unlimited power to hold unconstitutional everything which affects privacy. Certainly the Framers, well acquainted as they were with the excesses of governmental power, did not intend to grant this Court such omnipotent lawmaking authority as that. The history of governments proves that it is dangerous to freedom to repose such powers in courts."[119]

Despite the fact that Justice Black's dissent referred to the theory of original intent in constitutional interpretation and was critical of the expansion of the scope of the right to privacy, he claimed that the Court's approach was, in general, an example of a dangerous expansion of the meaning of the Constitution. By appealing to judicial restraint, Black observed the dangers and threats to the functioning of the country posed by leaving broad interpretive powers to the judicial branch. Being aware of Black's jurisprudence, it seems obvious that he was critical of Marshall's legitimate end approach and its promotion of the expansion of the meaning of several constitutional clauses and provisions, often resulting in the increase of the powers of the government.

---

118 *Ibid.* at 356, 357.

119 Black, dissenting. *Ibid.* at 367, 374.

As one of the consequences of the *Berger* and *Katz* decisions, as well as other important SCOTUS precedents, including *Miranda v. Arizona* – which determined the scope of the Fifth Amendment protection against self-incrimination[120] – less than a year later Congress passed a new law which partly referred to the scope of government surveillance. The Omnibus Crime Control and Safe Streets Act of 1968 was designed to achieve a double effect: to reduce the rate of crime, on the one hand, and to increase the effectiveness of law enforcement operations on the other. Among its various modifications in the functioning of the criminal justice system, the legislation introduced new principles guiding the imposition of surveillance measures, focusing mainly on the issue of wiretapping and electronic surveillance. In Title III of the document, Congress prohibited the unauthorized interception of wire, oral, or electronic communications by government agencies, and established procedures consistent with the Fourth Amendment in which government officers could obtain a warrant in order to conduct search and seizure without violating anyone's privacy.[121] As a result, minimum standards of privacy protection were established on the federal level which were also binding in all state jurisdictions. The only exceptions present in the Act of 1968 referred to special circumstances allowing for the initiation of interception without a warrant, such as a clear and present threat to the existence of the government, danger to someone's health or life, activities of organized crime, or national security reasons.[122] In the context of the right to privacy, the legislation confirmed the SCOTUS interpretation of the Fourth Amendment, by regulating the use and disclosure of evidence collected as a result of authorized surveillance.

The SCOTUS and Domestic Electronic Surveillance

The advancement of technology and the growing concern over security issues in the 1960s and 1970s increased the activity of the government in using electronic surveillance measures without judicial control. These issues

120 384 U.S. 436 (1966).
121 Title III of the *Omnibus Crime Control and Safe Streets Act*, 82 Stat. 197 (1968).
122 *Ibid.* § 2511.

will be thoroughly discussed in the next chapter, but there is a need to refer here to at least one dispute which raised constitutional concerns as to the character and scope of the right of the executive to authorize electronic surveillance in internal security matters without prior judicial approval. Such activity was challenged in 1972 in *United States v. U.S. District Court*, giving the Court the opportunity not only to present its interpretation of the Fourth Amendment's clauses with regard to the regulations of Omnibus Crime Control and Safe Streets Act, but also to differentiate between domestic and national security issues.

During a federal investigation concerning a conspiracy of members of the radical organization the White Panther Party, suspected of destroying government property and bombing a CIA office, law enforcement agents intercepted the conversations of some of its members via warrantless wiretapping. After the request from the defense to present the evidence collected by the prosecution, U.S. attorney general John Mitchell refused to disclose any surveillance-based material on the basis of the provisions of the 1968 Act. Furthermore, he claimed that the surveillance operation in question had been within the scope of the Fourth Amendment and could be conducted without a warrant due to the Omnibus legislation which allowed such a procedure in the case of the exception defined as a threat to the structure and existence of the government. The judge of the District Court for the Eastern District of Michigan, Damon Keith, rejected the argumentation of the government lawyers, ordering the disclosure of all information collected through the warrantless surveillance. The United States appealed to the Court of Appeals for the Sixth Circuit, which upheld the lower court's judgment, and the dispute was brought before the SCOTUS.

In a unanimous ruling, the justices confirmed the necessity to disclose the wiretapped communications as the surveillance measures imposed by the government were unconstitutional and violated the Fourth Amendment's Warrant Clause. According to the opinion written by Justice Lewis Powell, the procedures applied by the authorities had to be consistent with the Constitution, even if the issues at stake fell into the category of "domestic security":

> "History abundantly documents the tendency of Government -- however benevolent and benign its motive -- to view with suspicion those who most fervently dispute its policies. Fourth Amendment protections become the more necessary when the targets of official surveillance may be those suspected of unorthodoxy in their political beliefs. The danger to political dissent is acute where the Government attempts to act under so vague a concept as the power to protect "domestic security." Given the difficulty of defining the domestic security interest, the danger of abuse in acting to protect that interest becomes apparent."[123]

Consequently, Powell referred to the values of American democracy, including freedom and security, noticing the danger of the government's abuse of citizens' privacy during the conduct of electronic surveillance. The Court offered a balancing test of the conflicting values of people's free expression and privacy versus the necessity to protect domestic security on the part of the government. The vulnerability of the circumstances of the case, where federal officers were spying on U.S. citizens without judicial approval and control, forced Powell to use strong arguments against such a situation:

> "The price of lawful public dissent must not be a dread of subjection to an unchecked surveillance power. Nor must the fear of unauthorized official eavesdropping deter vigorous citizen dissent and discussion of Government action in private conversation. For private dissent, no less than open public discourse, is essential to our free society... As the Fourth Amendment is not absolute in its terms, our task is to examine and balance the basic values at stake in this case: the duty of Government to protect the domestic security, and the potential danger posed by unreasonable surveillance to individual privacy and free expression. If the legitimate need of Government to safeguard domestic security requires the use of electronic surveillance, the question is whether the needs of citizens for privacy and free expression may not be better protected by requiring a warrant before such surveillance is undertaken. We must also ask whether a warrant requirement would unduly frustrate the efforts of Government to protect itself from acts of subversion and overthrow directed against it."[124]

Analyzing the institutional and systemic aspects of government surveillance, the justices agreed that the impact of the executive branch, despite its crucial role in providing security to the country and its citizens, should be limited. One of the biggest threats to democracy and the principle of the separation

---

123 407 U.S. 297 (1972), at 314.
124 *Ibid.* at 314, 315.

of powers was the lack of judicial control over the process of obtaining warrants for the electronic surveillance of Americans:

> "These Fourth Amendment freedoms cannot properly be guaranteed if domestic security surveillances may be conducted solely within the discretion of the Executive Branch. The Fourth Amendment does not contemplate the executive officers of Government as neutral and disinterested magistrates. Their duty and responsibility are to enforce the laws, to investigate, and to prosecute... But those charged with this investigative and prosecutorial duty should not be the sole judges of when to utilize constitutionally sensitive means in pursuing their tasks. The historical judgment, which the Fourth Amendment accepts, is that unreviewed executive discretion may yield too readily to pressures to obtain incriminating evidence and overlook potential invasions of privacy and protected speech."[125]

The Court agreed with the government that issues related to domestic security should produce exceptions as compared to ordinary criminal investigations, but the justices disapproved of the possibility of leaving the whole procedure to the discretion of the executive. On the other hand, they raised arguments strengthening the role of the judiciary in supporting government policies aimed at strengthening the security of citizens:

> "There is no reason to believe that federal judges will be insensitive to or uncomprehending of the issues involved in domestic security cases. Certainly courts can recognize that domestic security surveillance involves different considerations from the surveillance of "ordinary crime." If the threat is too subtle or complex for our senior law enforcement officers to convey its significance to a court, one may question whether there is probable cause for surveillance."[126]

Furthermore, the SCOTUS differentiated between domestic and national security issues, affirming the possibility of applying a different standard to circumstances constituting "legitimate need of government for intelligence information", but even then the reasonableness of the search and seizure should be sustained.[127] In conclusion, the Court, once again, stressed the necessity to apply Fourth Amendment standards to electronic surveillance conducted by the authorities in cases relating to domestic security.

---

125 *Ibid.* at 316, 317.
126 *Ibid.* at 320.
127 *Ibid.* at 323.

As Lester observes, the *United States v. U.S. District Court* precedent became a crucial reference in disputes concerning domestic surveillance, as well as a leading guide for Congress in the establishment of appropriate standards of electronic surveillance.[128] Although the opinion did not determine the mode and character of foreign or national security surveillance, these issues were to become one of the biggest challenges of the coming years, especially in the context of congressional investigations into potential abuses of power by the executive. On the one hand, there were numerous allegations about the illegal surveillance measures conducted by the NSA, CIA, and FBI, and, on the other, the country was to witness the most serious investigation of people associated with the presidential administration suspected of the unauthorized planting of electronic surveillance devices which led to the so-called Watergate scandal and, as a consequence, to the biggest congressional investigation into the legality of government surveillance in U.S. history (see chapter 3).

In the same year, in *Laird v. Tatum*, the SCOTUS faced a challenge concerning the alleged surveillance of various political organizations by the U.S. Army. Although the justices dismissed the suit based on its lack of ripeness, Chief Justice Warren Burger openly admitted in the majority opinion that if there were cases of concrete injuries of U.S. citizens resulting from military-ordered surveillance, the Court would not hesitate to review them and limit such interception as unconstitutional, especially in times of peace:

> "The concerns of the Executive and Legislative Branches in response to disclosure of the Army surveillance activities -- and indeed the claims alleged in the complaint -- reflect a traditional and strong resistance of Americans to any military intrusion into civilian affairs. That tradition has deep roots in our history, and found early expression, for example, in the Third Amendment's explicit prohibition against quartering soldiers in private homes without consent, and ın the constitutional provisions for civilian control of the military. Those prohibitions are not directly presented by this case, but their philosophical underpinnings explain our traditional insistence on limitations on military operations in peacetime. Indeed, when presented with claims of judicially cognizable injury resulting from military

---

128 Genvieve Lester, *When Should State Secrets Stay Secret? Accountability, Democratic Governance, and Intelligence*, Cambridge University Press, New York 2015, p. 42.

> intrusion into the civilian sector, federal courts are fully empowered to consider claims of those asserting such injury; there is nothing in our Nation's history or in this Court's decided cases, including our holding today, that can properly be seen as giving any indication that actual or threatened injury by reason of unlawful activities of the military would go unnoticed or unremedied."[129]

Although the dispute did not bring any new approaches towards the SCOTUS' constitutional interpretation of domestic surveillance, it clearly drew a jurisdictional line between military and civilian operations, suggesting that Army-approved interception would receive a different kind of scrutiny in judicial proceedings.

In the late 1970s, in domestic surveillance cases the Court continued to promote the reasonable expectation of privacy concept, as in its famous ruling in *Smith v. Maryland* concerning the warrantless use of a telephone pen register by law enforcement officers in a pending criminal investigation. Based on information obtained by the police from the victim of a robbery who was threatened by the alleged robber over the phone, the officers collected information from the telephone company on the numbers dialed by the suspect thanks to the use of a pen register. After another phone call from the suspect to the victim, the police obtained a search warrant, as a result of which Smith was arrested and put on trial. Although he tried to challenge the procedure, which led to the search and his arrest on the basis of a warrantless pen register installation, Smith lost in state courts and the dispute was brought to the Supreme Court on appeal.

The divided SCOTUS presented a decision supporting the government's argumentation. According to the majority opinion written by Justice Harry Blackmun, the procedure of recording phone numbers through a pen register did not require a search warrant due to the fact that information about such numbers was given voluntarily to the phone companies by customers. In other words, there was no expectation of privacy to cover the numbers dialed into a telephone system, which meant a lack of the violation of the Fourth Amendment's warrant requirements. Speaking for the Court, Justice Blackmun claimed that the scope of Fourth Amendment's protection was not determined by the mode of operation of telephone companies:

---

129 408 U.S. 1 (1972), at 15, 16.

"The fortuity of whether or not the phone company in fact elects to make a quasi-permanent record of a particular number dialed does not, in our view, make any constitutional difference. Regardless of the phone company's election, petitioner voluntarily conveyed to it information that it had facilities for recording and that it was free to record. In these circumstances, petitioner assumed the risk that the information would be divulged to police. Under petitioner's theory, Fourth Amendment protection would exist, or not, depending on how the telephone company chose to define local-dialing zones, and depending on how it chose to bill its customers for local calls. Calls placed across town, or dialed directly, would be protected; calls placed across the river, or dialed with operator assistance, might not be. We are not inclined to make a crazy quilt of the Fourth Amendment, especially in circumstances where (as here) the pattern of protection would be dictated by billing practices of a private corporation. We therefore conclude that petitioner in all probability entertained no actual expectation of privacy in the phone numbers he dialed, and that, even if he did, his expectation was not "legitimate." The installation and use of a pen register, consequently, was not a "search," and no warrant was required."[130]

In a dissenting opinion, Justice Potter Stewart argued that a person who used a telephone has a reasonable expectation of privacy regarding the content of a call, and that any information connected to such a call, including the numbers dialed, should be protected by the Fourth Amendment. Accordingly, Justice Thurgood Marshall stated that registering the phone with a telephone company should not result in a potential governmental surveillance of telephone records, which were constitutionally protected by the Fourth Amendment:

"Privacy is not a discrete commodity, possessed absolutely or not at all. Those who disclose certain facts to a bank or phone company for a limited business purpose need not assume that this information will be released to other persons for other purposes."[131]

Furthermore, Marshall claimed that permitting the use of pen registers could limit fundamental freedoms, such as freedom of speech and freedom of political opinions:

"Permitting governmental access to telephone records on less than probable cause may thus impede certain forms of political affiliation and journalistic endeavor that are the hallmark of a truly free society. Particularly given the Government's

130 442 U.S. 735 (1979), at 745 746.
131 Marshall, dissenting. *Ibid.* at 749.

> previous reliance on warrantless telephonic surveillance to trace reporters' sources and monitor protected political activity, I am unwilling to insulate use of pen registers from independent judicial review."[132]

The *Smith* decision became one of the most important Court rulings on the issue of surveillance and the right to privacy. There are at least three reasoned conclusions in support of this argument. First, the main consequence of the precedent was the limitation of the right to privacy, and, more concretely, a narrowing of the scope of the reasonable expectation of privacy, contrary to the Court findings in the 1960s rulings. Second, the justices introduced the "third party doctrine", according to which collecting phone records or other data without probable cause or individual court review was still constitutional, thus expanding the surveillance measures that could be imposed by the government. And third, although the ruling was announced in 1979, it still serves as the main reference for the SCOTUS interpretation of the Fourth Amendment with regard to the collection of metadata by the government – a problem which became a leading concern in recent years, especially in the aftermath of the Snowden Affair and the growing scale of mass surveillance imposed on the population by the government.

The understanding of privacy with regard to the scope of the Fourth Amendment and government surveillance was the subject of the Court's adjudication in two 1986 cases, *California v. Ciraolo* and *Dow Chemical Co. v. United States*. The circumstances of the first dispute refer to the actions undertaken by state police, who used a plane to fly over the property of a person suspected of growing marijuana plants in order to take aerial photos as evidence of his criminal activity. On the basis of these aerial observations the police obtained a search warrant and entered Ciraolo's house, collecting evidence against him which was later used in a trial during which he pleaded guilty. On appeal to the Supreme Court, Ciraolo claimed that his Fourth Amendment rights had been violated by the police taking photos without a necessary warrant. In a narrow margin opinion, the SCOTUS rejected its earlier rationale established in *Katz* and limited the constitutional protection of private property, arguing that law enforcement officers could use the evidence gathered as a result of warrantless "naked

132 *Ibid.* at 751.

eye" surveillance of someone's premises. By referring to the common law curtilage doctrine, the Court found that there was no reasonable expectation of privacy during an external observation of someone's premises by the police:

> "In an age where private and commercial flight in the public airways is routine, it is unreasonable for respondent to expect that his marijuana plants were constitutionally protected from being observed with the naked eye from an altitude of 1,000 feet. The Fourth Amendment simply does not require the police traveling in the public airways at this altitude to obtain a warrant in order to observe what is visible to the naked eye."[133]

Similarly, the second dispute concerned aerial photographs of premises which were the property of the Dow Chemical Company and which were taken by the Environmental Protection Agency (EPA). The company filed suit against the Agency, challenging the inspection as an act of illegal surveillance on the basis of its expectation of privacy protected by the Fourth Amendment's Search and Seizure Clause. Lower courts reached contradictory verdicts, as the district court ruled in favor of Doe, and the court of appeals reversed the decision, arguing that aerial pictures did not violate the privacy of indoor property. Such an approach was affirmed by the SCOTUS majority, claiming that a warrant was not necessary in the case of surveillance activities of governmental agencies which covered an area not subject to protection from observation. In that context, the actions undertaken by the EPA were legitimized by the concept of the open fields doctrine, confirmed in the majority opinion authored by Chief Justice Warren Burger. The Court argued that when there was no reasonable expectation of privacy, as in the case of aerial pictures taken by the Agency, the Fourth Amendment protection of private persons and their premises did not apply:

> "We conclude that the open areas of an industrial plant complex with numerous plant structures spread over an area of 2,000 acres are not analogous to the "curtilage" of a dwelling for purposes of aerial surveillance; such an industrial complex is more comparable to an open field, and, as such, it is open to the view and observation of persons in aircraft lawfully in the public airspace immediately above or sufficiently near the area for the reach of cameras. We hold that the

133 476 U.S. 207 (1986), at 215.

> taking of aerial photographs of an industrial plant complex from navigable airspace is not a search prohibited by the Fourth Amendment."[134]

Fifteen years later, in *Kyllo v. United States*, the Court seemed to rethink that idea, at least with respect to the technology used to spy on a home. An agent of the Department of the Interior used a thermal-image scanner to analyze the heat emanating from Danny Kyllo's premises, in which he was suspected to be growing marijuana. After finding out that there were suspicious areas of heat in Kyllo's home and receiving information from other sources, the agent obtained a search warrant which resulted in the collection of evidence of illegal marijuana cultivation. The defendant claimed that his Fourth Amendment's rights had been violated by the government, which had conducted an unconstitutional search of his premises, but lower courts disagreed, and Kyllo was found guilty. The SCOTUS, on appeal, reviewed the constitutionality of the use of thermal-imaging devices as a source of collecting evidence in criminal investigations and reversed the lower court's verdict.

In another narrow margin decision, the justices made several references to the surveillance measures imposed by the government, claiming that "[i]t would be foolish to contend that the degree of privacy secured to citizens by the Fourth Amendment has been entirely unaffected by the advance of technology," and that "[t]he Fourth Amendment's protection of the home has never been tied to measurement of the quality or quantity of information obtained."[135] In the majority opinion announced by Justice Antonin Scalia, the Court extended the definition of "search" in the context of the surveillance tools used by the federal agent:

> "Where, as here, the Government uses a device that is not in general public use, to explore details of the home that would previously have been unknowable without physical intrusion, the surveillance is a "search" and is presumptively unreasonable without a warrant."[136]

The divisions between the justices were visible in the number and the language of the dissenting opinions produced in the dispute. Especially

---

134 476 U.S. 227 (1986), at 239.
135 533 U.S. 27 (2001), at 37.
136 *Ibid.* at 40.

important were the arguments raised by Justice John Paul Stevens in his dissent, acknowledging the public interest in ensuring that the government may effectively monitor what is happening within the society:

> "Notwithstanding the implications of today's decision, there is a strong public interest in avoiding constitutional litigation over the monitoring of emissions from homes, and over the inferences drawn from such monitoring. Just as "the police cannot reasonably be expected to avert their eyes from evidence of criminal activity that could have been observed by any member of the public," *Greenwood,* 486 U. S., at 41, so too public officials should not have to avert their senses or their equipment from detecting emissions in the public domain such as excessive heat, traces of smoke, suspicious odors, odorless gases, airborne particulates, or radioactive emissions, any of which could identify hazards to the community. In my judgment, monitoring such emissions with "sense-enhancing technology," *ante,* at 34, and drawing useful conclusions from such monitoring, is an entirely reasonable public service."[137]

One of the recent SCOTUS decisions focusing on the use of surveillance devices in the operation of law enforcement officers was *United States v. Jones*. Antoine Jones was suspected of drug trafficking and was surveilled by the police with the use of a GPS tracker which was installed on his car. The tracker was legally attached to the car on the basis of a warrant, but the document set time and geographical limits (D.C. area) which were exceeded by the scope of the surveillance conducted. The evidence collected as a result of the search was used against Jones in the court, but the jury acquitted him. After two years the government accused Jones again, and this time he was convicted of taking part in the distribution of drugs. On appeal the U.S. Court of Appeals for the District of Columbia Circuit overturned his conviction, and the case was brought to the Supreme Court. The main issue in the dispute concerned the constitutionality of warrantless surveillance with the use of the tracking device attached to Jones' car.

The SCOTUS confirmed that the actions carried out by the federal officers involved a search in the meaning of it present in the Fourth Amendment:

> "It is important to be clear about what occurred in this case: The Government physically occupied private property for the purpose of obtaining information. We have no doubt that such a physical intrusion would have been considered a "search" within the meaning of the Fourth Amendment when it was adopted."[138]

---

137 Stevens, dissenting. *Ibid.* at 45.

138 565 U.S. 400 (2012).

By attaching a GPS tracker to the defendant's vehicle for a longer time and in another location than was stipulated in the warrant, law enforcement officers violated his constitutional rights and conducted an unreasonable search and seizure. Surprisingly, however, despite a similar approach to the general conclusions in the case with regard to the unconstitutionality of the government's actions, some justices wrote concurring opinions offering different argumentation than the majority opinion signed by Scalia, who believed that installing a GPS tracker on Jones' car meant trespassing into his private sphere. Scalia claimed that the trespass doctrine should be the main reference in the Court's adjudication, contrary to the reasonable expectation of privacy approach, which was raised as an argument by a few other justices, including Samuel Alito and Sonia Sotomayor. Alito, who called the arguments raised by Scalia "artificial", stressed that physical intrusion was not a necessary element of effective surveillance, and that the unconstitutionality of the government's actions stemmed from Jones' reasonable expectation of privacy.[139] Sotomayor agreed with Alito's reasoning, though she expanded the expectation of privacy standard from objective to subjective, negating any type of warrantless electronic surveillance, even on a short-term basis.[140] In this way, by referring to different doctrines and different SCOTUS case-law the justices reached similar critical conclusions about the government's warrantless surveillance.

Just two years later the Court announced its decision in another case involving the collection of evidence by the government through the warrantless interception of digital data. In *Riley v. California* the justices reviewed a dispute in which a member of an organized crime group, David Leon Riley, was stopped in his car by the police after participating in a drive-by shooting, on the basis of his driving license having expired. During the standard search of the vehicle the police discovered two guns and arrested Riley, additionally analyzing the content of his mobile phone, which revealed crucial evidence of his gang membership and participation in the drive-by shooting. Based on the search of the phone and other evidence Riley was convicted and, on appeal, the case was brought to the Supreme

139 Alito, concurring. *Ibid.*
140 Sotomayor, concurring. *Ibid.*

Court. In a unanimous decision the Court declared that the search of Riley's mobile phone violated his Fourth Amendment rights. By analyzing judicial precedents referring to search procedures during arrest, the author of the opinion, Chief Justice John Roberts, Jr. argued that accessing the phone data exceeded the standard actions the police were entitled to perform without a warrant as a consequence of a lawful arrest. As one of the arguments, Roberts stressed that digital data cannot pose a direct threat to arresting officers:

> "Digital data stored on a cell phone cannot itself be used as a weapon to harm an arresting officer or to effectuate the arrestee's escape. Law enforcement officers remain free to examine the physical aspects of a phone to ensure that it will not be used as a weapon—say, to determine whether there is a razor blade hidden between the phone and its case. Once an officer has secured a phone and eliminated any potential physical threats, however, data on the phone can endanger no one."[141]

The Court presented the specific character of mobile phones which – due to their broad storage capacities and ability to convey new types of information – raise concerns over the right to privacy beyond other types of objects subject to police search:

> "One of the most notable distinguishing features of modern cell phones is their immense storage capacity. Before cell phones, a search of a person was limited by physical realities and tended as a general matter to constitute only a narrow intrusion on privacy ... The storage capacity of cell phones has several interrelated consequences for privacy. First, a cell phone collects in one place many distinct types of information—an address, a note, a prescription, a bank statement, a video—that reveal much more in combination than any isolated record. Second, a cell phone's capacity allows even just one type of information to convey far more than previously possible. The sum of an individual's private life can be reconstructed through a thousand photographs labeled with dates, locations, and descriptions; the same cannot be said of a photograph or two of loved ones tucked into a wallet. Third, the data on a phone can date back to the purchase of the phone, or even earlier."[142]

The above-mentioned part of the *Riley* opinion clearly shows how contemporary justices view the delicate character of the data stored

141 573 U.S. 373 (2014), at 383.
142 *Ibid.* at 390.

by people in the objects or devices they carry and use in everyday life. The privacy concerns raised by the Court prove that there is a special category for electronic searches due to the vulnerability of the data and the danger of accessing and using private information about suspects as a consequence of a search of their phones. At the same time, however, the justices unanimously declared in *Riley* that their concerns pertained to a case of warrantless search and did not limit the procedures police may apply which are consistent with the SCOTUS' interpretation of the Fourth Amendment:

> "We cannot deny that our decision today will have an impact on the ability of law enforcement to combat crime. Cell phones have become important tools in facilitating coordination and communication among members of criminal enterprises, and can provide valuable incriminating information about dangerous criminals. Privacy comes at a cost. Our holding, of course, is not that the information on a cell phone is immune from search; it is instead that a warrant is generally required before such a search, even when a cell phone is seized incident to arrest."[143]

Interestingly, just a few years later, in 2018, in *Carpenter v. United States*, in another dispute concerning the warrantless search of mobile phone records by the police, only five out of the nine justices upheld their reasoning as presented in *Riley*. After an arrest of four men, one of them, Timothy Carpenter, confessed to committing armed robberies and gave his own phone number and those of other arrested persons to the FBI. On the basis of this knowledge the agents obtained orders from magistrate judges to get access to the telecommunication records of the arrested based on specific provisions of the Stored Communications Act. The records contained information about the dates and times of calls, as well as the location of interlocutors, which resulted in the collection of evidence against Carpenter and charges being laid against him of the crime of armed robbery. During the trial, Carpenter claimed that the government was not entitled to access his communication records without a warrant, but both lower courts rejected his argumentation, and the case was brought to the SCOTUS.

In a narrow margin opinion, written by Chief Justice Roberts, a conservative who in this case joined with the liberal wing of justices, the Court ruled that

143 *Ibid.* at 398.

the government violated Carpenter's Fourth Amendment rights by obtaining the evidence through the illegal accessing of his mobile phone records. The majority reminded all involved that one of the fundamental standards guiding the interpretation of the Amendment is the reasonable expectation of privacy, which may be enjoyed also by the owners of mobile phones. Chief Justice Roberts devoted much time and space to explaining the nature of the information collected by the government, admitting that in the digital age it is difficult to apply the historical understanding of the scope of law enforcement powers in the context of search procedures. However, by referring to all the important precedents concerning the scope of the Fourth Amendment's Search and Seizure Clause, the Court chose not to extend the third-party doctrine shaped in *Smith v. Maryland*, arguing that access to information about the location of callers invades their privacy:

> "Given the unique nature of cell phone location information, the fact that the Government obtained the information from a third party does not overcome Carpenter's claim to Fourth Amendment protection. The Government's acquisition of the cell-site records was a search within the meaning of the Fourth Amendment."[144]

Carpenter was not the last SCOTUS ruling concerning the scope of government surveillance, but it seems crucial in the context of the constitutional meaning of the Fourth Amendment's Search and Seizure and Warrant clauses, with regard to contemporary domestic surveillance.

---

144 484 U.S. 19 (2018), at 30.

Chapter Three The National Security Paradigm in SCOTUS Surveillance Adjudication

The National Security Paradigm

In order to analyze the foreign intelligence surveillance case-law it is necessary to begin with a brief reference to the concept of national security in American politics, as the two issues are deeply interconnected. Foreign intelligence surveillance would not be a topic of such concern if the country's foreign policy was not built around the national security concept, which became the main legitimizer of the establishment of the intelligence network responsible for conducting surveillance on foreigners. Of course, national security matters were not limited to foreign relations only, as they also affected domestic affairs, but before analyzing the scope of national security policy and its impact on SCOTUS foreign intelligence adjudication, it is important to present some theoretical assumptions with reference to the evolving concept of U.S. national security.

According to Whitfield Diffie and Susan Landau, the essence of national security is the protection of the country, including the government and the people, against attack by foreign military forces, or other threats, most of which are foreign.[145] Diffie and Landau list several activities undertaken by the government in the area of national security:

> "[M]aintenance of military forces adequate to deter attacks on the U.S., repel invaders, control domestic unrest, and undertake other military actions that may be in the national interest; provision of intelligence on the capabilities and intentions of all powers, both friendly and hostile, sufficient to inform foreign policy and military actions... denying to foreign powers intelligence about the U.S. that would interfere with American diplomatic, military or trade objectives; enforcement of certain laws, in particular those governing espionage, terrorism and integrity of the national security community itself, and the movements of people and material across borders; maintenance of an industrial base and an

145 Whitfield Diffie, Susan Landau, *Privacy on the Line. The Politics of Wiretapping and Encryption*, The MIT Press, Cambridge 2007, p. 87.

infrastructure adequate to support essential government activities, including military forces, intelligence and relevant aspects of law enforcement"[146]

Although most of these activities affect the country's foreign policy, there are several examples of government operations affecting the area of domestic affairs. Today, it seems impossible to divide foreign from domestic powers, as the foreign policy actors are functioning in the governmental of separation of powers system and are acting within the framework of constitutional and legislative delegation of powers. Even if their decisions concern military or intelligence matters, they may have an impact on domestic policies – in the context of the constitution – such as on the scope of government powers and the rights of the people. Furthermore, it is the domestic law which determines the powers of institutions carrying out foreign policy and acting within the area of international relations.

To successfully pursue the goals of national security policy, government has to establish a system of institutions and procedures which can assure the effective functioning of the country in the area of foreign and domestic policy. George C. Edwards and Wallace E. Walker believe that there are at least four categories of functions the governments needs to perform in order to protect and advance national security interests: statecraft, national defense, foreign relations, and economic policy.[147] In the era of globalization all these functions are intertwined and are carried out by both traditional actors, such as heads of state, chief executives, and national legislators, and specialized institutions established to perform their duties for the purposes of national security, such as security and intelligence agencies. The evolution of the national security concept in the 20th century resulted in the growing institutionalization of political processes, resulting in the establishment and development of units fully responsible for pursuing the goals and policies of the country in all the areas related to security, broadly understood. As a consequence, the process known as securitization has emerged, involving these institutions in the transformation of traditional political matters into security issues, dominating the governmental agenda on the basis of

146 *Ibid.*, pp. 87–88.
147 See: George C. Edwards III, Wallace Earl Walker (eds.), *National Security and the U.S. Constitution. The Impact of the Political System*, The Johns Hopkins University Press, Baltimore 1988.

various security concerns.[148] Governments began implementing national security strategies, which included arrangements and activities pertaining to both foreign and domestic issues, recasting its activities into the language characteristic of the national security world.

Such processes would not be possible without a system through which countries could obtain information and knowledge, and analyze and use it for the sake of effective national security. That is how intelligence came onto the stage quickly, becoming both a tool for gaining knowledge and information and a factor enabling the decision-making of governments pursuing national security policies. As Artur Gruszczak rightly observes:

> "it is hard to imagine a strong, robust, effective government without a tailor-made knowledge management apparatus ancillary to the state and society. The importance of knowledge management, information analysis, data processing, and intelligence has been a notable feature of government policies and world politics, particularly since 9/11 and subsequent terrorist attacks all over the world. National security policies and international security cooperation arrangements have begun to highlight growing reliance on early warning, situation awareness, threat assessment and risk analysis… Intelligence has come to play a pivotal role in contemporary security policies and can determine governments' resilience to threats and hazards."[149]

There is no doubt that the country that led in the development of this process – of introducing the national security paradigm into its policies and building an intelligence community affecting its foreign policy and relations with other countries – was the United States of America.

The national security paradigm is deeply rooted in the American political system and has been used by every U.S. presidential administration since the 1940s as an element of foreign and domestic policy, as well as a rhetorical tool legitimizing concrete actions undertaken by the government. Officially, the term "national security" was used for the first time by President Franklin D. Roosevelt in the wake of WWII, although similar phrases existed earlier in American politics, such as "national defense" or simply "defense", and were used in various contexts from the late 18th century on[150]. It is easy

148 More on securitization see: Andrew W. Neal, *Security as Politics: Beyond the State of Exception*, Edinburgh University Press, Edinburgh 2020.

149 Artur Gruszczak, *Intelligence Security in the European Union. Building a Strategic Intelligence Community*, Palgrave Macmillan, London 2016, p. 2.

150 See: Athan G. Theoharis, *Abuse of Power…*, op. cit.

to recall that soon after the establishment of the new country, the first President, George Washington, warned against the possible negative impact of foreign states on U.S. affairs in his famous *Farewell Address*:

> "Against the insidious wiles of foreign influence (I conjure you to believe me, fellow-citizens) the jealousy of a free people ought to be constantly awake, since history and experience prove that foreign influence is one of the most baneful foes of republican government"[151]

There are many examples in 19th century U.S. history of how the government shaped its foreign and domestic policies with regard to security issues, by announcing and acting in pursuance of presidential doctrines, such as the Monroe Doctrine of 1823, or by conducting wars aimed at the expansion of the U.S. territory, such as the U.S.-Mexican war. Interestingly, during this period the SCOTUS was not actively involved in adjudicating in disputes pertaining to foreign policy matters (apart from the Marshall Court rulings which, as we have seen, strengthened the scope of federal power at the expense of the states) and rarely focused on security or defense issues. The outbreak of the Civil War changed the situation, as the government's actions affected the scope of the rights of the people, leading to constitutional conflicts which could be resolved by the courts. The most famous issue of a constitutional character was provoked by President Abraham Lincoln's suspension of the writ of habeas corpus, which the Chief Executive justified with reference to the conduct of the war. Despite the critique from Lincoln's political opponents, including Chief Justice Roger Taney, who even issued a decision in *Ex parte Merryman* claiming the President had violated the Constitution (though he did that as a judge presiding in the United States Circuit Court for the District of Maryland)[152], Lincoln did not follow Taney's order and continued his practice of suspending writs of habeas corpus. The *Merryman* dispute did not reach the Supreme Court, so the justices did not have a chance to issue a ruling concerning the constitutionality of Lincoln's war powers, but in 1866, in *Ex parte Milligan*, the SCOTUS decided on

151 *George Washington's Farewell Address* available at https://www.educatingforamericandemocracy.org/primary-source/george-washingtons-farewell-address-1797/ .

152 17 F. Cas. 144 (1861).

another controversial aspect of the scope of presidential powers exercised during the Civil War.

The dispute was a result of the operation of military tribunals established by the government to try people suspected of conspiracy against the Union, and the facts of the case referred to Lambdin P. Milligan and two other people who were charged with conspiracy and inciting rebellion during the war. Following their convictions, they appealed to higher courts and Milligan's case reached the Supreme Court, which announced its ruling in 1866. In a narrow margin decision authored by Justice David Davis, the Court declared the operation of military tribunals unconstitutional with regard to their jurisdiction over civilians, who had to be tried by civil courts. In this unique example of judicial objection to actions undertaken by the government during wartime, Davis stressed the danger such actions may have posed to the freedom and security of U.S. citizens, rejecting the possibility of imposing different constitutional standards in times of war and peace:

> "These securities for personal liberty thus embodied were such as wisdom and experience had demonstrated to be necessary for the protection of those accused of crime. And so strong was the sense of the country of their importance, and so jealous were the people that these rights, highly prized, might be denied them by implication, that, when the original Constitution was proposed for adoption, it encountered severe opposition, and, but for the belief that it would be so amended as to embrace them, it would never have been ratified.
>
> Time has proven the discernment of our ancestors, for even these provisions, expressed in such plain English words that it would seem the ingenuity of man could not evade them, are now, after the lapse of more than seventy years, sought to be avoided. Those great and good men foresaw that troublous times would arise when rulers and people would become restive under restraint, and seek by sharp and decisive measures to accomplish ends deemed just and proper, and that the principles of constitutional liberty would be in peril unless established by irrepealable law. The history of the world had taught them that what was done in the past might be attempted in the future. The Constitution of the United States is a law for rulers and people, equally in war and in peace, and covers with the shield of its protection all classes of men, at all times and under all circumstances. No doctrine involving more pernicious consequences was ever invented by the wit of man than that any of its provisions can be suspended during any of the great exigencies of government. Such a doctrine leads directly to anarchy or despotism, but the theory of necessity on which it is based is false, for the government, within the Constitution, has all the powers granted to it which are necessary to preserve

its existence, as has been happily proved by the result of the great effort to throw off its just authority."[153]

Ex parte Milligan was the only Court decision to oppose so strongly the growth of executive powers during times of war, and definitely one of the few SCOTUS precedents in the second part of the 19th century referring to the issues related to the country's security. Another ruling worth analysis is *Chae Chan Ping v. United States*, known also as the Chinese Exclusion Case, concerning the challenges connected to Asian immigration to the United States in the 1870s and 1880s. As a result of congressional legislation which limited the immigration of Chinese laborers, including a ban on the immigrants' re-entry, a Chinese citizen who used to live in California but left for China for a certain period of time could not return, and therefore he sued the U.S. government for violation of international treaties between the two countries. On appeal, the Supreme Court upheld the legislation, despite its inconsistency with international law, unanimously holding that it was the role of U.S. government to shape and pursue immigration policy which affected the security of the country and the people. In a unanimous decision, the justices acknowledged the federal government's right to use its powers in the name of protection and security:

> "To preserve its independence, and give security against foreign aggression and encroachment, is the highest duty of every nation, and to attain these ends nearly all other considerations are to be subordinated. It matters not in what form such aggression and encroachment come, whether from the foreign nation acting in its national character, or from vast hordes of its people crowding in upon us. The government, possessing the powers which are to be exercised for protection and security, is clothed with authority to determine the occasion on which the powers shall be called forth, and its determinations, so far as the subjects affected are concerned, are necessarily conclusive upon all its departments and officers."[154]

Throughout this period, especially at the end of the century and the beginning of the next, American foreign policy was slowly becoming involved in the affairs of other countries, including its occupation of the Philippines and interventions in Central America, which serves as proof of the replacement of isolationism with interventionism. Already at the

---

153 71 U.S. 2 (1866), at 120, 121.
154 130 U.S. 581 (1889), at 606.

beginning of the 20th century there were ideas among politicians and diplomats as to the establishment of a council of national defense, and the outbreak of WWI only strengthened the interest of the U.S. government in pursuing active defense and foreign policies.[155]

The early years of the interwar period marked a significant involvement of the Court in determining the scope of government war policies in relation to the rights and freedoms of individuals. After the U.S. entered the war Congress implemented the Espionage Act, which prohibited the obstruction of military recruitment and punished those who opposed the mobilization. When Charles Schenck and other members of Socialist Party circulated materials criticizing the government's involvement in the war, they were arrested and Schenck was convicted for violating the Espionage Act. In 1919, in *Schenck v. United States*, the Supreme Court reviewed the case and upheld Schenk's conviction on the basis of the constitutionality of the congressional legislation. The majority opinion authored by Justice Oliver Wendell Holmes introduced the so-called clear and present danger test, determining the scope of the constitutional freedom of speech in times of war and threats to the country's security:

> "The question in every case is whether the words used are used in such circumstances and are of such a nature as to create a clear and present danger that they will bring about the substantive evils that Congress has a right to prevent. It is a question of proximity and degree. When a nation is at war, many things that might be said in time of peace are such a hindrance to its effort that their utterance will not be endured so long as men fight, and that no Court could regard them as protected by any constitutional right. It seems to be admitted that, if an actual obstruction of the recruiting service were proved, liability for words that produced that effect might be enforced."[156]

According to Holmes, the interest of the government in protecting the country and its citizens at such times outweighed the protection the Constitution provided to individuals based on their freedom of speech. Although there was no direct reference to national defense or security, the

---

155 Marcus G. Raskin, A. Carl LeVan, *The National Security State and the Tragedy of Empire* in: *In Democracy's Shadow. The Secret World of National Security*, Marcus G. Raskin, A. Carl LeVan (eds.), Nation Books, New York 2005, pp. 7–19.

156 249 U.S. 47 (1919), at 52.

Court's decision played an important role in setting a standard for future cases affecting issues of national security.

Security became even a stronger concern for the government in the interwar period when the first Red Scare occurred as a consequence of Bolshevik Revolution and the growth of the popularity of far-left movements and anarchist organizations in America. As a result, the government introduced actions aimed at limiting the impact of the radical movements on politics and society, such as the so-called Palmer Raids, led by Attorney General A. Mitchell Palmer. One of the two main activities initiated by Mitchell were illegal searches and seizures resulting in warrantless arrests, and large-scale deportations of people suspected of sharing views inconsistent with the government's policies.[157] Some of these actions were challenged in the courts but none of these disputes reached the Supreme Court, which would have given the justices an opportunity to determine the constitutionality of the government's activities. In the meantime, the SCOTUS announced its decision in *Olmstead v. United States*, which, as mentioned earlier, affected future legislation concerning wiretapping, as in 1934 when Congress implemented a new law known as the Communications Act, prohibiting the illegal interception of the communications of private persons. This did not prevent President Roosevelt from issuing two secret directives in 1936 and 1939 expanding the powers of the FBI, which played a role in both law enforcement and intelligence activity during WWII.[158] As a result, the Agency was involved in extensive wiretapping, which was justified by presidential directives and the conduct of war but which could not be used as evidence in courts.

For obvious reasons national defense, which turned into national security during WWII, was used as a justification for government policies in both domestic and foreign relations. The national security paradigm was guiding not only the military operations in Europe and in the Pacific, but also government actions domestically, such as the establishment of the internment camps for Japanese citizens and Japanese Americans. These camps, which were created on the basis of Roosevelt's executive orders,

157 See: Christopher M. Finan, *From the Palmer Raids to the Patriot Act: A History for the Fight for Free Speech in America*, Beacon Press, Boston 2008.

158 Athan G. Theoharis, *Abuse of Power...*, op. cit., p. 3.

provoked several court challenges, some of which, including *Hirabayashi v. United States* and *Korematsu v. United States*, reached the SCOTUS. Both disputes were initiated by Japanese Americans who claimed that their constitutional rights had been violated by the government, which forced them to stay in internment camps or adapt to a curfew, and both Court decisions upheld the constitutionality of their internment. The majority opinions referred to the findings and arguments raised by the military, which convinced the justices about the danger the presence of Japanese Americans represented for the United States, it being at war with Japan. Writing for the majority in *Korematsu*, a case in which a Japanese American challenged Roosevelt's executive order, Justice Hugo Black declared that the most appropriate standard to apply in cases concerning racial inequalities is strict scrutiny, but due to the circumstances of war the government's establishment of internment camps in which to hold American citizens of Japanese ancestry was legitimate:

> "Korematsu was not excluded from the Military Area because of hostility to him or his race. He was excluded because we are at war with the Japanese Empire, because the properly constituted military authorities feared an invasion of our West Coast and felt constrained to take proper security measures, because they decided that the military urgency of the situation demanded that all citizens of Japanese ancestry be segregated from the West Coast temporarily, and, finally, because Congress, reposing its confidence in this time of war in our military leaders -- as inevitably it must -- determined that they should have the power to do just this."[159]

Similarly, in *Hirabayashi*, a dispute pertaining to the violation of a curfew during the period of the operation of the internment camps by a Japanese American student, the Court, in a unanimous opinion authored by Justice Harlan F. Stone, claimed that:

> "We cannot reject as unfounded the judgment of the military authorities and of Congress that there were disloyal members of that population, whose number and strength could not be precisely and quickly ascertained. We cannot say that the war-making branches of the Government did not have ground for believing that, in a critical hour, such persons could not readily be isolated and separately dealt with, and constituted a menace to the national defense and safety which demanded that prompt and adequate measures be taken to guard against it."[160]

---

159 323 U.S. 214 (1944), at 223, 224.
160 320 U.S. 81 (1943), at 99.

Despite the critical evaluation of both these precedents in the following decades, the reasoning offered by the justices played a significant role in determining the future standards of scrutiny in national security cases which affected the scope of the rights and freedoms of individuals.

As Athan Theoharis argues, President Roosevelt looked at national security from the perspective of defense policy, whereas his successor, Harry S. Truman, extended the scope and meaning of national security, which referred not only to foreign affairs but also to domestic issues.[161] Similar conclusions are presented by Michael Glennon, who observes that under Truman's governance Congress enacted the National Security Act of 1947, which unified the military under a new Department of Defense led by a secretary of defense, established the Central Intelligence Agency, created the modern Joint Chiefs of Staff, and introduced the National Security Council (NSC). Furthermore, President Truman was responsible for issuing a secret directive establishing the National Security Agency, which was intended to monitor communications abroad in the name of national security.[162] Interestingly, the NSA was not the first-ever U.S. foreign surveillance institution in history, as it substituted for the Armed Forces Security Agency (AFSA) which functioned from 1949, and its predecessor functioning during the times of WWII, the Signal Intelligence Service (SIS).[163]

All of the initiatives of Truman's administration were consistent with the new presidential doctrine in foreign affairs aimed at containment of the expansion and influence of the Soviet Union, which marked the beginning of the Cold War era. In this way, in the late 1940s and early 1950s the national security system was implemented and one of the main roles of the institutions operating within the system was to collect information about potential threats to the government and American society. Not surprisingly, the SCOTUS also played an important role in strengthening the interest of the government in preserving and expanding the operation of the national security apparatus.

---

161 Athan G. Theoharis, *Abuse of Power...*, op. cit., p. 31.

162 Michael J. Glennon, *National Security...*, op. cit., 12–13.

163 See: James L. Gilbert, John P. Finnegan, *U.S. Army Signals Intelligence in World War II: A Documentary History*, Center of Military History, Washington D.C. 1993.

The majority of cases adjudicated by the Supreme Court in the first two decades of the Cold War era concerned the constitutionality of federal legislation or operations of the executive connected with the anti-communist sentiments within the U.S. government. The justices supported the rhetoric and argumentation used by the authorities, which resulted in the expansion of their powers at the expense of the constitutional rights and freedom of the people. In that context, the Court decisions may be divided into two groups: rulings which upheld congressional national security legislation, and precedents which confirmed the scope of presidential powers in the area of foreign policy.

The first group of rulings was a consequence of the implementation of congressional acts regarding Cold War limitations of certain rights and freedoms, which were challenged in courts by individuals and civil rights organizations. By the mid-1950s Congress had already passed the following laws: requiring non-citizen adult residents to register with the U.S. government (the Alien Registration Act, known also as the Smith Act), requiring professionals to sign affidavits swearing that they were not members of the Communist party (the Labor-Management Relations Act, known as the Taft-Hartley Act), investigating persons engaged in un-American activities and authorizing concentration camps in emergency situations (the Internal Security Act, known as the McCarran Act) and criminalizing membership of the Communist Party of the United States (the Communist Control Act).[164] The existence of such legal provisions resulted in numerous prosecutions and deportations of people suspected of radical activities, loyalty oath requirements, and freewheeling investigations by several congressional committees which seemed to violate the fundamental rights of American citizens.

In *American Communications Association v. Douds*, in which the Court considered the constitutionality of the Taft-Hartley Act, the majority, led by Chief Justice Fred M. Vinson, held that communist groups were capable of engaging in different kinds of subversive actions, such as industrial sabotage or political strikes, thus weakening the national economy. The justices

164 *The Alien Registration Act* 54 U.S. 670 (1940); *The Labor Management Relations Act* 61 Stat. 136 (1947); *The Internal Security Act* 64 Stat. 987 (1950); and *The Communist Control Act* 68 U.S. 775 (1954).

upheld the legislation, defining it as a necessary means of the protection of the national economy, which, in turn, had a positive effect on safeguarding national security. In the words of the Vinson, balancing the values of freedom of speech and national security concerns led to the prioritization of the latter, as the public interest was more important than the rights of the individual. However, the role of judiciary in providing balance in this context was difficult, and sometimes impossible, to fulfill:

> "The task of this Court to maintain a balance between liberty and authority is never done, because new conditions today upset the equilibriums of yesterday. The seesaw between freedom and power makes up most of the history of governments, which, as Bryce points out, on a long view consists of repeating a painful cycle from anarchy to tyranny and back again. The Court's day-to-day task is to reject as false, claims in the name of civil liberty which, if granted, would paralyze or impair authority to defend existence of our society, and to reject as false, claims in the name of security which would undermine our freedoms and open the way to oppression. These are the competing considerations involved in judging any measures which government may take to suppress or disadvantage its opponents and critics."[165]

In *Dennis v. United States*, a case against eleven people accused of conspiracy and infringement of the Smith Act - which made it unlawful to conspire, to teach and advocate the destruction of the United States government - the Court found the defendants guilty of teaching communist ideology and actively advocating its ideas. According to the majority of the justices, communist advocacy was dangerous for U.S. national security, and it was the role of the government to implement laws which would ensure the effective protection of the country and its citizens against the threats posed by communism:

> "The obvious purpose of the statute is to protect existing Government not from change by peaceable, lawful and constitutional means, but from change by violence, revolution and terrorism. That it is within the power of the Congress to protect the Government of the United States from armed rebellion is a proposition which requires little discussion ... The question with which we are concerned here is not whether Congress has such power, but whether the means which it has employed conflict with the First and Fifth Amendments to the Constitution."[166]

---

165 339 U.S. 382 (1950), at 445.
166 341 U.S. 494 (1951), at 501.

Acknowledging the importance of the constitutional protection of freedom of speech, the Court claimed that the government had selected a proper means for the protection of national security, as the activities undertaken by subjects challenging the law constituted a clear and present danger to the United States:

> "We hold that §§ 2(a)(1), 2(a)(3) and 3 of the Smith Act do not inherently, or as construed or applied in the instant case, violate the First Amendment and other provisions of the Bill of Rights, or the First and Fifth Amendments because of indefiniteness. Petitioners intended to overthrow the Government of the United States as speedily as the circumstances would permit. Their conspiracy to organize the Communist Party and to teach and advocate the overthrow of the Government of the United States by force and violence created a "clear and present danger" of an attempt to overthrow the Government by force and violence. They were properly and constitutionally convicted for violation of the Smith Act."[167]

A similar decision was made in *United States ex rel. Knauff v. Shaughnessy*, where the SCOTUS acknowledged the inherent power of the executive and legislative branches to deport immigrants deemed to be threatening national security. As a consequence, the justices limited the scope of judicial review of actions of the government pertaining to the exclusion of immigrants from the United States.[168] Generally, the early years of the Cold War, which also mark the period of the leadership of the Court of Fred M. Vinson, proved that the judicial branch staunchly supported the policy of the government, in which security outweighed freedom. After a change in the Court's membership it became more liberal; this was also visible in adjudication in civil rights case-law, starting from the second part of the 1950s, when the fears of the Red Scare had eased a little. SCOTUS decisions in three disputes in particular - *Watkins v. United* States, *Yates v. United States* and *United States v. Robel* - may serve as examples of a change in its approach to the rights and freedoms of individuals; however, national security concerns still remained an important point of reference in the Court's decision-making.

In *Watkins* the SCOTUS prohibited congressional committees from asking questions which would be irrelevant to the legislation that these

167 *Ibid.* at 516.
168 338 U.S. 537 (1950).

committees were considering raising to the status of law. Testifying before the House Committee on Un-American Activities, a labor organizer refused to share information about the people who had left the Communist Party, arguing that such questions violated the scope of government powers. In a 6-1 opinion authored by Chief Justice Earl Warren, the Court held that Congress had operated beyond its power and that Watkins' conviction violated the due process of law.[169] In *Yates*, the SCOTUS reviewed the conviction of several leaders of the Californian branch of the Communist Party for conspiracy against the U.S. government. By reversing the lower court's verdict, the majority led by Justice John Marshall Harlan II argued that the Smith Act, which was the basis for the conviction, did not refer to abstract cases but to concrete conspiracy actions and initiatives which had to be proven by the government. Six of the justices were convinced that the circumstances of the dispute produced abstract principles rather than a real danger to national security.[170]

Ten years later, in *United States v. Robel*, the SCOTUS overturned the conviction of Communist Party member Eugene Robel for violation of the federal law prohibiting employment in so-called defense facilities, on the basis of the government's violation of the First Amendment. In the majority opinion, written by Chief Justice Earl Warren, the Court stressed the importance of protecting the First Amendment's values against the concept of national defense, presented in the dispute as an argument legitimizing the necessary limitation of freedom of speech and freedom of association:

> "Yet, this concept of "national defense" cannot be deemed an end in itself, justifying any exercise of legislative power designed to promote such a goal. Implicit in the term "national defense" is the notion of defending those values and ideals which set this Nation apart. For almost two centuries, our country has taken singular pride in the democratic ideals enshrined in its Constitution, and the most cherished of those ideals have found expression in the First Amendment. It would indeed be ironic if, in the name of national defense, we would sanction the subversion of one of those liberties -- the freedom of association -- which makes the defense of the Nation worthwhile."[171]

169 354 U.S. 178 (1957).
170 354 U.S. 298 (1957).
171 389 U.S. 258 (1967), at 264.

On the other hand, the adjudication of SCOTUS in cases concerning the powers of the presidency in national security matters was limited due to the reluctance of the Court to plunge into the political domain and determine those matters of foreign affairs which were reserved for the executive. Already in 1930s and 1940s the justices had an opportunity to express their opinions about the scope of presidential foreign powers in such cases as *United States v. Curtiss-Wright Export Corp.*, *United States v. Belmont*, and *United States v. Pink*.

In the first of these disputes, the Court reviewed the role of Congress and the president in foreign policy matters, challenged by a company which sold airplanes to countries involved in the Chaco War in Latin America and thus violated the federal laws prohibiting such activity. The main source of regulating the operations of private companies with respect to an international conflict was presidential proclamation, which was the result of the delegation of powers in the area of foreign affairs to the chief executive. The Curtiss-Wright Export Corporation claimed that the Resolution was unconstitutional as it illegally delegated legislative power to the president. The SCOTUS decided the case in 1936, confirming the broad powers of the federal government and especially the chief executive in conducting foreign policy. According to the majority of the justices, Congress did not exceed its delegation powers, because in the area of foreign affairs the federal government had a broad remit. The Court introduced the sole-organ doctrine concerning the role of the president in foreign affairs, which meant not only the potential of a future expansion of the executive powers in the area of foreign policy, but also a limitation of congressional control over the way in which presidents pursued that policy:

> "Not only, as we have shown, is the federal power over external affairs in origin and essential character different from that over internal affairs, but participation in the exercise of the power is significantly limited. In this vast external realm, with its important, complicated, delicate and manifold problems, the President alone has the power to speak or listen as a representative of the nation. He makes treaties with the advice and consent of the Senate; but he alone negotiates. Into the field of negotiation the Senate cannot intrude, and Congress itself is powerless to invade it."[172]

---

172 299 U.S. 304 (1936), at 319.

Despite the fact that the Court's opinion did not refer directly to national security or national defense, it seems obvious that by determining the dominating role of the president within foreign policy matters the justices laid foundations for the acknowledgment of a similar role of the executive within future national security issues.

The other two precedents of the pre-Cold War era concerned U.S.-Soviet relations from the perspective of the agreements signed by the two countries and the role of federal and state governments in affecting foreign policy issues. In *United States v. Belmont,* the SCOTUS declared that the U.S. government could recover deposits from former Russian corporations based on the substance of the agreement signed by President Franklin D. Roosevelt and Soviet foreign affairs minister Maxim Litvinov, known as Roosevelt-Litvinov Accords, which superseded New York law's neglecting such a procedure. The justices argued that federal government had the predominant power over state governments and laws in the area of foreign policy, and that presidential executive agreements, even if they were not signed at the level of international treaties, were an important source of law regarding foreign affairs.[173] This approach was confirmed five years later in *United States v. Pink*, where the Court sustained the leading role of the federal government in shaping and determining the conduct of foreign affairs; state governments were not, on the other hand, to have a role in regulating matters concerning foreign policy.[174]

By the time the Cold War had begun the Supreme Court had already defined the role of presidents and the executive branch within foreign affairs; therefore, it could be assumed that a similar approach would be taken by the justices with regard to national the security issues that pertained to a large extent to the country's foreign policy. In the early years of the conflict, however, there were not many occasions on which the Court could determine the constitutionality of presidential actions and, if they did occur, the justices decided to impose certain limitations on the powers of the chief executive. Such a situation took place in the early 1950s, when the SCOTUS adjudicated in a dispute over the attempted seizure of steel

173 301 U.S. 324 (1937).
174 315 U.S. 203 (1942).

mills by President Harry Truman in connection with the pending Korean War. The President issued an executive order which directed the Secretary of Commerce to seize and operate private steel mills located in different areas of the United States in order to prevent a national strike in the steel industry which could affect the conduct of the military conflict in Korea. In 1952, in a 6-3 decision in *Youngstown Sheet and Tube Company v. Sawyer*, the Supreme Court declared that the President had overused his powers by issuing the order and trying to seize private property. Although the executive order referred numerous times to national security arguments, the justices rejected Truman's argumentation based on his commander-in-chief powers, especially since there was no statutory delegation from Congress allowing the president to take possession of private property. Writing for the majority, Justice Hugo Black expressed his concern over the arguments raised by President Truman, believing that the role of the judicial branch was to limit the unconstitutional exceeding of any of its powers on the part of the government:

> "It is not a pleasant judicial duty to find that the President has exceeded his powers, and still less so when his purposes were dictated by concern for the Nation's wellbeing, in the assured conviction that he acted to avert danger. But it would stultify one's faith in our people to entertain even a momentary fear that the patriotism and the wisdom of the President and the Congress, as well as the long view of the immediate parties in interest, will not find ready accommodation for differences on matters which, however close to their concern and however intrinsically important, are overshadowed by the awesome issues which confront the world."[175]

The majority opinion did not neglect, however, the possibility of legalizing actions of the executive which could even limit the right to property of private people and entities provided that wartime policy, public safety, national security, or other similar circumstances were at stake:

> "Congress deemed seizure so drastic a power as to require that it be carefully circumscribed whenever the President was vested with this extraordinary authority. The power to seize has uniformly been given only for a limited period or for a defined emergency, or has been repealed after a short period. Its exercise has been restricted to particular circumstances such as "time of war or when war

175 343 U.S. 579 (1952), at 614.

> is imminent," the needs of "public safety" or of "national security or defense," or "urgent and impending need." "[176]

Not for the first time, and not for the last, the SCOTUS referred to national security arguments which could legitimize certain activities undertaken by other branches of government, despite showing reluctance to extend presidential powers beyond a certain constitutional limit. Still, *Youngstown* did not overrule any of the former Court decisions which recognized the broad powers of U.S. government in foreign policy matters, and the SCOTUS rulings limiting the rights of individuals during the early decades of the Cold War prove that the majority of justices were ready to sacrifice constitutional freedoms for the sake of expanding the powers of the government and strengthening the security of the country. In the following years there were several Court decisions which acknowledged the power of the president and the executive in foreign affairs and national security areas, such as *Zemel v. Rusk*, *Goldwater v. Carter* and *Dames & Moore v. Regan*.[177] The legitimate end of U.S. foreign policy and national security outweighed the needs of the constitutional protection of the First, Fourth, and Fifth Amendments' freedoms, despite the means applied by the government. As time showed, one of the most intrusive means used in the name of national security was surveillance, which was effective on the one hand, but uncontrolled and thus unlimited on the other.

Surveillance in the Name of National Security

Until the 1970s national security had not only been the core paradigm of U.S. foreign and domestic policy, legitimizing the expansion of power of the leading surveillance and intelligence agencies such as FBI, CIA, and NSA, but it also became the main justification for the overwhelming culture of secrecy surrounding the activities undertaken by the executive. Although the problem of secrecy with regard to SCOTUS adjudication will be addressed later in the chapter, it is worth stressing here that the majority of government spying programs, as well as surveillance practices, were kept far from public knowledge. Given the character of the work of the

---

176 *Ibid.* at 598.
177 381 U.S. 1 (1965); 444 U.S. 996 (1979); 453 U.S. 654 (1981).

intelligence and law enforcement communities, it seems obvious that the fewer witnesses to their activities the better for their effective and successful operation; therefore, the general approach of the government in the early years of Cold War was socially and politically accepted. Problem began to occur with the release of certain information and documents related to the functioning of the FBI, CIA, and NSA, accompanied by a number of scandals connected with the illegal surveillance measures adopted by these agencies. It turned out that the emergence of the national security system had resulted in the conducting of uncontrolled intelligence activities which led to the overuse of their powers by government institutions and violations of the rights and freedoms of American citizens.

As Athan Theoharis points out, "secrecy had enabled FBI, CIA and NSA officials to avoid public scrutiny of their abuses of power throughout the WWI and cold war years."[178] The culture of secrecy in which the national security apparatus operated was revealed at the beginning of 1970s in a series of press leaks and investigations which undermined trust in government. First, in 1970 radical activists released secret FBI documents, disclosing to the public information about a large-scale counterintelligence program monitoring of members of activist groups and other organizations in order to discredit and neutralize them. Then, a few years later, public opinion was shocked by the results of an independent investigation conducted by the press exposing the Watergate scandal, which was the result of an attempt to set up an illegal wiretap involving high-ranking officers of the Nixon administration. In 1974 American citizens were once again shocked by press publications revealing an illegal CIA surveillance project the purpose of which was to uncover foreign influence on civil rights movements. And finally, during his 1975 testimony before a House committee, Attorney General Edward Levi disclosed that FBI Director Edgar J. Hoover had collected information on the personal and political activities of American politicians, including members of Congress.[179] All of these events led to the reaction of Congress and establishment of two committees to investigate

178 Athan G. Theoharis, *Abuse of Power...*, op. cit., p. 141.
179 See: *Ibid.*, pp. 141–142; Morton H. Halperin, Daniel Hoffman, *Freedom v. National Security. Secrecy and Surveillance*, Chelsea House Publishers, New York 1977.

the potentially illegal activities of the FBI, CIA, and NSA – the Church and Pike Committees.

The investigations and hearings conducted by the House and Senate Committees resulted in the collection of information concerning illegal practices of government agencies engaged in establishing a system of national security surveillance based on intercepting the communications of American citizens. Among the most significant secret activities of the federal agencies revealed during the investigation there were two NSA, two CIA and one FBI program. The National Security Agency conducted a project in cooperation with communications-transmission companies which accumulated and reviewed the telegraphic data of U.S. citizens without judicial approval (SHAMROCK), and also operated a program monitoring the foreign communications and international communications of Americans (MINARET). At the same time the Central Intelligence Agency launched a program intercepting the mail content and address data of people sending letters to communist countries (HTLINGUAL), and imposed domestic surveillance measures which affected U.S. politicians and activists in the name of determining the presence of foreign influence (MHCHAOS). Finally, the FBI was operating a counterintelligence program which surveilled thousands of political organizations and public persons involved in activities defined as subversive (COINTELPRO).[180]

It turned out that surveillance measures became a very effective tool of government agencies' control of the communications and activities of U.S. citizens, often resulting in intimidation, discrediting, or blackmail, and leading to obvious violations of the civil rights of Americans. Among the constitutional rights which were limited by these national security surveillance operations were freedom of speech, of the press, of assembly, and of association, the ban on unreasonable searches and seizures, and due process of law[181]. The scale of abuses was reflected in the findings of the Church Committee, which asked the following rhetorical questions:

---

180 See: Athan G. Theoharis, *Abuse of Power...*, op. cit.; John Prados, *The Family Jewels...*, op. cit.; Daniel J. Solove, *Nothing to Hide...*, op. cit.

181 See: Mary L. Dudziak, *Cold War Civil Rights: Race and Image of American Democracy*, Princeton University Press, Princeton 2000.

> "What is a valid national secret? Assassination plots? The overthrow of an elected democratic government? Drug testing or unwitting American citizens? Obtaining millions of private cables? Massive domestic spying by the CIA and the military? The illegal opening of a mail? Attempts by the agency of a government to blackmail a civil rights leader? These have occurred and each has been withheld from scrutiny by the public and the Congress by the label secret intelligence".[182]

The reports prepared by the investigative committees left no doubt as to the illegal nature of government activities which were operated in total secrecy, beyond any control on the part of the other branches of government:

> "Too many people have been spied upon by too many Government agencies and too much information has been collected. The Government has often undertaken the secret surveillance of citizens on the basis of their political beliefs, even when those beliefs pose no threat of violence or illegal acts on behalf of a hostile foreign power."[183]

As a result of these reports Congress decided to equip the committees with permanent oversight powers with which to control the foreign intelligence and counterintelligence activities undertaken by the intelligence community[184]. Congress also expanded the powers of judicial committees of both houses to oversee the actions of domestic surveillance agencies[185]. Furthermore, in 1978 Congress implemented the Foreign Intelligence Surveillance Act (FISA), introducing a higher degree of judicial scrutiny of national security surveillance measures. As a result of the legislation, the Foreign Intelligence Surveillance Court (FISC) was established to grant warrants for the surveillance of the people who, based on the probable cause standard, were suspected of being foreign agents[186]. The means of the appointment of FISC judges, as well as the length of their tenure, was aimed at producing a system of judicial checks on the activities of institutions engaging in surveillance without violating the sensitive character of the

---

182 Jason R. Arnold, *Secrecy in the Sunshine Era. The Promise and Failures of U.S. Open Government Laws*, University Press of Kansas, Lawrence 2014, pp. 17–18.

183 Daniel J. Solove, *Nothing to Hide...*, op. cit., p. 10.

184 Mary Graham, *Presidents' Secrets...*, op. cit., pp. 5–6.

185 See: Michael J. Glennon, *National Security...*, op. cit.; Daniel J. Solove, *Nothing to Hide...*, op. cit.

186 *Foreign Intelligence Surveillance Act* 92 U.S. 1783 (1978).

cases discussed. On the other hand, the special court had to operate on the basis of information and documents provided solely by the executive, which made its proceedings and decision-making process dependent on the value and relevance of the data shared.[187] Obviously, in order to protect national security the FISC judges met behind closed doors and issued confidential rulings, which means that secrecy has played a central role in its operation. In the period under review, the SCOTUS was not involved directly in the process of controlling the foreign surveillance measures imposed by the government, leaving that field to congressional committees and the FISA Court.

In the 1980s the national security paradigm was still the leading reference point in shaping U.S. foreign and domestic policy, especially during Ronald Reagan's presidency. For the Republican chief executive the main role of the federal executive was to strengthen America's impact abroad, as well as its economy, as a guarantee of dominance in the bipolar Cold War world, but the President was also active in implementing new regulations determining the scope of government surveillance. As early as in 1980, Reagan issued an executive order expanding the National Security Agency's powers and allowing its interception of foreign communications. The document set guidelines for the collection of foreign intelligence, as it referred to

> "all means, consistent with applicable federal law and this EO, and with full consideration of the rights of the U.S. persons, shall be used to obtain reliable intelligence information to protect the United States and its interests".[188]

Although Reagan's order included a general reference to the rights of the American people, it did not specify which rights it protected and to what extent, promoting rather a Marshall-type approach towards the scope of the powers of government. The legitimate end of obtaining reliable intelligence information allowed the executive to select the means which ensured the pursuit of a successful and effective national security policy.

The executive order required the establishment of procedures, to be approved by the attorney general, through which to manage the collection of foreign intelligence materials, which not only strengthened the powers

187 Genvieve Lester, *When Should State...*, op. cit., pp. 174–177.
188 Executive Order 12333, December 4, 1981.

of the NSA but also equipped other executive institutions with control over said procedures, limiting the possible judicial review of these actions.[189] As time showed, the law introduced by President Reagan became the legitimization for new intelligence surveillance programs falling into the category of signals intelligence collection. Although the majority of these programs were launched in the post-9/11 reality, national security was one of the leading paradigms of Bill Clinton's presidency, which was reflected in his National Security Strategy of Engagement and Enlargement of 1996, as well as the National Security Strategy for a New Century, announced in 1999: "Protecting the security of our nation – our people, our territory and our way of life – is my foremost mission and constitutional duty".[190] In both these documents the President acknowledged the development of science and technology as the key factor in shaping the future of U.S. national security policy. Among the many factors serving as the conditions that would enable greater security, the documents listed different types of surveillance measures, including effective foreign surveillance and intelligence collection.[191] As a proof of such an approach, as early as in 1993 Clinton issued a directive under which the NSA developed a special chip to be installed in the phones of U.S. citizens, designed to enable intelligence operatives to eavesdrop on their conversations. Despite the termination of the program after its disclosure in a press leak, the legitimate end of national security stemming mainly from terrorist threats led to numerous attempts to expand the surveillance powers of the government.

As Jan-Henrik Kuntze notes:

> "In the 1980s and 1990s concerns about serious terrorist threats grew enormously. This led to proliferation of the norm of security and the preventive approach to security. Nonetheless, and although the security norm led to massive spending by intelligence agencies and to new efforts of surveillance by broadening the term terrorist, the norm of privacy was present and was not weakened by legislative acts."[192]

189 Laura K. Donoghue, *The Future of Foreign Intelligence. Privacy and Surveillance in a Digital Age*, Oxford University Press, New York 2016, p. 12.

190 *A National Security Strategy for a New Century*, available at: https://clinton whitehouse3.archives.gov/WH/EOP/NSC/Strategy/ .

191 See: Jason R. Arnold, *Secrecy in the Sunshine...*, op. cit.

192 Jan-Hendrik Kuntze, *The Abolishment of the Right to Privacy? The USA, Mass Surveillance and the Spiral Model*, Tectum Verlag, Baden-Baden 2018, p. 72.

If the end of the 20th century marked a significant increase in the government's surveillance activity in the name of national security, the terrorist attacks of 9/11 resulted in the concentration of all the efforts being made to strengthen the national security system, including the establishment of new surveillance programs which would prevent such dramatic events in the future.

Less than a month after the Al-Qaeda members hijacked and crashed four U.S. airplanes, killing more than 3,000 people, the Bush administration initiated a secret warrantless foreign intelligence surveillance program, which intercepted the communications of U.S. citizens without the approval of FISC or Congress. The program, called Stellar Wind, allowed the bulk collection of metadata from large databases storing different types of communications of Americans, such as telephone conversations, e-mails, financial transactions, and other types of activities conducted on the Internet.[193] Despite voices in the Department of Justice raising doubts about the legality of the program, as well as the 2005 and 2006 press articles revealing its unlimited character, Stellar Wind was not officially terminated until 2007. Until then, the program had lacked any judicial or congressional supervision, allowing the NSA to select targets for monitoring, control the surveillance process, and impose limitations to the right to privacy.[194]

In 2007 the government decided to launch a new program to monitor the data of the users of the most important American Internet providers, which, after a few years of operation, included among others Apple, Facebook, Google, Microsoft, Skype, Yahoo and YouTube. The purpose of the PRISM program was to intercept the various data (such as e-mails, chats, photographs, but also log-ins and stored files) necessary to reveal the terrorist activities of both foreign nationals and American citizens. The Agency collected, stored, and analyzed billions of data items on U.S. persons, which were kept in secret, in order to provide the information necessary to limit the terrorist threat[195]. Unlike Stellar Wind, the PRISM program was

193 Timothy J. Edgar, *Beyond Snowden…*, op. cit., pp. 39–41.
194 Victor M. Hansen, Lawrence Friedman, *The Case for Congress. Separation of Powers and the War on Terror*, Routledge, New York 2016, p. 42.
195 John Prados, *The Family Jewels…*, op. cit., p. 340.

authorized by Congress, which implemented the so-called Section 702 in the Protect America Act of 2007[196].

For the Bush administration, the national security paradigm was at the center of foreign and domestic policy, legitimizing all warrantless interception programs operating under the name of the Presidential Surveillance Program (later called the Terrorist Surveillance Program). Their common feature was the expansion of the powers of law enforcement and intelligence agencies, as well as the lack of congressional oversight and judicial review, except for the FISC procedures which in any case proved ineffective. As Peter Shane observes, this lack of accountability meant that "millions of Americans were potentially subject to the electronic surveillance of their telephone calls and e-mails without any sort of judicial warrant".[197]

The Bush administration operated most of its surveillance programs in secrecy, claiming that this provided greater effectiveness in the achievement of their aims, but also referring to an interpretation of the Constitution which confirmed the right of the president to apply any means necessary for the successful imposition of national security measures. Although the theory was derived from a direct reading of the text of the Constitution, its proponents prepared a document the role of which was the legitimization of the expansion of presidential prerogatives in the area of foreign and domestic policy, at the expanse of checks and balances and the rights of the people. The memorandum, produced by the Office of Legal Counsel, was assumed by lawyers to sanction an almost unlimited power of the chief executive in determining the scope of government surveillance, claiming that as the commander-in-chief operating in a time of emergency only the president could ensure the use of the best measures for providing security to the American people.[198] As an argument strengthening this approach, its authors argued that unitary executive theory, derived from the constitutional delegation of powers to the president in Article Two, produced a system which was swift, quick, less formalized, and – above all – effective.[199]

196 *Protect America Act* 121 U.S. 552 (2007).

197 Peter M. Shane, *Madison's Nightmare...*, op. cit., p. 83.

198 See: Eric E. Posner, Adrian Vermeule, *Terror in the Balance...*, op. cit.

199 See: Edward Goldfarb (ed.), *After Snowden...*, op. cit.; Michael J. Glennon, *National Security...*, op. cit.;

National security concerns were also discussed in the legislative branch, proving that in the first weeks after 9/11 Congress did not remain inactive, implementing in 2001 crucial legislation aimed at strengthening security and equipping law enforcement with broad powers. This was called the U.S.A. Patriot Act. The legislation covered a broad range of issues relating to domestic and national security policies, such as surveillance procedures, money laundering, border protection, investigating terrorism, increased information sharing, strengthening criminal laws against terrorism, and improving intelligence. One of the consequences of the legislation was the establishment of new surveillance measures which could be used by law enforcement in their investigations of criminals threatening the security of the country and the American people. Among the various provisions determining the relations among executive agencies, the Act introduced National Security Letters (NSL), to be issued without judicial control by FBI, and roving wiretaps focusing on individual persons rather than the devices they used[200]. The Patriot Act served also as a basis for NSA surveillance, which used Section 215, amended in 2006, to obtain warrants from FISC, which authorized the bulk collection of the telephone records of U.S. and foreign citizens. By defining a "seed number" used by a person who, according to the standard of reasonable suspicion, was suspected of being a foreign terrorist (level one), government agents could analyze all of the numbers associated with the seed number (level two), as well as the numbers associated with all numbers from level two (level three). Such an interpretation of the Patriot Act guaranteed that hundreds or thousands of numbers could be analyzed with regard to one seed number, providing for the almost infinite collection of data concerning U.S. citizens[201].

Among the long-lasting consequences of 9/11 were the structural and competence changes in the operation of the executive branch, as well as of the intelligence community. The analysis of the reasons which led to the terrorist attacks, as well as the post-9/11 reports, including the report of the 9/11 Commission, clearly pointed out intelligence and law

200 *The Uniting and Strengthening America by Providing Appropriate Tools Required to Intercept and Obstruct Terrorism Act – The USA Patriot Act*, 115 Stat. 272 (2001).

201 See: Chris Edelson, *Power Without Constraint...*, op. cit.

enforcement failures, an inability to properly understand and process information obtained through surveillance, an inability to effectively use the legal tools available, and a serious problem with the coordination of the work and communication among the leading institutions devoted to the protection of national security.[202] In response the government initiated a number of reforms which reorganized and restructured the administration, including the establishment of the Department of Homeland Security and the transfer of some powers from the Department of Justice offices to the new unit. However, the most serious changes were implemented within the Intelligence Community, via the introduction of the Director of National Intelligence (DNI) as the head of the Community, which was the principal recommendation of the 9/11 Commission. By moving the leadership from the CIA director to a new institution, the government wanted to enhance the coordination of the work of different federal intelligence agencies located in various federal departments, and to ensure the DNI's independence from any other agency, as well as the White House.[203] The DNI, along with the Office of the DNI, was responsible among the various coordinating and controlling powers for shaping the direction of intelligence activities, such as defining the means by which the Intelligence Community would effectively purse national security policies, as well as collect the information necessary to successfully protect the country and its citizens from external threats.

Despite the rhetoric of the presidential campaign of 2008, in which Barack Obama promised to end the extensive national security surveillance which limited the rights of Americans and to pursue his policies with greater transparency than his predecessor, after winning the election President Obama continued most of the Bush administration's policies in that respect. On the one hand, after reviewing the scope and character of surveillance programs his government decided to modify some of them, including the bulk interception of metadata from leading communication companies

202 Stephen J. Schulhofer, *The Enemy Within. Intelligence Gathering, Law Enforcement, and Civil Liberties in the Wake of September 11*, Century Foundation Press, New York 2002, pp. 31–32.

203 Timothy J. Edgar, *Beyond Snowden...*, op. cit., pp. 28–29.

under the PRISM program.[204] On the other hand, during Obama's tenure National Security Letters were actively used, resulting in the collection of extensive data and information about the customers of U.S. companies. The administration also played a crucial role in supporting the extension of certain legislative provisions which strengthened the surveillance powers of law enforcement and intelligence agencies, such as the Patriot Act and the FISA Amendments Act.[205]

During President Obama's second term the issue of NSA surveillance became the top of the headlines when former NSA contractor Edward Snowden released, in 2013, numerous documents proving the existence of the massive uncontrolled interception of the data of U.S. citizens. Thousands of pages of classified documents revealed the scope of secretive NSA surveillance programs, producing political and social tensions in the United States and all over the world, especially among U.S. allies outraged by the unlimited interception activities practiced by American intelligence agencies. Apart from diplomatic tensions, internal investigations conducted in a few countries, and the unsuccessful efforts of the U.S. government to arrest Snowden, the main topic of public debate in the United States became the scope of government surveillance powers, as well as the call for greater transparency. Both the President and Congress initiated actions which were aimed at protecting the rights of Americans and limiting the bulk collection of metadata, such as issuing presidential directives, establishing independent commissions, and enacting congressional legislation. One such initiative, the USA Freedom Act, ended the domestic bulk collection and introduced a reform of FISC, making its role more significant and its procedures more effective.[206]

---

204 See: Kathryn Olmsted, *Terror Tuesdays: How Obama Refined Bush's Counterterrorism Policies* in: *The Presidency of Barack Obama. A First Historical Assessment*, Julian E. Zelizer (ed.), Princeton University Press, Princeton 2018, pp. 212–226.

205 See: Mary Graham, *Presidents' Secrets…*, op. cit.; Michael J. Glennon, *National Security…*, op. cit.

206 *The Uniting and Strengthening America by Fulfilling Rights and Ensuring Effective Discipline over Monitoring Act – the USA Freedom Act*, 129 Stat. 268 (2015).

Unsurprisingly the next administration, led by President Donald Trump, used the national security paradigm in both its foreign and domestic policies, supporting the continuation of surveillance programs and imposing new measures aimed at providing stronger security at American borders. The President was a strong proponent of secrecy in the context of his communications and activities undertaken within the executive branch, criticizing any attempts at whistleblowing and the leaking of classified national security documents. Among various initiatives in that respect, President Trump ordered the building of a wall on the U.S.-Mexican border, for which he lobbied during the 2016 presidential campaign, and issued an executive order banning the entrance of citizens of seven nations to the United States, justifying it with national security reasons.[207] Paradoxically, surveillance became a highly criticized issue by Trump when he raised accusations against his predecessor of using illegal wiretapping during the 2016 campaign. These accusations were the result of the investigation conducted by the FBI into the possible cooperation between Trump campaign officials and Russian intelligence.[208] Although these accusations were not confirmed, the problem of the powers of law enforcement and intelligence agencies was still highly discussed among U.S. politicians and citizens.

In 2017 President Trump announced his administration's New National Security Strategy for a New Era, in which he listed four primary national interests: protecting the homeland, promoting American prosperity, preserving peace through strength, and advancing American influence. The document was full of references to American values, including security and freedom, but it mainly invoked the principles Trump understood as elements of the "America First" program, determining the most crucial exterior and interior threats to American democracy. Unsurprisingly the Strategy focused on the need to control the borders and the immigration system, prevent the impact of biological threats and pandemics, combat

207 See: Paweł Laidler, "To Divide and Rule: Political Impact of President Trump's U.S.-Mexico Border Wall Initiative", *Politeja* 6(81), 2022, pp. 253–278; Michael Nelson, *Trump: The First Two Years*, University of Virginia Press, Charlottesville 2018.

208 Michael V. Hayden, *The Assault…*, op. cit., pp. 139–141.

terrorist organizations, and increase cybersecurity. However, the only context in which the document related to surveillance was devoted to China, which was defined as a country spreading its authoritarian features, such as corruption and surveillance.[209]

Trump's attitude towards the scope of national security could also be viewed in the way he approached the matter of employment within the executive branch, limiting federal hiring with exceptions for national security and public safety, thereby being responsible for the growth of such institutions as Department of Defense and Department of Homeland Security.[210] In the area of legislation, Trump's administration supported passing the reauthorization of Section 702 of FISA, which was labelled during the debate in Congress as a safeguard for civil liberties and an assurance of greater transparency, but, in reality, expanded the government's powers to conduct foreign intelligence surveillance of non-U.S. citizens.[211]

The change in the White House which occurred as a consequence of the 2020 presidential election could be compared to the political circumstances of the 2008 election, when a Democrat supporting greater transparency and the protection of the rights of individuals replaced a Republican who had implemented measures expanding the power of the executive in the name of national security policy. Furthermore, similarly to Bush and Obama, the differences between Trump and Biden came down to rhetoric, while in practice Democratic presidents tend to follow the paths paved by their predecessors. One significant distinction of Joe Biden as a President compared to Barack Obama was his enormous experience in foreign policy matters and his earlier service in the U.S. government in various roles, in which he had always supported the country's national security policy. Paradoxically, even if Biden wanted to promote a new approach towards security issues, focusing more on the scope of the rights and freedoms of individuals rather than strengthening the powers of the government, it turned out to be impossible due to the international and domestic circumstances determining the character of his presidency. During his tenure, Biden faced

209 *A New National Security Strategy for a New Era*, available at: https://trumpwhitehouse.archives.gov/articles/new-national-security-strategy-new-era/ .
210 Michael Nelson, *Trump: The First Two Years...*, op. cit., p. 52.
211 See: Jack Goldsmith, *Power and Constraint...*, op. cit.

the Covid-19 pandemic, which required redefining the goals and measures of national security strategy, and he became involved in two international conflicts which dominated U.S. foreign policy under his governance.

Most significantly, the outbreak of the pandemic, resulting in more than 100 million Covid-19 infections and around 1.2 million deaths in the United States[212], became a fundamental concern of the government and American people, pushing other issues to the margins of political and social reality. It forced the Biden administration to approach national security from different angle and announce huge investments and costly measures which could effectively fight the pandemic. The American Rescue Plan of 2021 aimed at improving the capacity of federal and state governments to identify Covid-19 mutations and monitor the circulation of variants, strengthening the national bioinformatics infrastructure and establishing units having expertise in genomic epidemiology. In the proposed area of operation of these units the document assumed the development of surveillance tools to better track pathogens, but also to serve the public health system in a broader perspective.[213] Even if the syndromic and virological surveillance imposed by the government seemed a necessary means with which to end the spread of the pandemic, the new digital surveillance measures, such as telephone apps, location data, and electronic tags designed to monitor the activities and movements of U.S. citizens, raised a number of privacy concerns. For example, in order to enhance the effectiveness of the monitoring of the spread of the virus, the Center for Disease Control and Prevention of the Department of Health and Human Services cooperated with airlines to obtain data on passengers and monitor their travel information.[214] In this way, during the first two years of Biden's presidency Covid-19 played a crucial role in defining the scope of national security policy, as well as

212 Coronavirus Resource Center, The Johns Hopkins University & Medicine, available at: https://coronavirus.jhu.edu/region/united-states .

213 *Biden Administration Announces $1.7 Billion Investment to Fight Covid-19 Variants*, available at: https://www.whitehouse.gov/briefing-room/statements-releases/2021/04/16/fact-sheet-biden-administration-announces-1-7-billion-investment-to-fight-covid-19-variants/ .

214 Order of the Centers for Disease Control and Prevention, Department of Health and Human Services, available at: https://www.cdc.gov/port-health/media/pdfs/CDC-Global-Contact-Tracing-Order-10-25-2021-p.pdf .

expanding the government surveillance of American citizens. Health issues which did not dominate within the national security argument suddenly became the leading concern of the government and the people in the context of their security.

The support of the United States given to Ukraine as a consequence of the Russian invasion of it became the leading aspect of Biden's national security strategy from 2022, producing tensions in Congress over the proper scope of American help for a Ukrainian nation fighting against its oppressor. At the same time, in the area of surveillance, the Biden administration acted in line with all earlier administrations, upholding and even expanding the scope of government surveillance powers by signing reauthorizations of FISA, especially in the context of its Section 702. As a result, despite numerous references to the need to protect citizens' right to privacy, the government supported a law which permitted the collection and storing of different types of communications of Americans and using them without probable cause.[215]

All post-9/11 presidents, then, supported by congressional legislation, have contributed to the establishment of a national security system and intelligence network that have conducted secret surveillance of foreign and American citizens and thus potentially limited the constitutional rights of the latter. The word 'potentially' has not been used here by accident: the key remaining question refers to the role of the Supreme Court – the institution responsible for judicial review and the main interpreter of the Constitution – in the process of legitimizing national security surveillance.

Post-9/11 SCOTUS Rulings

SCOTUS adjudication in the 21st century has produced many fundamental precedents regarding the scope of the powers of the executive and legislative branches and federal-state relations, as well as the constitutional interpretation of the rights and freedoms of individuals, such as freedom

---

215 *Biden Signs Reauthorization of Surveillance Program Into Law Despite Privacy Concerns*, National Public Radio, April 24, 2024, available at: https://www.npr.org/2024/04/20/1246076114/senate-passes-reauthorization-surveillance-program-fisa .

of speech, of religion, the right to bear arms, the right to privacy, equal protection under the law, and procedural rights in criminal cases, including the Fourth Amendment's protections against searches and seizures (see chapter two). There have also been decisions concerning government powers in the area of national security, especially in the context of the post-9/11 operations of the U.S. government and their impact on the rights of foreign and American citizens. Hardly any ruling, however, has referred to foreign intelligence or national security surveillance – issues which determined the character of the actions of intelligence agencies.

The discussion about the constitutionality of the actions of the executive performed in the name of national security became a subject of judicial concern in the first decade of the 21st century, as a result of the conduct of the Bush administration's War on Terror. Yaser Esam Hamdi, a U.S. citizen, who, after being captured in Afghanistan and classified as an enemy combatant was detained by the U.S. government, claimed his right of habeas corpus, and had his case brought before the SCOTUS. In 2004, in *Hamdi v. Rumsfeld*, in a per curiam opinion presented by justice Sandra Day O'Connor, the Court declared that the government had the power to detain persons defined as enemy combatants who threatened the national security, even if they were U.S. citizens; however, it also said that such a power could not be exercised without limits:

> "[A]s critical as the Government's interest may be in detaining those who actually pose an immediate threat to the national security of the United States during ongoing international conflict, history and common sense teach us that an unchecked system of detention carries the potential to become a means for oppression and abuse of others who do not present that sort of threat."[216]

Despite the acknowledgment of the broad power of the executive, the justices guaranteed that U.S. citizens who were detained were entitled to due process rights and had a right to a fair trial before an impartial court. By balancing the needs of national security and the constitutional protection of individual freedoms, the Court appealed to the judicial branch to consider both types of arguments when deciding similar disputes:

---

216 542 U.S. 507 (2004), at 530.

> "We have no reason to doubt that courts faced with these sensitive matters will pay proper heed both to the matters of national security that might arise in an individual case and to the constitutional limitations safeguarding essential liberties that remain vibrant even in times of security concerns."[217]

At the same time *Hamdi* was decided, the Supreme Court ruled in two other Guantanamo Bay detention disputes, *Rasul v. Bush* and *Al Odah v. United States*, which were combined under the name of the first one. The cases referred to questions of jurisdiction pertaining to foreign nationals who were detained by the United States and sought petition for writ of habeas corpus in U.S. courts to determine the legality of their detention. Despite the objection of the Bush administration, which claimed the federal courts lacked jurisdiction in the matter, in a 6-3 decision the Court reversed the lower courts' decisions, holding that the right to habeas corpus was not dependent on nationality, and that U.S. control over the detention camps gave the detainees the power to file suits in American courts challenging the constitutionality of their status.[218]

If *Hamdi* and *Rasul* can be viewed as rulings which only partially limited executive power in times of national security concerns, the SCOTUS decision in *Hamdan v. Rumsfeld* went a step further. During the U.S. intervention in Afghanistan in 2001, a Yemeni citizen, Salim Ahmed Hamdan, was captured and put in the detention camp in Guantanamo Bay. He was later tried before a military commission established by the Department of Defense, but he was granted the right to habeas corpus and, finally, the dispute was adjudicated by federal judiciary. After winning in the District Court and losing in U.S. Court of Appeals for the District of Columbia Circuit, Hamdan appealed to the Supreme Court, which ruled in his favor in 2006. In a 5-3 opinion authored by Justice John Paul Stevens, the Court declared that the president did not have the power to establish military commissions under either U.S. law – the Constitution, congressional legislation, and military justice law – or international law, such as the Geneva Conventions.[219] Similarly, two years later, in *Boumediene v. Bush*, a dispute reviewing the constitutionality of the suspension of habeas corpus

217 *Ibid.* at 539.
218 542 U.S. 466 (2004).
219 548 U.S. 557 (2006).

by the Military Commissions Act of 2006, the Court held that a presidential memorandum was insufficient to override state law, and that the chief executive lacks the independent power to convert a non-self-executing treaty into a self-executing treaty. In a 5-4 ruling, the majority of the justices acknowledged the right of habeas corpus of detainees held in U.S. military bases such as Guantanamo.[220] Both rulings imposed certain limitations on the authority of the president in matters concerning national security, but they did not deprive the executive of the leading role in these matters.

Somewhat different conclusions, especially with regard to the scope of executive powers in national security matters, may be derived from the SCOTUS ruling in *Trump v. Hawaii*, a dispute concerning a travel ban imposed by the President as a consequence of legal acts issued by him in 2017. Fulfilling one of his campaign promises, Donald Trump issued two executive orders and a proclamation which restricted travel into the United States of nationals of seven Muslim countries, as well as refugees without valid documents.[221] As the main argument legitimizing the ban on the entrance of foreigners, Trump's administration argued that it was "in the national interest to restrict the entry of aliens who could not be vetted with adequate information – both to protect national security and public safety, and to induce improvement by their home countries." The Supreme Court adjudicated in the dispute in 2018, checking the constitutionality of Trump's proclamation, which was challenged by several states, including Hawaii, on the basis of a violation of the First Amendment's Free Establishment clause. In a narrow margin decision, made along ideological lines, the Court upheld the travel ban, holding that the president may issue laws which are intended to protect national security:

> "Under these circumstances, the Government has set forth a sufficient national security justification to survive rational basis review. We express no view on the sound- ness of the policy. We simply hold today that plaintiffs have not demonstrated a likelihood of success on the merits of their constitutional claim."[222]

---

220 553 U.S. 723 (2008).

221 Executive Order 13769, January 27, 2017; Executive Order 13780, March 6, 2017; Proclamation 9645, September 24, 2017.

222 585 U.S. 17–965 (2018).

Apart from the national security disputes pertaining to the status of detainees or the scope of presidential executive orders, the SCOTUS has been reluctant to actively participate in cases regarding foreign intelligence surveillance, despite press leaks, political debates, and the concerns of the American society over the scope of NSA surveillance of U.S. citizens. Following the implementation of the Patriot Act and other post-9/11 legislation expanding the surveillance powers of the intelligence agencies, until 2013 the Court did not adjudicate in any dispute over the constitutionality of NSA surveillance. Then, the justices had the opportunity to review a challenge to the FISA Amendments Act of 2008 which was brought by Amnesty International and many other groups including civil rights organizations, journalists, and lawyers. The challenge concerned the law which authorized U.S. foreign intelligence electronic surveillance of foreigners outside the United States, which – according to the petitioners – violated several provisions of the Constitution, including Article Three and the First and Fourth Amendments. The District Court for the Southern District of New York ruled that the petitioners did not have standing to sue the government, as they asked abstract questions not being subject themselves of the negative consequences of the surveillance. On appeal, the U.S. Court of Appeals for the Second Circuit rejected this argumentation, holding that reasonable fear of such negative consequences as the cost of ensuring the confidentiality of international communications was enough to prove their standing. The Supreme Court was divided as to the final assessment of the case, but the majority consisting of five justices overruled the Court of Appeals decision, arguing that the organizations and individuals who challenged the legislation did not have a legal standing.

Justice Samuel A. Alito, who wrote the majority opinion in *Clapper v. Amnesty International USA*, analyzed the scope and character of NSA surveillance, trying to determine the potential impact of these measures on the functioning of the challengers. In his opinion Alito referred often to the speculative character of the challenge, as well as to various forms of surveillance which can be imposed by the government on foreign nationals:

> "First, it is speculative whether the Government will imminently target communications to which respondents are parties... Yet respondents have no actual knowledge of the Government's §1881a targeting practices. Instead, respondents merely speculate and make assumptions about whether their

communications with their foreign contacts will be acquired under §1881a... Simply put, respondents can only speculate as to how the Attorney General and the Director of National Intelligence will exercise their discretion in determining which communications to target. Second, even if respondents could demonstrate that the targeting of their foreign contacts is imminent, respondents can only speculate as to whether the Government will seek to use §1881aauthorized surveillance (rather than other methods) to do so. The Government has numerous other methods of conducting surveillance, none of which is challenged here. Even after the enactment of the FISA Amendments Act, for example, the Government may still conduct electronic surveillance of persons abroad under the older provisions of FISA so long as it satisfies the applicable requirements, including a demonstration of probable cause to believe that the person is a foreign power or agent of a foreign power."[223]

Claiming that the secret character of the surveillance programs made it impossible for their targets to be aware of their scope, the justices rejected the arguments, stressing the high probability of these groups being subject to government surveillance. By analyzing different theories of standing and its interpretation in earlier Court adjudication, Alito reminded his readers that only concrete, not abstract, injury can justify the right to sue the government:

"We hold that respondents lack Article III standing because they cannot demonstrate that the future injury they purportedly fear is certainly impending and because they cannot manufacture standing by incurring costs in anticipation of non-imminent harm."[224]

Interestingly, lower federal courts were more active in confirming the legal standing of petitioners and imposing judicial review of the surveillance programs undertaken by executive agencies, although the rulings announced by these courts were often contradictory. Later the same year, when *Clapper v. Amnesty International USA* was decided, two district courts reviewed the constitutionality of NSA surveillance and reached different verdicts. The U.S. District Court for the District of Columbia ruled against the NSA's bulk metadata collection program in *Klayman v. Obama*, whereas the U.S. District Court for the Southern District of New York declared the constitutionality of the program in *ACLU v. Clapper*. Both disputes were

223 568 U.S. 398 (2013).
224 *Ibid.*

effects of the Snowden affair and growing public concern over the scope of government surveillance powers.

The first dispute, *Klayman v. Obama*, combined two suits challenging the constitutionality of NSA surveillance affecting the privacy rights of the customers of various communications companies. Judge Richard J. Leon called the NSA bulk metadata collection program an indiscriminate and arbitrary invasion of the privacy rights of U.S. citizens which, according to him, violated the Fourth Amendment. He argued that the extent to which the government was collecting data and information about its citizens led to a high probability that everyone's communication could be subject to NSA monitoring:

> "Because the Government can use daily metadata collection to engage in repetitive, surreptitious surveillance of a citizen's private goings on, the NSA database implicates the Fourth Amendment each time a government official monitors it."[225]

Leon was the first federal judge to determine the scope of the program, which he found not only unconstitutional but also ineffective. Two years later, reviewing the dispute once again, focusing this time on jurisdictional grounds, Leon stressed that although he respected the government's power to protect national security, there was also a strong need to support the constitutional rights of U.S. citizens who were being surveilled in an uncontrolled way:

> "With the Government's authority to operate the Bulk Telephony Metadata Program quickly coming to an end, this case is perhaps the last chapter in the Judiciary's evaluation of this particular Program's compatibility with the Constitution. It will not, however, be the last chapter in the ongoing struggle to balance privacy rights and national security interests under our Constitution in an age of evolving technological wizardry. Although this Court appreciates zealousness with which the Government seeks to protect the citizens of our Nation, that same Government bears just as great responsibility to protect the individual liberties of this very citizens." [226]

In *ACLU v. Clapper*, another case challenging the constitutionality of NSA bulk metadata collection, Judge William Pauley of the U.S. District Court

225 957 F. Supp 2d.1 (2013).
226 142 F. Supp. 3d.172 (2015).

for the Southern District of New York ruled for the government, finding no violation of citizens' right to privacy and arguing that the plaintiffs did not enjoy a reasonable expectation of privacy while providing information to third parties, such as telecommunications companies. Pauley claimed that all of the procedures imposed by the Agency were consistent with congressional legislation, including the Patriot Act and the FISA Amendments Act, and that they were a legitimate means to an end, which was the protection of United States against terrorist attacks:

> "No doubt, the bulk telephony metadata collection program vacuums up information about virtually every telephone call to, from, or within the United States. That is by design, as it allows the NSA to detect relationships so attenuated and ephemeral they would otherwise escape notice. As the September 11th attacks demonstrate, the cost of missing such a thread can be horrific. Technology allowed al-Qaeda to operate decentralized and plot international terrorist attacks remotely. The bulk telephony metadata collection program represents the Government's counter-punch: connecting fragmented and fleeting communications to re-construct and eliminate al-Qaeda's terror network."[227]

However, the appeal of the ACLU to the U.S. Court of Appeals for the Second Circuit proved successful, as it overruled the lower court's ruling, holding that the bulk telephone metadata program was unconstitutional because the NSA had exceeded its authority based on Section 215 of the Patriot Act.[228] Both the *Klayman* and *ACLU* disputes did not reach the Supreme Court, as in 2015 Congress adopted the Freedom Act, which prohibited the bulk collection of the records of U.S. citizens' phone calls.

Since 2015, the SCOTUS has not issued any ruling in which it would limit the scope of the foreign intelligence surveillance conducted by the U.S. government. There were several attempts to bring suits to the Court challenging particular programs or actions undertaken by the National Security Agency in the process of the surveillance of U.S. citizens, but the Court remained consistent in its approach to the lack of legal standing of the challengers or the necessarily secretive character of the programs and national security documents. Such an approach may be evidence of Court's reluctance to engage in national security and foreign surveillance

---

227 959 F.Supp.2d 724 (2013).
228 *ACLU v. Clapper*, 14-42 2d.Cir (2015).

disputes, leaving the regulation of the issue to Congress, while also silently approving the placing of potential limitations on the constitutional right to privacy and other freedoms of U.S. citizens. To fully understand the silence or reluctance of the justices to adjudicate in national security surveillance cases it is important to acknowledge the importance of two doctrines raised by the government as a legitimization of broader powers of the executive: the executive privilege and the state secrets privilege. SCOTUS rulings concerning the scope of these doctrines may fully reveal why the legitimate end approach prevails in justices' interpretation of the national security powers of the government.

The SCOTUS and Executive Privilege

Executive privilege is one of the main doctrines invoked by U.S. presidents in the process of legitimizing their surveillance powers, especially with regard to national security policy and foreign surveillance. It refers to the possibility of chief executives withholding information and not sharing it with the members of the other two branches of government or the public. The main arguments in support of the privilege stem from the need for confidentiality in presidential communications and the power to act in secrecy in order to ensure the effectiveness of executive policies. In a system of government based on the separation of powers, it seems crucial that the three leading institutions of respective branches – the president, Congress, and the Supreme Court – cooperate not only by performing common functions or imposing checks and controls on each other, but that they also share crucial information concerning the operation of the government. However, the idea of executive privilege lies in a conviction shared by many U.S. presidents in history, that the exceptional position of the federal executive in the system of government, and the necessity to conduct effective domestic and foreign policy, allows chief executives to enjoy immunity from the encroachment of legislative and judicial institutions into the area of presidential prerogatives.

The sources of executive privilege date back to the beginnings of American statehood. Already during the Philadelphia convention, while discussing the structure and scope of presidential powers, the Founding Fathers referred to the executive branch as the one possessing "the powers of secrecy, vigor, and dispatch".[229] During President George Washington's tenure a discussion occurred as to the scope of his executive power to withhold documents, out of congressional reach. The President rejected the request from Congress to disclose documents related to the expedition against the Indians led by General St. Clair, stating that "the executive ought to communicate such papers as the public good would permit, and ought to refuse those, the disclosure of which would injure the public"[230] As Louis Fisher argues, the dispute over the documents relating to St. Clair's expedition helped to establish the principle of executive privilege, and the significance of Washington's argumentation, which referred to the public instead of the executive branch, set a principle for the following decades of preserving the confidentiality of the actions of the executive.[231]

The issue was indirectly brought up by John Marshall in *Marbury v. Madison* when he set the limits of judicial review, declaring that the judiciary should not plunge into the political relations between the president and his executive officers:

> "By the Constitution of the United States, the President is invested with certain important political powers, in the exercise of which he is to use his own discretion, and is accountable only to his country in his political character and to his own conscience. To aid him in the performance of these duties, he is authorized to appoint certain officers, who act by his authority and in conformity with his orders. In such cases, their acts are his acts; and whatever opinion may be entertained of the manner in which executive discretion may be used, still there exists, and can exist, no power to control that discretion. The subjects are political. They respect the nation, not individual rights, and, being entrusted to the Executive, the decision of the Executive is conclusive. The application of this remark will be perceived by adverting to the act of Congress for establishing the Department of Foreign Affairs. This officer, as his duties were prescribed by that act, is to conform precisely to the will of the President. He is the mere organ by whom that will is communicated. The acts of such an officer, as an officer, can never be examinable by the Courts."[232]

---

229 Max Farrand (ed), *Records of the Federal Convention of 1787. Vol. I*, Yale University Press, New Haven 1966.

230 Francis E. Rourke, *Secrecy and Publicity*, Johns Hopkins University Press, Baltimore 1961, p. 65.

231 Louis Fisher, *The Supreme Court and Congress. Rival Interpretations*, CQ Press, Washington D.C. 2009, p. 10.

232 5 U.S. 137 (1803), at 165, 166.

Although the Marshall Court did not refer to the principle of executive privilege, it clearly stated where the boundaries of the interference of the judicial branch lay when it came to the confidentiality of political relations within the executive. Such an approach refers to the same rationale used by the proponents of executive privilege – that there is a constitutional need to impose limitations on actions undertaken by other branches of government, including the Supreme Court and Congress. This was reflected in the famous trial of Vice-President Aaron Burr, in which John Marshall was the presiding judge and President Thomas Jefferson was a key witness. Marshall subpoenaed Jefferson, making him appear before the court, but he did not force the President to present all the relevant documents during the trial, as both Marshall and Jefferson agreed that there was a form of executive privilege protecting the confidentiality of presidential communications.[233]

There is, however, a problem with reconciling the need for the confidentiality of presidential actions, including the possibility of withholding presidential communication, with the approach presented by Congress acknowledging its power to demand information from the president about executive actions and policies. As David Frost points out, "among the most important of Congress' checks on the executive branch is Congress' power to investigate and oversee the actions of the executive."[234] The investigatory powers of the legislative branch have become one of the main tools used by Congress to collect information about the operations of the executive, although they are not expressed in the Constitution. However, reading from its spirit rather than letter, the justices were able to define the scope of congressional power to investigate and obtain necessary information from the executive, which happened in *McGrain v. Daugherty*. In a unanimous decision concerning a failure to appear before a congressional investigative committee, the Court declared an implied power of the federal legislature to carry out an investigation and call witnesses to give testimonies.[235] In that context, there seems to

233 See: John C. Yoo, "The First Claim: The Burr Trial, United States v. Nixon, and Presidential Power", *Minnesota Law Review* 83, 1999, pp. 1435–1474.

234 David B. Frost, *Classified. A History of Secrecy in the United States Government*, McFarland and Company, Jefferson 2017, 145.

235 273 U.S. 135 (1927).

be a conflict between the congressional need to get access to information, and presidential executive privilege protecting the access of outside actors to valuable information withheld by the executive branch. Regardless of the above-mentioned tensions, the scope of executive privilege became the main issue in SCOTUS adjudication in the milestone case *United States v. Nixon*, decided in 1974. The decision belongs to the pantheon of rulings regarding the scope of the separation of powers doctrine, and, especially, the character and limits of the powers of the judiciary, as well as the extent to which executive privilege may be exercised by the president. It is also significant from the perspective of the main purposes of this research, as the analysis of it may bring interesting conclusions with respect to the role of the national security paradigm in Supreme Court rulings, including surveillance case-law.

The facts of the dispute concern the events known as the Watergate scandal, as mentioned above – the burglary of the Watergate hotel in Washington in an attempt to install illegal surveillance devices during the 1972 Democratic National Convention, which was to nominate the party's presidential candidate. The possible involvement in the burglary of high-ranking officials in Richard Nixon's campaign was revealed by the *Washington Post* as a consequence of an independent investigation conducted by journalists of the newspaper, who obtained information from an undercover FBI officer.[236] Evidence subsequently collected by federal law enforcement led to the accusation of involvement in the plot of seven people, including the former Attorney General and the chief of the Committee to Re-elect President Nixon, John Mitchell. During the *U.S. v. Mitchell, et.al.* trial, the District Court came into possession of information that President Nixon had recorded conversations in the Oval Office and was in possession the tapes which could shed new light on the circumstances of the dispute. The court requested that the President hand over the tapes as important evidence in a pending litigation, but he refused and justified his decision by invoking executive privilege. When the dispute reached the Supreme Court the justices had to balance two contradictory values: presidential

236 See: Carl Bernstein, Bob Woodward, *All the President's Men: The Greatest Reporting Story of All Time*, Simon & Schuster, New York 2014.

privilege and judicial intrusion into the powers of the executive. Writing for the Court, which reached a unanimous decision, Chief Justice Warren Burger emphasized the importance of the privilege for the proper operation of the government:

> "The expectation of a President to the confidentiality of his conversations and correspondence, like the claim of confidentiality of judicial deliberations, for example, has all the values to which we accord deference for the privacy of all citizens and, added to those values, is the necessity for protection of the public interest in candid, objective, and even blunt or harsh opinions in Presidential decision making. A President and those who assist him must be free to explore alternatives in the process of shaping policies and making decisions, and to do so in a way many would be unwilling to express except privately. These are the considerations justifying a presumptive privilege for Presidential communications. The privilege is fundamental to the operation of Government, and inextricably rooted in the separation of powers under the Constitution."[237]

Despite affirming the value of the privilege, Burger argued that it was never meant to be absolute, as the principles of separation of powers and checks and balances ensured that each branch could impose certain means of controlling the others, such as judicial review exercised by the Court. The SCOTUS questioned the arguments via which President Nixon tried to legitimize the absolutist character of the privilege, referring to the public interest as the main justification for the need to protect the confidentiality of his communication:

> "However, neither the doctrine of separation of powers nor the need for confidentiality of high-level communications, without more, can sustain an absolute, unqualified Presidential privilege of immunity from judicial process under all circumstances. The President's need for complete candor and objectivity from advisers calls for great deference from the courts. However, when the privilege depends solely on the broad, undifferentiated claim of public interest in the confidentiality of such conversations, a confrontation with other values arises."[238]

Paradoxically, the reasoning offered by Nixon was contrary to the values of the criminal justice system, especially since there was a pending dispute in which evidence was necessary to determine its outcome. By referring to

---

237 418 U.S. 683 (1974), at 708.
238 *Ibid.* at 706.

the famous quote from *Berger v. United States*, the Chief Justice Burger reiterated the main purposes of criminal justice system, that "guilt shall not escape, or innocence suffer", and that:

> "The ends of criminal justice would be defeated if judgments were to be founded on a partial or speculative presentation of the facts. The very integrity of the judicial system and public confidence in the system depend on full disclosure of all the facts, within the framework of the rules of evidence. To ensure that justice is done, it is imperative to the function of courts that compulsory process be available for the production of evidence needed either by the prosecution or by the defense."[239]

As a result, the Court declared that executive privilege, although important for the operation of the executive, could not override the interests of a pending criminal trial, and that President Nixon was obliged to release the tapes to the District Court for the needs of the Watergate litigation. By acknowledging the presidential general power of executive privilege, the justices presented the circumstances which could legitimize the possibility of withholding the content of the tapes:

> "Absent a claim of need to protect military, diplomatic, or sensitive national security secrets, we find it difficult to accept the argument that even the very important interest in confidentiality of Presidential communications is significantly diminished by production of such material for *in camera* inspection with all the protection that a district court will be obliged to provide."[240]

In the above quoted part, the Court clearly listed three types of circumstances which could justify the secrecy of presidential actions and communication: military, diplomatic, and sensitive national security secrets. One may wonder if that part of the opinion was not created just to strengthen the argumentation in support of the value of executive privilege, as it referred to issues which Nixon did not raise in his defense of it. On the other hand, such an approach correlates with the arguments presented in earlier SCOTUS opinions, were the defense of the country and its national security became the main justification for upholding the powers of the government. Furthermore, the analysis of this part of Court's reasoning has served in subsequent years as a crucial point of reference in disputes

239 *Ibid.* at 709.
240 *Ibid.* at 706.

which did not raise questions concerning presidential executive privilege, not to mention the fact that Burger's argumentation corresponds with John Marshall's approach from *McCulloch* and can be understood as defining the scope of the powers of the executive in the area of national security policy. If claims of military, diplomatic, and national security imperatives may justify the confidentiality of presidential communication, they may also justify various activities undertaken by the chief executive and the institutions subordinate to him, including those involved in government surveillance. It is just a matter of which means the government chooses.

Of course, the justices did not directly reach such conclusions, but the fact that the circumstances of the case resulted both from an attempt to conduct illegal surveillance, as well as the existence of the tapes that were secretly recorded by the President in the Oval Office, strengthens the feeling that *Nixon* was not just a case determining the character of presidential executive privilege. Instead, it should be read as a strong suggestion of the judicial branch that its executive counterpart may act with more freedom once it has invoked national security arguments. Such an approach, understood in the context of *McCulloch*, guarantees that if the "end" of the government is to protect national security, then it is legitimate when the means used to ensure the effective security of the country are within the letter and spirit of the Constitution. Not surprisingly, the constitutionality of such means has to be determined by the judiciary, which Burger recalled at the beginning of his opinion by reaffirming the *Marbury* holding. In this way the spirit of Marshall's argumentation helped the mid-1970s SCOTUS to decide about the scope of presidential powers, which were limited as to the circumstances of the particular case, but in reality could be expanded by the legitimization of government national security claims.

The executive privilege argument has been present in subsequent opinions written by the Supreme Court justices, some of which were concurring, and some dissenting, still playing an important role in understanding the scope of the doctrine, especially in the context of the national security powers of the executive. As one of the common features of executive privilege the argument of confidentiality and secrecy has become significant. As David Frost rightly notes:

> "The executive privilege affects the scope of the separation of powers doctrine by granting the presidents and their executive agencies a certain sphere of

> sovereignty from encroachments of Congress or the courts. Such sovereignty is especially necessary with regard to surveillance measures, where confidentiality refers to both the actions of the executive, and often to the lack of information about the existence of concrete program."[241]

From that perspective, not only national security as a rhetorical tool or an element of government policy, but confidentiality as a value assuring the effectiveness of the authorities' pursuit of their goals remains at the center of the argumentation used by those who would like to justify certain actions of the executive, including the imposition of broad surveillance measures. The analysis of SCOTUS adjudication shows that secrecy has played a significant role in supporting the operations of the executive, especially in the area of national security and government surveillance. The main arguments raised by the justices were often based on the state secrets privilege.

The SCOTUS and the State Secrets Privilege

The state secrets privilege has been part of the U.S. constitutional system since its inception, which is not surprising considering the references made by the Founding Fathers to the need for the executive to operate in secret. Although it is a broader concept than the executive privilege, which refers to the confidentiality of presidential actions and communications, both doctrines have been used in courts to protect certain classified information from being revealed to the public, usually in disputes involving governmental officials or specific actions of the authorities which affected the scope of the rights and freedoms of individuals. The most important case to confirm the importance of the doctrine for American constitutionalism was the 1950's dispute *United States v. Reynolds*, but already in the late 19th century the Supreme Court was involved in shaping the character and scope of the concept which later was defined as the state secrets privilege.

In *Totten v. United States,* the justices analyzed the issue of whether the judiciary had the power to determine the legal aspects of oral contracts of government spies, or whether judicial review of these documents was impossible due to their secret character. The dispute concerned the potential recovery of expenses incurred during William Lloyd's service as a spy for

241 David B. Frost, *Classified. A History...*, op. cit., p. 145.

Abraham Lincoln's administration. The interests of Lloyd's family, he already being deceased, were represented by the executor of his estate, Enoch Totten, who sued the government in the United States Court of Claims. This Court suggested that the claims should be dismissed on the basis of the character of the contract. Similarly, in a unanimous decision authored by Justice Stephen J. Field, the SCOTUS affirmed the dismissal of the case, holding that judicial review of the contract was impossible as it would result in the disclosure of state secrets. By comparing different types of contracts and confidential relations occurring within the participants of various social relations, Justice Field stressed the importance of contracts for secret services with the government:

> "It may be stated as a general principle that public policy forbids the maintenance of any suit in a court of justice the trial of which would inevitably lead to the disclosure of matters which the law itself regards as confidential and respecting which it will not allow the confidence to be violated. On this principle, suits cannot be maintained which would require a disclosure of the confidences of the confessional, or those between husband and wife, or of communications by a client to his counsel for professional advice, or of a patient to his physician for a similar purpose. Much greater reason exists for the application of the principle to cases of contract for secret services with the government, as the existence of a contract of that kind is itself a fact not to be disclosed."[242]

Even if the state secrets privilege was not yet established, the arguments referring to the secrecy of government operations had been raised and had gained constitutional significance. Despite the narrow character of the opinion, as it concerned the protection of the confidentially of contracts in the area of espionage, the *Totten* principle has been followed in the 20th century Court's adjudication, as well in 21st century decisions which have even expanded the meaning of the precedent. Interestingly, in the second half of the 20th century the state secrets privilege was raised in more than 50 cases, whereas in the first fifteen years of the 21st century it was used in almost 40 disputes and was approved by the judiciary on most occasions.[243] Out of all the SCOTUS decisions determining the character of the doctrine, the most significant was the ruling in *Unites States v. Reynolds*, announced

---

242 92 U.S. 105 (1875), at 107.

243 Barry Siegel, *Judging the State Secrets: Who Decides – and How?* in: *After Snowden...*, op. cit.

in 1953 in the first phase of the Cold War, however, already in late 1940s the justices acknowledged the limited scope of judicial intrusion into presidents' foreign affairs powers:

> "The President, both as Commander-in-Chief and as the Nation's organ for foreign affairs, has available intelligence services whose reports are not and ought not to be published to the world. It would be intolerable that courts, without the relevant information, should review and perhaps nullify actions of the Executive taken on information properly held secret."[244]

Five years later, the *Reynolds* case reached the SCOTUS. The dispute was the result of an accident involving a B-29 bomber with military and civilian personnel on board which was testing secret equipment for the Army. Three widows whose husbands died in the crash applied to have access to the investigation report analyzing and explaining the circumstances related to the accident, as well as the possible cause of it. The Air Force refused to release the report due to the fact that it contained information concerning the secret equipment on board the aircraft and therefore that its publication could threaten U.S. national security. Lower courts found in favor of the widows, claiming that the government had an obligation to disclose the report to the judges. The case was brought to the Supreme Court, which analyzed the powers of the executive to withhold secret information related to its operation, as well as the power of the judiciary to determine the validity of an invocation of the state secrets privilege.

In the majority opinion authored by Chief Justice Fred Vinson and signed by five other justices, the Court begun with the assertion of the source and scope of executive power in the area of foreign affairs. Then, by referring to the history of the state secrets privilege, both in England and in the United States, the Court identified the principles and procedures guiding the use of the privilege by government institutions, as well as the role of judges in defining the appropriateness the authorities' invoking of the privilege:

> "Judicial experience with the privilege which protects military and state secrets has been limited in this country. English experience has been more extensive, but still relatively slight compared with other evidentiary privileges. Nevertheless, the principles which control the application of the privilege emerge quite clearly

---

244 *Chicago & Southern Airlines, Inc. v. Waterman S.S. Corp.* 333 U.S. 103 (1948), at 111.

from the available precedents. The privilege belongs to the Government, and must be asserted by it; it can neither be claimed nor waived by a private party. It is not to be lightly invoked. There must be formal claim of privilege, lodged by the head of the department which has control over the matter, after actual personal consideration by that officer. The court itself must determine whether the circumstances are appropriate for the claim of privilege, and yet do so without forcing a disclosure of the very thing the privilege is designed to protect."[245]

Furthermore, as Chief Justice Vinson observed, the controlling role of the judiciary had certain limits stemming from the character of the privilege and from the reasons which justified the lack of disclosure of the documents, among which the most crucial were national security concerns and the military interest:

"Judicial control over the evidence in a case cannot be abdicated to the caprice of executive officers. Yet we will not go so far as to say that the court may automatically require a complete disclosure to the judge before the claim of privilege will be accepted in any case. It may be possible to satisfy the court, from all the circumstances of the case, that there is a reasonable danger that compulsion of the evidence will expose military matters which, in the interest of national security, should not be divulged. When this is the case, the occasion for the privilege is appropriate, and the court should not jeopardize the security which the privilege is meant to protect by insisting upon an examination of the evidence, even by the judge alone, in chambers."[246]

The national security and the defense of American interests became the main concern of the Court, which acknowledged the circumstances of U.S. foreign policy at the beginning of the 1950s. The justices not only approved the necessity of maintaining secrecy with regard to the equipment carried by the airplane, but expanded the protection of the government's privilege to all cases in which a reasonable danger to country's security was present:

"In the instant case, we cannot escape judicial notice that this is a time of vigorous preparation for national defense. Experience in the past has made it common knowledge that air power is one of the most potent weapons in our scheme of defense, and that newly developing electronic devices have greatly enhanced the effective use of air power. It is equally apparent that these electronic devices must be kept secret if their full military advantage is to be exploited

245 345 U.S. 1 (1953), at 7.
246 *Ibid.* at 9.

> in the national interests. On the record before the trial court, it appeared that this accident occurred to a military plane which had gone aloft to test secret electronic equipment. Certainly there was a reasonable danger that the accident investigation report would contain references to the secret electronic equipment which was the primary concern of the mission."[247]

Therefore, if the government wanted to withhold information or documents on the basis of the state secrets privilege, it had to justify its operation with reasonable arguments, but not necessarily disclose the information or documents in a judicial proceeding. In such a way, the courts were equipped with theoretical control of the actions undertaken by the executive, as the government did not exercise an exclusive authority in invoking the privilege. In practice, however, judges or justices had limited access to the materials being subject to the application of this privilege. This meant, according to Victor Hansen and Lawrence Friedman, that the privilege could be exercised at the sole discretion of the chief executive, who was in the best position to know when the disclosure of protected information would have an adverse impact on national security interests.[248] The SCOTUS therefore legitimized the government's invoking of the privilege in every single situation in which it reasonably argued that the disclosure of information or documents was impossible due to national security concerns.

Interestingly, as revealed half century later, the text of the report contained information that the bomber had mechanical defects which could have led to the crash. It turned out that the arguments used by the authorities were not honest, as they hid information about the mistakes made by the Army, rather than protecting the U.S. from reasonable danger.[249] In that context, the words used by Judge Albert Maris of the U.S. Court of Appeals for the Third Circuit, who criticized the government's position in the *Reynolds* case, take on a special meaning. Writing an opinion in which he supported the claims of the widows of the military officers killed in the crash, he stressed that the refusal to disclose the contents of the report was "to assert a privilege against any disclosure of records merely because they might

---

247 *Ibid.* at 10.

248 Victor M. Hansen, Lawrence Friedman, *The Case for Congress...*, op. cit., p. 97.

249 Louis Fisher, *Supreme Court Expansion...*, op. cit., p. 125.

prove embarrassing".[250] Maris' arguments were quoted by the three justices who dissented in *Reynolds* – Hugo Black, Felix Frankfurter and Robert Jackson – but the precedent set by the SCOTUS remained in force over the following decades, affirming the significance of the state secrets privilege for the operation of the executive within the national security framework.

However, the Supreme Court did not invoke the state secrets privilege in every Cold War-relevant ruling, or other argumentation based on the need for secrecy, even if the government tried to legitimize its operations by making national security arguments. In *New York Times Co. v. United States* – a dispute known as the "Pentagon Papers" case – the SCOTUS defended the right of the media to publish documents relating to government war operations in spite of a presidential argument referring to the protection of national security. The issue concerned the efforts of two newspapers of record, the *New York Times* and the *Washington Post*, to publish classified documents regarding the activities of the U.S. Army in Vietnam. President Nixon, stressing the classified character of the information, wanted to impose prior restraint to prevent the publication of the articles. In a per curiam opinion the justices rejected the President's claims, raising the importance of the First Amendment's guarantees of freedom of speech and of the press. They argued that prior restraint would be legitimate only if President Nixon was able to prove his claims about serious national security concerns rather than just refer to the "broad, vague generality" of the word 'security'. As the Court declared:

> "[W]e are asked to hold that, despite the First Amendment's emphatic command, the Executive Branch, the Congress, and the Judiciary can make laws enjoining publication of current news and abridging freedom of the press in the name of "national security." The Government does not even attempt to rely on any act of Congress. Instead, it makes the bold and dangerously far-reaching contention that the courts should take it upon themselves to "make" a law abridging freedom of the press in the name of equity, presidential power and national security, even when the representatives of the people in Congress have adhered to the command of the First Amendment and refused to make such a law."[251]

250 Frederick A.O. Schwartz, jr., *Democracy in the Dark: The Seduction of Government Secrecy*, The New Press, New York 2015, p. 206.
251 403 U.S. 713 (1971), at 718.

Interestingly, the concurring opinion signed by Justices Potter Stewart and Byron White focused on the challenges presented by the secrecy issue in the context of the operation of the executive branch. On the one hand, the justices pointed out the indispensable character of confidentiality and secrecy for national security policies, claiming that "in the area of basic national defense, the frequent need for absolute secrecy is ... self-evident". On the other hand, however, they stressed that:

> "If the Constitution gives the Executive a large degree of unshared power in the conduct of foreign affairs and the maintenance of our national defense, then, under the Constitution, the Executive must have the largely unshared duty to determine and preserve the degree of internal security necessary to exercise that power successfully. It is an awesome responsibility, requiring judgment and wisdom of a high order ... [M]oral, political, and practical considerations would dictate that a very first principle of that wisdom would be an insistence upon avoiding secrecy for its own sake. For when everything is classified, then nothing is classified, and the system becomes one to be disregarded by the cynical or the careless, and to be manipulated by those intent on self-protection or self-promotion. I should suppose, in short, that the hallmark of a truly effective internal security system would be the maximum possible disclosure, recognizing that secrecy can best be preserved only when credibility is truly maintained."[252]

At the beginning of the 21st century, in the post-9/11 period, the U.S. executive strengthened its support of the state secrets privilege, during the presidency of George W. Bush. As Laura K. Donoghue notes, the Bush administration used the privilege in a very broad context to prevent litigants from challenging executive branch actions, including the transfer of suspects to other countries for interrogation and torture, warrantless surveillance conducted by the NSA, and other executive initiatives.[253] As a consequence the executive sought dismissals in many civil cases which were brought to lower federal courts; none of them, however, reached the Supreme Court. In most of these cases, however, district and circuit courts found the government's arguments invoking state secrets privilege to be reasonable, for example as in *El Masri v. United States*, a dispute in which the plaintiff accused the government of illegal detention and the infliction

---

252 Stewart, concurring. *Ibid.* at 728, 729.

253 Laura K. Donoghue, "The Shadow of State Secrets", *University of Pennsylvania Law Reviews* 159, 2010, p. 79.

of torture, and in *Arar v. Ashcroft, et.al.*, a case involving a Canadian citizen who was interrogated by the FBI and sent to Syria, where he suffered torture.[254] Contrarily to the federal judiciary, Congress considered in 2008 adopting legislation to regulate and limit the state secrets privilege, but the Bush administration lobbied to prevent the implementation of the law as an unconstitutional interference the executive's right to operate in secrecy.[255]

The change in the White House which occurred with Barack Obama's victory in the 2008 presidential election did not significantly change U.S. policy towards the state secrets privilege. Despite a memorandum of attorney general Eric Holder, who promised to limit the use of the privilege - invoking it only in necessary cases having a negative impact on national security - the Obama administration continued to invoke the doctrine in judicial disputes involving extraordinary rendition, warrantless surveillance, and cases in which individuals challenged the right of the government to place them on the no-fly list.[256] This approach could be observed in the government's argumentation in *Mohamed v. Jeppesen Dataplan, Inc.* (a case brought by five victims of extraordinary renditions, in which the state secrets privilege argument was approved), *Jewel v. N.S.A.* (a class action lawsuit against the NSA's warrantless surveillance – privilege partly approved), *Shubert v. Obama* (a class action against NSA dragnet surveillance – privilege rejected), and *Al-Aulaqi v. Obama* (a challenge to the government's asserted authority to carry out targeted killings of U.S. citizens – privilege approved).[257] All of these disputes were adjudicated in lower federal courts and, despite their different outcomes, none of the losing parties were granted certiorari from the Supreme Court. Still, in the first decade of the 21st century there were cases concerning the state secrets privilege which did reach the highest judicial instance, although the facts of these disputes resembled those from *Totten v. United States*.

First, in 2005, in *Tenet v. Doe* the SCOTUS reviewed an appeal stemming from a dispute in which people engaged in the CIA's espionage activities

---

254 479 F.3d 296 (2007); 585 F.3d 559 (2009).

255 Heidi Kitrosser, *Reclaiming Accountability...*, op. cit., p. 4.

256 Chris Edelson, *Power Without Constraint...*, op. cit., p. 153.

257 Christina Wells, "State Secrets and Executive Accountability", *Constitutional Commentary* 26, 2010, pp. 626–628.

challenged the government over the lack of enforcement of their contracts. Similarly to the *Totten* ruling, a unanimous Court confirmed that the secrecy of espionage contracts serves the interest of the state and therefore legitimizes the government to be beyond the reach of judicial review, arguing that "[t]he possibility that a suit may proceed and an espionage relationship may be revealed, if the state secrets privilege is found not to apply, is unacceptable".[258] Then, a few years later, in *General Dynamics Corp. v. United States*, the justices strengthened the *Totten* and *Tenet* holdings by preventing a private military entity from using the contract it signed with the government as evidence in a dispute over potential damages for the problems with the enforcement of this contract. The main reasoning behind the verdict related to the state secrets privilege as a justification for a non-disclosure of documents signed between the government and private contractor who should have been aware of the risk stemming from such a relationship.[259]

Apart from the above-mentioned SCOTUS decisions which defined the scope of the state secrets privilege with regard to contracts regarding military, defense, or – more broadly – security issues, in recent years the Court has issued important decisions determining the current status of the privilege, including *United States v. Zubaydah* and *F.B.I. v. Fazaga*. The first dispute referred to Abu Zubaydah, who was detained in Pakistan and later in Guantanamo Bay, but claimed that he was also held in a secret CIA detention center in Poland. During the trial in lower courts, Zubaydah demanded that the government disclose information about the secret detention site, but the authorities denied such a possibility by hiding behind the state secrets privilege. The U.S. Court of Appeals for the Ninth Circuit decided for Zubaydah, arguing that there was no reasonable danger to the national security and that the government should release the information demanded. In a 7-2 ruling authored by Justice Stephen Breyer, the SCOTUS reversed the lower court's decision based on the government's argumentation for withholding information about the Agency's secret detention camps:

258 544 U.S. 1 (2005).
259 563 U.S. 478 (2011).

> "The Government argues that the privilege should apply because Zubaydah's discovery request could force former CIA contractors to confirm the location of the detention site and that confirmation would itself significantly harm national security interests. In our view, the Government has provided sufficient support for its claim of harm to warrant application of the privilege."[260]

It is hard to ignore the impression that the 2022 Court followed the principle of stare decisis and applied the reasoning from the almost 70-year-old precedent, confirming the role of the judiciary in determining whether the state secrets privilege should be invoked, and leaving it, at the same time, to the discretion to the government to present national security arguments which could ensure success in the eyes of a majority of justices.

Just one day later, the SCOTUS decided another case which partly referred to the state secrets privilege, but mainly concerned the legality of electronic surveillance. In *F.B.I. v. Fazaga* the justices were required to determine whether the Foreign Surveillance Intelligence Act of 1978 limited the scope of the state secrets doctrine, thus authorizing courts to force the executive to disclose necessary evidence which the government had treated as privileged. The facts of the dispute concerned a covert FBI surveillance program collecting information about the activities of an Islamic Center in Irvine, California. Referring to religious freedom, the right to privacy and due process of law, three Muslim residents sued the Agency for violation the Constitution, but during the trial the government invoked state secrets privilege to prevent the court gaining access to the documents necessary to determine the character of the surveillance program. The District Court approved most of the arguments presented by the legal representatives of the FBI, but the U.S. Court of Appeals for the Ninth Circuit reversed the decision, claiming that the judges could have access to the privileged evidence in the dispute. On appeal, the Supreme Court unanimously confirmed the right of the government to invoke the state secrets privilege, arguing that the FISA provisions did not preclude the use of the privilege. The justices agreed with the FBI's argumentation that the legislation analyzed here did not apply to disputes which challenged the Agency's surveillance methods:

260 595 U.S. 20–827 (2022).

> "The text of FISA weighs heavily against the argument that Congress intended FISA to displace the state secrets privilege. The absence of any reference to the state secrets privilege in FISA is strong evidence that the availability of the privilege was not altered when Congress passed the Act. Regardless of whether the state secrets privilege is rooted only in the common law (as respondents argue) or also in the Constitution (as the Government argues), the privilege should not be held to have been abrogated or limited unless Congress has at least used clear statutory language."[261]

By quoting the findings of the *Reynolds* Court, the author of the majority opinion, Justice Samuel Alito, reminded his readers that in disputes concerning the state secrets privilege, "the central question is not whether the evidence in question was lawfully obtained but whether its disclosure would harm national-security interests."[262] Therefore, once again the SCOTUS declared the constitutionality of the government's use of the privilege, strengthening the reasonable danger standard as a basis for the limitation on both private parties suing the government and the presentation of national security-sensitive evidence in court. National security arguments have served continuously as a legitimate end of government operations, and all means which have been labelled as appropriate, or constitutional, have been applied within an overwhelming spirit of secrecy.

261 595 U.S. 20–828 (2022).
262 *Ibid.*

Chapter Four The Legitimization of Surveillance

The Consequences of SCOTUS Surveillance Decisions

The analysis of Supreme Court adjudication pertaining to both domestic and foreign intelligence, or national security surveillance, brings various research conclusions that have serious consequences for the functioning of the government, including relations among its various branches and the nature of the policies that have been implemented, but also for fundamental values that affect American society, such as the scope of the rights and freedoms of individuals and the relations between the society and the government. Before discussing the most important of these conclusions, it seems indispensable to point out that SCOTUS adjudication in surveillance cases may be divided into two major groups of disputes: cases in which the justices decided to issue rulings which determined the constitutionality of challenged actions or legislation (including the interpretation of the Fourth Amendment with regard to domestic surveillance, and the scope of the fundamental constitutional rights of individuals), and disputes which the Court accepted for consideration but declined to resolve in the way expected by the challengers due to the imposition of certain judicial self-restraint procedures or other doctrines and privileges (such as lack of standing or ripeness, executive privilege or state secrets doctrine).

However, it is worth stressing the fact that there have also been a significant number of cases decided by lower courts which did not reach the Supreme Court for various reasons, including justices' reluctance to address the legal challenges raised in these disputes. It is impossible to determine the number of such cases, but careful analysis of SCOTUS adjudication and the arguments used by justices in a number of opinions pertaining to issues other than surveillance explains why in certain areas of constitutional law the Court was more passive. It is by no means only the nature of judicial restraint, but also the conviction among the justices, that some issues should not be reviewed by the judicial branch because they constitute political questions and therefore fall within the powers reserved for the other branches, or that they should remain confidential. The power of secrecy will be discussed below, but it must be emphasized here, before any further elaboration, that the research conclusions should consider both the results of the rulings issued by the Supreme Court *as well* as the consequences of the lack of Court decisions in the area of government surveillance. Such an approach stems from the fact that judicial restraint may be understood as a certain form of judicial activism, proving that there are always legal and political consequences of SCOTUS inactivity and silence. The lack of a decision is also a decision – there are always beneficiaries and victims of disputes in which justices decide not to intervene, which brings not only individual consequences for the parties to the dispute but also reveals the real attitude of justices, who have the discretionary power to determine the cases in which they want to adjudicate. Furthermore, inactivity or a reluctance to issue a ruling in a dispute raising important issues may also position the Court in relation to the two other branches of government, thereby influencing the character of the separation of powers and the system of checks and balances.

Considering the importance of judicial restraint and judicial activism, one should focus on the precedents which shaped the contemporary understanding of the scope of the constitutionality of U.S. government surveillance. The analysis conducted in chapters two and three focused on several dozen SCOTUS decisions which determined various aspects connected with the changing meaning of the Search and Seizure and Warrant Clauses of the Fourth Amendment, such as the scope of the right to privacy, the reasonableness of search and seizure conducted by law enforcement agencies, the conditions set for obtaining a warrant, the exceptions of warrantless searches and seizures, the constitutionality of the surveillance tools used by the authorities, the necessary balance between freedom and security, the scope of national security surveillance, the executive privilege and state secret doctrines limiting the suits in government surveillance cases, ideological attitudes of justices in adjudication concerning surveillance, the arguments supporting and limiting the expansion of the powers of the government, the level of control of the executive by the other branches, and other issues the examination of which can help us to understand the current constitutional status of government surveillance. The Court's involvement in constitutional debates about the meaning of the Fourth Amendment occurred in different moments of history with varying intensity, depending on the political circumstances of domestic and international reality, the actions undertaken by individuals or organizations challenging the procedures imposed by the government, the growth of technology and changing character of surveillance tools, and, most often, initiatives undertaken by law enforcement or national security institutions responsible for protecting the society from inner and outer threats.

The main purpose of the analysis was to determine how the Supreme Court legitimized the expansion of powers of the government with regard to domestic and foreign intelligence surveillance. I wanted to examine the character of SCOTUS surveillance adjudication from the perspective of the *McCulloch v. Maryland* ruling, focusing especially on the legitimate end approach, trying to define the purposes of government surveillance and the means used by the authorities to legitimize their need to expand their powers. In that context, not only the majority opinions, but also concurring and dissenting opinions of justices also required analysis in order to bring in the full range of arguments used by the justices to expand or limit government surveillance powers. The research was conducted mainly with reference to 20th and early-21st century history, including domestic and international events which determined the character of the U.S. government's politics, resulting in several challenges to executive action and congressional legislation in the area of criminal justice and national security. However, the nature of the research determined the necessity to focus also on early 19th century SCOTUS jurisprudence from the era of the Marshall Court, as its legacy turned out to be significant for subsequent generations of justices in their constitutional interpretation. Adopting such a perspective allowed the obtaining of research results which have produced important conclusions as to the character of government surveillance and the role of the Supreme Court in shaping the domestic and national security policy of the United States. The list below consists of the most important issues, in the estimation of the author, which can be derived from the analysis of SCOTUS adjudication in surveillance disputes:

1. The Court has balanced the need to provide security with the protection of the freedom of individuals, by raising crucial arguments in support of both values and applying different standards if disputes concerned domestic or foreign intelligence surveillance.

2. The justices have expanded government powers in surveillance-related cases, which meant strengthening the position of the executive branch in relation to the legislative and judicial branches, thus affecting the separation of powers and checks and balances system.
3. As a result of its surveillance-relevant adjudication, the SCOTUS has played an important role in legitimizing, sustaining, and developing the overwhelming culture of secrecy shrouding the operation of the government, on the one hand, and hampering the social need for transparency on the other.
4. Although ideology has played a decisive role in the direction of Court's adjudication in the majority of cases regarding the scope of the rights and freedoms of individuals, as well as federal-state relations, in disputes concerning government surveillance the conservative and liberal justices have often been unified in their approach towards the expansion of government powers.
5. The text of the Fourth Amendment and its interpretation by the Supreme Court raises concerns as to the possible adaptation of the Constitution to the contemporary government surveillance reality resulting mainly from the enhancement of technology and the methods of collecting data used by the authorities.
6. The 20th and 21st century the SCOTUS, either by issuing rulings in surveillance cases which expanded the powers of the government, or via the silent approval of such expansion, legitimized the functioning of a national security surveillance state operating in an era of endless emergency.

Balancing the Values

The majority of SCOTUS decisions regarding the scope of government surveillance focus on the tensions between the values of freedom and security. The Founding Fathers were aware, from the beginning, of difficult tensions between the need to provide safety and freedom when they were defining the future character of the Constitution and the features of the political system. They believed that it was impossible to provide full security without giving up some freedoms, and, accordingly, that full freedom did not always ensure the level of safety demanded by the people. Such an approach was reflected in Alexander Hamilton's essay in which he discussed the consequences of hostilities between states:

"Safety from external danger is the most powerful director of national conduct. Even the ardent love of liberty will, after a time, give way to its dictates. The violent destruction of life and property incident to war; the continual effort and alarm attendant on a state of continual danger, will compel nations the most attached to liberty, to resort for repose and security to institutions which have a tendency to destroy their civil and political rights. To be more safe, they, at length, become willing to run the risk of being less free."[263]

The analysis of the Constitution confirms that both values had a significant meaning for the members of the Philadelphia Convention, as both freedom and security were mentioned, directly or indirectly, in the part of Preamble referring to the purposes of the document:

"We the People of the United States, in Order to form a more perfect Union, establish Justice, ensure domestic Tranquility, provide for the common defense, promote the general Welfare, and secure the Blessings of Liberty to ourselves and our Posterity, do ordain and establish this Constitution for the United States of America."[264]

As a matter of fact, the purposes underlying the establishment of the Constitution, expressed in such phrases as justice, tranquility, common defense, and securing the blessings of liberty, considered the importance of both the security of the country and the people, as well as the protection of the rights and freedoms of individuals. Even if the main text of the Constitution did not refer directly to security or freedom, the meaning of the Preamble and the character of the powers granted to the federal and state governments clearly ensured that these values laid the foundation of American constitutionalism from the time of its inception. The implementation of the Bill of Rights after their ratification in 1791 fixed the shortcomings of the first seven Articles, which had been the subject of thorough debates and disputes in Philadelphia. As a consequence of the adoption of the Bill of Rights and subsequent amendments introduced in the 19th and 20th centuries, the words freedom and security, in various versions and forms, appeared several times in the Constitution, strengthening the Preamble's announcements as to the role of the government in establishing and preserving these values in the United States.

---

263 Alexander Hamilton, *Federalist no. 8* in *The Federalist Papers*, James Madison, Alexander Hamilton, John Jay (eds.), U.S. Imports, New York 1999.

264 Preamble to the U.S. Constitution.

The significant role of freedom and security as values of American constitutionalism would not be possible without the active role of the judicial branch in interpreting the Constitution, including the meaning and character of both values in the functioning of the country and the people. It is not surprising that many Supreme Court rulings in which the justices interpreted the Constitution concerned the scope of freedom and security, understood in different contexts and from different perspectives. While in the 19th century SCOTUS adjudication determined the role of the federal government in protecting the rights of individuals, it was the 20th century Court which opened a new dimension in the constitutional interpretation of these values. The process of incorporation of the Bill of Rights on the states expanded not only the number of addressees of the constitutional limitations imposed on the government, but also the scope of the protection provided by the document, determining which rights and freedoms had a fundamental character. This was possible due to the Court's interpretation of the Fourteenth Amendment, and especially its Due Process Clause, which prohibited the authorities from depriving people of their life, liberty, and property without constitutionally approved procedural or substantive means being applied.[265] In the process initiated in 1920s, most of the freedoms expressed in the first ten amendments or derived from their essence were defined by the SCOTUS as fundamental and, therefore, binding within state jurisdictions.

It seems obvious that the expansion of the powers of the government resulting from the circumstances of foreign and domestic policies presented new threats to the functioning of the country, and that the rights of the people would become a major challenge for a judiciary responsible for solving disputes stemming from conflicting values. Even if the justices did not expressly declare that the tension between freedom and security always produced serious pressure on their constitutional meanings, they often imposed balancing tests which reflected the character of a dispute and the arguments used by the parties to it. A similar situation occurred in the analyzed cases regarding government surveillance, where the necessity

265 See: Raoul Berger, *Government by Judiciary: The Transformation of the Fourteenth Amendment*, Liberty Fund, New York 1997.

to prevent crimes and foreign threats to the country's security clashed with the need to protect the individual rights and freedoms of American citizens. These tensions were clearly expressed by the justices in the majority opinion in *United States v. U.S. District Court*, where the Court offered a balancing test weighing the values of freedom and security. On the one hand, the justices noticed a serious threat to the constitutional rights of U.S. citizens, mainly the First Amendment's freedom of expression and the Fourth Amendment's right to privacy, but, on the other, they acknowledged the power of the government to protect domestic security issues and elements which affected the functioning of the country and the society. Weighing arguments in support of both values, the Court considered the "legitimate need of government for intelligence information" but also "the potential danger posed by unreasonable surveillance" to the constitutional rights of the people. Searching for the best solution which would not eliminate any of the values from proper protection, the justices suggested that "the needs of citizens for privacy and free expression" may require the government to obtain a warrant which would legitimize surveillance and the collection of evidence.[266] The SCOTUS rationale was built on the conviction that the Fourth Amendment leaves space for the co-existence of both the security of the people and individual freedoms, which the justices found in the proper interpretation of the Warrant Clause.

In the majority of the case-law analyzed in the preceding chapters the freedom-security tensions were balanced by the justices even if there was no exact reference to these values, or when they were expressed by other values which were in conflict. Freedom, or liberty, was understood as a guarantee derived from the First Amendment (freedom of expression, of religion, of the press, as well as the right to associate and to assemble), the Fourth Amendment (right to privacy, freedom from unreasonable search and seizure), and the Fifth and Fourteenth Amendment's due process of law. On the other hand, security could refer to domestic or foreign threats to the proper functioning of the country and the necessary security-led actions of the government in terms of maintaining the confidentiality of its communications and operations, but also the security of the people from

266 407 U.S. 297 (1972).

encroachments into their rights and freedoms by the government and other actors. In such a context, security and freedom may overlap, referring in fact to the same needs of the society: to feel free and secure at the same time. As Viet Dinh observes, "security and freedom are not rivals in the universe of possible goods; rather they are interrelated, mutually reinforcing goods. Security is the very precondition of freedom."[267] Such a perspective seems especially significant in the reading of the Fourth Amendment, which refers to both the security and freedom of the people, understood as a guarantee of the protection of the right to privacy. Privacy is the key value distinguished in the Amendment and the role of the government is not only to acknowledge that right but also to impose such measures aiming at protecting people's security as do not violate the necessary scope of citizens' privacy. And here the Supreme Court steps in by balancing the government's need to provide security with people's right to go about their business in privacy.

Therefore, the legitimate end of government surveillance is the result of the Court's balancing between the arguments used in support of the measures which need to be undertaken in order to achieve the demanded level of security with those referring to the necessity of providing a certain level of protection of citizens' right to privacy. Since the beginning of the 20th century the SCOTUS has created several standards of privacy protection by applying different modes of interpretation of the Fourth Amendment and establishing various theories explaining the scope of government surveillance, including the trespass doctrine (*Olmstead v. United States*), the reasonable expectation of privacy (*Katz v. United States*), or the third party doctrine (*Smith v. Maryland*). The analysis of the Court's adjudication in disputes concerning domestic surveillance, from the perspective of the differentiation between the public space and private sphere, shows the evolution of justices' approach towards the scope of government intrusion into the privacy of individuals:

> "Thus, government is able to use, without infringing Fourth Amendment interests, any type of technology, generally available or not, if the target is located in a public space or on curtilage that is viewed from an area outside the curtilage.

---

267 Viet D. Dinh, "Liberty and the Rule of Law After September 11", *Journal of Law and Policy* 19(1), 2005, pp. 31–38.

> Second, even the home is not protected from surveillance with devices that are in general public use. Thirdly, even if very sophisticated technology may be used to view activities that take place in the home if it merely duplicates what a law enforcement officer could have seen with the naked eye from a lawful vantage point."[268]

In the area of domestic interception conducted by law enforcement agencies in the realization of their investigative powers, the standard has usually been higher than in surveillance operations undertaken as a part of national security policy justified by the authorities. For example, the Court introduced, in *Weeks v. United States* and *Mapp v. Ohio,* the exclusionary rule determining which evidence collected by law enforcement officers did not meet the criteria of reasonable search and seizure and could not be used in judicial proceedings. The justices also determined the conditions that needed to be met in order to obtain warrants to impose surveillance measures defining reasonable grounds for probable cause, thus limiting the scope of the government's interception of the communications of private persons (*Berger v. United States*, *Katz v. United States*). These examples prove that in the area of domestic surveillance the SCOTUS was very cautious in allowing the government to enter the private worlds of American citizens, expanding constitutional protection of their rights and freedoms.

The results of the balancing tests applied by the justices were dependent on national and international realities determined by the political, economic, military, and security factors surrounding these circumstances. Both U.S. domestic and foreign policy had a crucial impact on the direction of government surveillance, creating an environment in which it was easier for law enforcement and intelligence agencies to impose new surveillance measures. The securitization of most of the areas of the government's operations legitimized the establishment of a system in which security arguments outweighed the necessity to protect individual freedoms. The application of the national security paradigm on the part of presidents, their administrations and the executive and intelligence agencies, as well as Congress in its creation of new legislation, determined the rhetoric of

268 Christopher Slobogin, *Is the Fourth Amendment Relevant in a Technological Age?* in *Constitution 3.0*, Jeffrey Rosen, Benjamin Wittes (eds.), Brookings Institution, Washington DC 2011, p. 16.

everyday politics and the character of legal regulations and their enforcement. Unsurprisingly, in times of security threats and emergency concerns, the SCOTUS took the side of the government by approving the surveillance measures it could employ and expanding the powers of the institutions responsible for providing security; and, to the contrary, the willingness of the Court to protect the constitutional rights and freedoms of the people, although it accompanied justices' constitutional considerations, was greater in times of peace or when national security arguments were not dominating government rhetoric.

For the justices such an approach was consistent with their role as constitutional interpreters. Even if not all of the members of the Court approved the limitations of the scope of the rights and freedoms of the American people, the vast majority accepted the expansion of the government's powers in periods which were determined to be times of war, or times of emergency, such as in *Shenck*, *Korematsu*, *Hirabayashi*, and *Dennis*. Situations in which the justices did not differentiate between times of war and peace, treating the necessity to protect the rights and freedoms of individuals regardless of the military and political circumstances, were rare. One such exception can be observed in the SCOTUS post-civil war ruling in *Ex parte Milligan*, which proves that 19th century adjudication was conducted in different circumstances than those in which the 20th century Court made decisions during the two World Wars, the Red Scare, the Cold War, and the War on Terror. The external and internal threats occurring in these periods were used as the main factor in the government's argumentation justifying the use of more restrictive means of surveillance. In such circumstances the majority of justices legitimized tipping the scales in favor of security, thus limiting the scope of the constitutional protection of privacy, and even those who opposed the expansion of government powers were aware of the need to protect the security of the country. Rather than criticizing the direction of the government policies, they observed the attitude of American society at large, which shared the national security concerns. Such an approach was expressed in the words of Justice Hugo Black, who wrote a dissenting opinion in *Dennis v. United States* when the Court approved a limiting of freedom of speech during the Cold War:

> "Public opinion being what it now is, few will protest the conviction of these Communist petitioners. There is hope, however, that, in calmer times, when

> present pressures, passions and fears subside, this or some later Court will restore the First Amendment liberties to the high preferred place where they belong in a free society."[269]

As can be observed in Black's opinion, the civil rights advocates should have hoped that after the times of increased security the scales would move towards the constitutional protection of the freedoms of individuals, providing a proper balance between the two values. Black also justified the direction of the Court's adjudication by referring to public opinion, which may suggest that one of the factors determining the tipping of the scales in the process of balancing security and freedom is views of American citizens, who expect the government to act effectively to diminish external and internal threats. At least, such an attitude may be derived from the analysis of public opinion polls conducted in periods of increased social concerns connected with such threats. During the early phase of the Cold War a vast majority of Americans defined the Soviet Union as the major threat to U.S. security, approving of the anti-communist legislation and measures undertaken by the presidents in question, and such a situation changed at the turn 1980s and 90s with the collapse of the bipolar world.[270] Following the 9/11 terrorist attacks the polls indicated that many citizens were ready to relinquish some of their freedoms for stronger security, and that they were able to approve of the anti-terrorist measures imposed by the government. For example, a Pew Research Center survey found that in the aftermath of Sep 11 "only a third of Americans worried that the government's new anti-terrorist laws would excessively restrict civil liberties". Similarly, another poll in early 2002 found that about 78 % U.S. citizens declared themselves "more willing to give up certain freedoms to improve safety and security".[271] In 2006, after press leaks about the secret NSA programs monitoring millions of overseas and domestic phone calls in search of potential terrorists, polls indicated that while 63 % of Americans felt the program was an "acceptable way to fight terrorism", only 37 %

269 Black, dissenting. 341 U.S. 494 (1951), at 581.

270 Alvin Richman, "Poll Trends: Changing American Attitudes Toward the Soviet Union", *The Public Opinion Quarterly* 55(1), 1991, pp. 135–148.

271 Christian Parenti, *The Soft Cage...*, op. cit., p. 184.

disagreed.[272] Not surprisingly, in the aftermath of the Snowden Affair, when the leaked documents revealed excessive government surveillance affecting the scope of citizens' right to privacy, the distrust of the authorities grew, with four out of five citizens negatively evaluating secret surveillance programs.[273] However, according to public opinion polls conducted in recent years, the majority of Americans put safety and security within their main concerns, listing the threat of terrorism as one of the three top public priorities.[274]

In that context, the legitimate end of government surveillance was strengthened by the Court's references to the needs and expectations reflected by public opinion approving various types of limitations to the scope of rights and freedoms during times of increased threat. The same public opinion believed that said limitations were only temporary; however, the institutions which benefitted from increased security were reluctant to let go of the power they gained.

The Superiority of the Executive

The analysis of SCOTUS surveillance adjudication leads to the obvious conclusion that its justices have presented a different approach towards the scope of government powers and the status of rights and freedoms of individuals in disputes concerning domestic and national security surveillance. Whereas in the first group of rulings, the Court was reluctant to expand the surveillance competences of the government at the expense of the right to privacy, in national security cases the interest of the government has outweighed the constitutional protection of individual rights. As was presented in chapter three, such an approach has been characteristic not only in disputes pertaining to the general national security paradigm, but also in cases specifically concerning government foreign intelligence and national security surveillance. However, not only the national security area but also

272 Christopher Slobogin, *Is the Fourth Amendment…*, op. cit., p. 20.

273 Edward Jay Epstein, *How America Lost Its Secrets. Edward Snowden, the Man and the Theft.* Alfred A. Knopf, New York, 2017, p. 303.

274 Pew Research Center, *Terrorism: Public Opinion Polls 2018–2022*, available at https://www.pewresearch.org/topic/politics-policy/political-issues/defense-national-security/terrorism/ .

domestic policy issues have produced several challenges to the scope of government powers with regard to procedural and substantive aspects of the surveillance of U.S. citizens. Each decision in which the justices redefined the meaning of the Search and Seizure and Warrant Clauses resulted in the position of the surveilling institutions being changed in relation with regards to other governmental units. In a broader context, the branches which were beneficiaries of SCOTUS surveillance adjudication strengthened their position in relation to others, affecting the character of the separation of powers and the checks and balances system.

The SCOTUS became an effective legitimizer of the increase of governmental powers in surveillance disputes, especially those concerning national security issues, which means that the main branch which benefited from the Court's rulings was the executive. The approach taken by the Court that led to this stems from at least three factors. First, the nature of executive power as reflected in Article Two equips the president and his subordinates with the means necessary to execute or enforce the law, among which there are surveillance measures that can be imposed to ensure the effective prevention of crimes or successful investigations leading to the reinforcement of security. Second, the position of presidents in foreign policy matters evolved both with the change of the paradigm and announcement of presidential doctrines defining the position of the United States in international relations, and with the Court's willingness to confirm the primary role of the chief executive in determining the direction of U.S. foreign policy and choosing the means by which that policy is implemented. Third, the executive has the most secretive character of all three branches, derived from the character of its powers and the growing demand for confidentiality among the institutions responsible for the effective execution of the law.

The first argument is too simple to warrant thorough discussion. The idea of dividing power into three branches of government assumed the existence of subjects responsible for the execution of the law created by the legislative department. It is hard to imagine that the power to impose surveillance measures would not be assumed by the executive branch, which "is the only organ of the government with the resources, power, and flexibility to respond to threats to national security"[275]; and, according to Marshall's legitimate end approach, that could choose the best means with which to reach the goals for which it was established in the political system: the faithful execution of the laws. In that respect, the Founding Fathers had no doubt that the operation of the executive would be connected with the operation of the two other branches of government – the legislative, in the procedure through which the head of state approves of the laws implemented in the legislative process, and the judicial, in the procedural collaboration between the law enforcement institutions and courts. Therefore, in the context of the surveillance powers of the federal government the president could have an impact on the acts created by Congress which referred to the scope of government surveillance powers, and law enforcement officers were forced to cooperate with judges in order to legalize the searches and seizures they conducted. Still, the initiative belonged to the executive.

The analysis of the use of the veto power of U.S. presidents proves that there was no important congressional legislation concerning government surveillance which would be blocked by chief executives. Regardless of this, if it was focusing on domestic surveillance (as in the Omnibus Crime and Control Act), national security surveillance (as in the Foreign Intelligence Surveillance Act), or both, as is the case with the Patriot Act and Freedom Act, presidents always supported the legislation which expanded the powers of the executive in the area of surveillance. Similarly, the number of judicial approvals of warrants on the basis of which the executive agencies could impose surveillance seems very optimistic for the law enforcement and intelligence institutions. Of course, it is very difficult to assess the real percentage of cases in which the courts approved or rejected warrant requests, but at least in the area of foreign intelligence these figures are easy to track. According to the data as of the end of 2023, of the 42,213 NSA requests for warrants in foreign intelligence cases, only 336 were rejected by the Foreign Intelligence Surveillance Court, which makes the government successful in more than 99 % of cases.[276]

275 Eric E. Posner, Adrian Vermeule, *Terror in the Balance*..., op. cit., p. 4.

276 *Foreign Intelligence Surveillance Act Court Orders 1979–2022*, Electronic Privacy Information Center, available at: https://epic.org/foreign-intelligence-surveillance-court-fisc/fisa-stats/ .

On the other hand, the SCOTUS rulings in domestic surveillance cases determining the scope of the Warrant Clause show the willingness of the justices to adhere not only to the probable cause standard, but also the reasonable suspicion of law enforcement officers (*Terry v. Ohio*), thus leaving more space for the executive to determine the basis for search and seizure. Similarly, since the fundamental rulings concerning the scope of Fourth Amendment, such as *Katz* and *Mapp,* in which the Court limited governmental surveillance powers, there have been many examples of exemptions which justices discerned in the Constitution as enabling law enforcement to impose warrantless surveillance. This all leads to the clear conclusion that the character of the executive powers gives the president and law enforcement a good deal of discretion in deciding whether to investigate or not, and which instruments to apply in order to effectively achieve the goals for which this branch was founded. The nature of executive power not only ensures that decisions about whether to impose surveillance measures are on the side of the president, law enforcement, and intelligence units, but also guarantees that the executive branch will do everything it can to strengthen its surveillance powers at the expense of other branches.

The second argument is also logical, considering both the evolution of the United States' position in international relations, from the Monroe doctrine's isolationism through Wilsonian idealism to Cold War interventionism, as well as the history of SCOTUS rulings referring to the scope of American president's power to act in foreign affairs situations. As was presented in chapter three, the justices did not have any doubt in confirming the leading role of presidents in shaping U.S. foreign policy and determining the means to be used by chief executives in their activities affecting foreign affairs. Despite the fact that in some disputes the Court prevented presidents from going beyond their constitutional duties (*Youngstown*, *Hamdi*, *Hamdan*), the majority of rulings approved the broad discretionary power of chief executives in choosing the manner of their pursuit of foreign policy goals. It is worth noting that the expansion of presidential powers was achieved by just a few SCOTUS precedents, and that in the majority of cases the Court did not take a direct position, thereby silently legitimizing the actions taken by the executive. The analysis of the judicial interpretation of presidents' powers proves that the biggest change appeared in the area of war powers, observed both during the Cold War period and the post-9/11 War on

of powers to the executive without effective control or oversight made Congress only partly responsible for the growth of executive surveillance powers. The scale of possible overuse of power in that area could be seen during the investigations conducted by the Church and Pike Committees in the mid-1970s, or after press and whistleblower leaks in the first two decades of the 21st century. Still, the results stemming from these investigations did not fundamentally change the approach in which the authorities had to be equipped with broad surveillance powers in order to successfully fulfill their constitutional duties.

It is important to acknowledge the fact that the SCOTUS did not only fail to limit any serious surveillance legislation, but that it even went a step further by both expanding the executive's powers in that respect, or silently approving such an expansion. The results of this research show that there has been no Court ruling that would significantly limit the scope of executive surveillance powers, and no decision which would impose stronger congressional or judicial checks on the initiatives undertaken by presidents in the area of foreign and national security surveillance. It was Congress which established systemic solutions for control of the surveillance activities of the executive, namely the NSA, such as stable congressional intelligence committees and the Foreign Intelligence Surveillance Court, but due to the necessity of them operating in secrecy the impact of these entities on the functioning of the Agency is limited. This stems from a special relationship in this area between the executive and legislative branches:

> "While conflict between the branches is built into the structure of the governmental separation of powers, conflict with regard to intelligence oversight is unique. It is one area where government goals are seen to be diametrically opposed, with the executive wanting and needing to maintain secrecy, while the legislative branch demands information, transparency, and relative openness."[285]

Without neglecting the significance of the tensions between secrecy and openness, which are inherent in the nature of said relationship, it is important to note that they constitute only one of many reasons which make the relations among the branches of government difficult with regard to surveillance policies. All of these reasons, including the nature

285 Genevieve Lester, *When Should State Secrets...*, op. cit., p. 5.

of the executive powers, congressional legislation delegating power to the executive, limited congressional and judicial control and oversight, and the judiciary's expansion of executive powers were directly or indirectly the result of the Supreme Court's approach towards government surveillance. If subsequent generations of justices, both conservative and liberal, had not issued rulings allowing for the gradual expansion of the powers of presidents, or, from the other perspective, if the majority of justices of the 20th and 21st century Courts had decided to impose significant limitations on executive power, there would be less discussion about the scope of government surveillance. And the position of the executive branch within the separation of powers and checks and balances system would remain untouched. As Robert Pallitto and William Weaver argue:

> "The judiciary has a legitimate and crucial goal of providing accountability for presidential and executive actions, but it has prostrated itself before the altar of national security and, through its neglect of duty, has allowed a substantial and unchecked increase in presidential power. This increase threatens the balance of power among the branches of government and puts citizens' constitutional rights and civil liberties at risk."[286]

Another interesting approach to these matters is presented by Amanda DiPaolo. Her research findings show that when liberties are limited during national emergencies, the judiciary, more often than not, will defer to the political branches of government when they are working together. DiPaolo believes that courts see things from the perspective of the separation of powers rather than any other constitutional limitations and follow the congressional authorization of the executive's activities. Furthermore, she claims that cases concerning war powers become questions of procedure rather than substance, and, therefore, that federal courts often decide these cases based on statutory claims by looking at the delegation of powers to the president by Congress.[287] Such a perspective is partly consistent with what Robert Dahl wrote in the 1950s, calling the Supreme Court a "national policy maker", referring to the Cold War period, when all three branches were cooperating to successfully limit the impact of the Red Scare and

---

286 Robert M. Pallitto, William G. Weaver, *Presidential Secrecy...*, op. cit., p. 79.
287 Amanda DiPaolo, *Zones of Twilight. Wartime Presidential Powers and Federal Court Decision Making*. Lexington Books, Lanham 2010, p. 2.

crucial legacy in building a wall around the presidency and preventing the public disclosure of confidential communications between chief executives and their subordinate officers, especially in cases of military, diplomatic, or national security concerns. The precedent was established in the middle of a quest for transparency as announced by Congress, as a consequence of the serious abuses of power by executive and intelligence agencies directly resulting from a dispute over the imposition of illegal surveillance measures on the part of the government. Despite the significant role of the press in revealing the Watergate scandal, and the social expectation that the truth about the president's involvement in the eavesdropping controversy should be disclosed, the Court did not bow to demands for full disclosure, defending the right of the executive to hide behind the privilege of confidentiality. Despite limiting the scope of the privilege, the justices – acknowledged the importance of secrecy for the operation of government in certain politically sensitive areas.

The justices were also responsible for strengthening the meaning of the state secrets doctrine, which was used by the executive as the main argument in disputes in which citizens' or civil rights organizations demanded access to information held by the authorities. Since *United States v. Reynolds*, the Court has officially recognized the privilege protecting the government from releasing information or data which it considered crucial from the perspective of national security or foreign policy matters. As has been observed in different cases, the justices often applied the state secrets doctrine without having full access to the information on the basis of which the privilege was invoked. Therefore, the secrecy established by the SCOTUS was a result of the rulings in which the arguments raised in support of greater confidentiality of government operations were based on partial evidence which could not be disclosed due to the requirements of national security or other legitimate interests of the United States. In other words, the justices approved of the government's reasoning to use secrecy as a justification for embedding more secrecy in the American political and social reality. Such an approach was especially visible with regard to rulings in disputes involving government surveillance.

Based on the philosophy that there is information which courts "cannot review ... or interpret", the privilege has been used by the government to impose surveillance programs in the name of a broader protection of national security. In a system in which state secrets privilege exists, transparency seems impossible to achieve as citizens are not empowered to find out the whole truth about the actions of a government hiding behind arguments about the need for confidentiality. Since the national security paradigm has dominated U.S. foreign and domestic policy, there has been hardly any president who did not refer to state secrets privilege in a judicial dispute in which citizens claimed that it was necessary that sensitive information be disclosed. Even during the tenures of Democratic presidents, who have often admitted that government operations need to be more transparent, it was clear that the judiciary would support executive claims of state secrets privilege in cases pertaining to national security surveillance.[289]

The problem with the culture of secrecy is that the approach of active politicians towards it depends on their position within the government – while being in opposition they often claim adherence to transparency, whereas when serving in an administration they become more prone to upholding the arguments supporting an increase in secrecy. For example, at the beginning of his presidency Barack Obama referred to the need to diminish the scope of secrecy in the operation of the government:

> "Whenever possible, my administration will make all information available to the American people so that they can make informed judgments and hold us accountable. But the most sensitive national security measures – defending our troops at war, protecting sources and methods, safeguarding confidential actions to keep the American people safe – cannot simply be an open book. Whenever we cannot release certain information to the public for valid national security reasons, I will insist that there is oversight of my actions – by Congress or the courts. When I release something publicly or keep something secret, I will tell you why."[290]

However, in the following years the presidential rhetoric was replaced by actions legitimizing secret surveillance programs and litigation in which the administration invoked state secrets privilege to protect precious information from being disclosed to the public. Consequently, the Supreme Court deepened the meaning of the state secrets privilege in *United States*

289 See: Chris Edelson, *Power Without Constraint…*, op. cit.
290 Mary Graham, *Presidents' Secrets…*, op. cit., p. 181.

v. Zubaydah, confirming the right of the government to withhold information about sensitive foreign or national security matters, and in *F.B.I. v. Fazaga*, rejecting the claim that the Foreign Intelligence Surveillance Act limits the application of the state secrets doctrine. It seems that, despite conflicting approaches towards the meaning of the Constitution, both Democratic and Republican politicians, as well as liberal and conservative justices, have participated in the establishment of a national security state by sharing one timeless conviction: that only a certain scope of secrecy can assure its proper functioning. To use language characteristic of sports, we might say that both branches, executive and judicial, regardless of their blue and red jerseys, have been playing on the same team, sponsored by the word 'secrecy' in a game in which rules were kept, at least in part, secret.

Similarly, secrecy has also been a core value guiding the process whereby the NSA obtains a warrant from the judges of the Foreign Intelligence Surveillance Court. It seems difficult to reach a fully objective conclusion in a judicial procedure which assumes that the deciding subject lacks full information about the circumstances of the dispute or has limited access to documents due to the necessity to keep them classified. If the Agency files a warrant request as an element of a pending investigation legitimized by a concrete surveillance program, without having access to the full information about the program, its character, and the probable cause of the national security danger caused by the surveilled subject, the FISC judge operates in a blurred reality. Such a system assumes possible mistakes or flaws, although potential violations of the Constitution and personal privacy are at stake. And even if the fundamental idea behind FISA is to enhance the control and oversight of certain type of government surveillance which may affect U.S. citizens' Fourth Amendment rights, the imperfection of the legislation stems from the lack of access of controlling subjects to crucial information or documents. On the other hand, secrecy forces the judicial branch to trust the government in determining the legality of its operations, which can be directly observed in the nature of FISA court procedures and decisions. Paradoxically, trust among branches of government may become a source of social distrust of the authorities, as they establish together a system in which secrecy is defined as a guarantee of the successful completion of certain policies. The problem occurs when the government overuses its powers, acting behind the scenes and beyond the effective control of the institutions that should guarantee that such overuse never occurs.

Both arguments, in support of and against secrecy, raised by various participants in the American political and social spheres, bring important but not fully convincing conclusions. Despite the fact that secrecy was present in the operation of the executive from the beginning of American statehood, even before the American Revolution there were voices warning against the negative consequences of a government operating in secret. John Adams, criticizing the implementation of the Stamp Act by the British parliament in 1765, argued that:

> "liberty cannot be preserved without a general knowledge among the people, who have a right, from the frame of their nature, to knowledge... they have a right, an indisputable, unalienable, indefeasible, divine right to that most dreaded and envied kind of knowledge. I mean, of the characters and conduct of their rulers".[291]

Other Founding Fathers were also of the opinion that open government might better secure the protection of the rights and freedoms of Americans, and that was one of the reasons for the adoption of the First Amendment, which served as a guarantee of the freedom of expression, as well as the right of citizens to be informed.

In the 19th century the issue of secrecy did not become a major concern of the judicial branch, but soon after, at the beginning of the 20th century, Justice Louis D. Brandeis warned against the negative consequences of secrecy, declaring that "sunlight is said to be the best of disinfectants", and "electric light the most efficient policeman".[292] This argument did not, however, prevent the growth of the classification of documents relating to the functioning of the government in the period that followed, with the expansion of the executive's powers in the area of foreign affairs and national security. The scope of the problem was later observed by Justice Potter Stewart, who wrote the concurring opinion in the *New York Times Co. v. United States* arguing that:

---

291 Jason R. Arnold, *Secrecy in the Sunshine Era...*, op. cit., pp. 31–32.

292 Louis D. Brandeis, *Other People's Money and How the Bankers Use It*, 1914, available at: https://archive.org/stream/otherpeoplesmone00bran/otherpeoplesmone00bran_djvu.txt .

> "when everything is classified, then nothing is classified, and the system becomes one to be disregarded by the cynical or the careless, and to be manipulated by those intent on self-protection and self-promotion... The hallmark of a truly effective internal security system would be the maximum possible disclosure, recognizing that secrecy can best be preserved when credibility is truly maintained".[293]

A similar approach could be observed in Judge Learned Hand's opinion in *United States v. Coplon*, in which he stressed that "few weapons in the arsenal of freedom [we]re more useful than the power to compel a government to disclose the evidence on which it s[ought] to forfeit liberty of its citizens."[294] All three elements of the judicial branch acknowledged the need for a broader disclosure of information concerning the operation of the government as a guarantee of ensuring the real liberty of the people and credibility of the authorities. In this perspective secrecy may be understood and treated as a serious threat to American democracy.

In his quest for transparency, Senator Daniel Patrick Moynihan noticed the dangers stemming from the secrecy of the national security government and suggested that an opposing culture of openness could be established:

> "We are not going to put an end to secrecy, nor should we. It is at times legitimate and necessary. But a culture of secrecy, a culture of the sort that we associate with Hoover need not remain the norm in American government as regards national security. It is possible to conceive that a competing culture of openness might develop, and that it could assert and demonstrate greater efficiency."[295]

For the Founding Fathers, judges, and some politicians the main domestic source of danger to the effective functioning of the country lay in the overuse of secrecy as a legitimization of various policies and operations labelled as consistent with national security concerns or the public interest in providing safety to American citizens. On the other hand, among the proponents of broader secrecy in government operations, especially in the area of surveillance, there are now mainly politicians and officers responsible for implementing security policies or imposing security measures who explain the need for confidentiality with an argument about the growing

---

293 Stewart, concurring. 403 U.S. 713 (1971), at 729.

294 185 F.2d 629 (1950), at 638.

295 Daniel Patrick Moynihan, *Secrecy: The American Experience*, Yale University Press, New Haven 1998, p. 221.

effectiveness of government operations, including surveillance programs. Such an approach was presented by Attorney General Alberto Gonzales, shortly after the press leak of information about the secret NSA programs in 2005, who stated:

> "our enemy is listening, and I cannot help but wonder if they are not shaking their heads in amazement at the thought that anyone would imperil such a sensitive program by leaking its existence in the first place, and smiling at the prospect that we might now disclose even more or perhaps even unilaterally disarm ourselves of a key tool in the war on terror."[296]

But even in domestic surveillance there has been a need to provide more secrecy rather than disclosure, which was observed as early as at the beginning of 1940s by Attorney General Robert Jackson, who later became an Associate Justice of the Supreme Court:

> "Disclosure of confidential data in law enforcement files might tip off criminals under investigation, could embarrass and might even endanger confidential informants, and, in view of the erroneous information and malicious gossip "might also be the grossest kind of injustice to innocent individuals".[297]

James Ross Arnold presents crucial arguments advanced by the proponents of secrecy who were responsible for pursuing the national security policy of the country and developing the contemporary modes of data collection known as the mosaic theory:

> "Defenders of the American secrecy system often justify its enormity and excesses by citing national security needs. The risks and harms from excessive secrecy they argue, pale in comparison to those that would result from disclosing information potentially useful to malicious enemies. We may not even know what information would be useful, they argue, and therefore, the government's heavy hand is warranted ... Mosaic theorists therefore defend overprotection of sensitive information, and they advocate secrecy even when transparency rules require openness."[298]

William J. Stuntz goes further and calls for more secrecy, which would ensure "effective, active government – government that innovates, that protects people who need protecting, that acts aggressively when action is

---

296 Daniel J. Solove, *Nothing to Hide...*, op. cit., p. 33.
297 Francis E. Rourke, *Secrecy and Publicity...*, op. cit., p. 33.
298 James R. Arnold, *Secrecy in the Sunshine Era...*, op. cit., p. 26.

needed." According to him, privacy and transparency make it harder for government officials to act resourcefully:

> "For most officials most of the time, the key choice is not between doing right and doing wrong, but between doing something and doing nothing. Doing nothing is usually easier – less likely to generate bad headlines and critical blog posts".[299]

Effectiveness has become most frequently invoked argument in the defense of the culture of secrecy, and opponents of greater transparency claim that without the operations carried out in secret the government would not be able to achieve the level of security the public demands. They argue that, especially in the area of national security, there is a need to give up on dreams of greater openness and disclosure, similar to the widely accepted weakening of the broad constitutional protection of rights and freedoms of individuals. Instead, people may feel secure in being able to meet their basic social needs thanks to the preventive or reactive operations of the law enforcement or intelligence agencies fighting effectively against various types of internal and external threat. And, as many of them point out, it is better to feel safe than sorry.

Such arguments are congruent with the general approach of the SCOTUS, which has supported, in most of cases, the government in building a national security state which would not be able to operate effectively without remaining largely secret, which has been especially necessary in applying surveillance measures to subjects threatening the safety of the American people. Despite being sensitive to issues concerning constitutional rights and individual freedoms, the justices took the part of the government in protecting secrecy as a value that ensures the effective fulfillment of its duties; on the scale of justice, that of security outweighed that of freedom.

The truth is that the culture of secrecy resulting in the excessive classification of the surveillance policies observed in the contemporary U.S. political system, no matter how it is explained or justified, may bring a lot of negative consequences not only to political subjects, but also to the society and the system in general. In the debate concerning the proper scope of government secret surveillance, at least four counter arguments

299 William J. Stuntz, "Secret Service: Against Privacy and Transparency", *New Republic*, Apr 7, 2006, pp. 12–15.

appear: the potential of the abuse the power by the institutions acting in secret, limitations on the rights and freedoms of individuals imposed by secret surveillance programs, the lack of effective control and oversight by the legislative and judicial branch, and the deterioration of trust. According to Steven Aftergood,

> "the secrecy system does not exist in some kind of abstract isolation. It is an ordinary, bureaucratic artifact that is subject to pressure on many levels – political, legal, sociological, international, and others. It is constantly undergoing changes due to press reporting and leaks (unauthorized disclosures), budget appropriations and congressional oversight, FOIA requests and lawsuits, and foreign government disclosures, errors, whistleblowers, financial pressures, and – not least important – an ideological or tactical preference for disclosure – or the opposite – on the part of senior officials."[300]

The history of U.S. secret surveillance in the 20th century proves that secrecy served to hide illegal operations carried out by government officials, such as warrantless eavesdropping on political opponents, social activists, or organizations during the Cold War era. It also allowed for a limitation of certain rights of the people, such as freedom of speech, the right to be informed, the right to privacy and due process of law. The SCOTUS played a crucial role in legitimizing the establishment of secret surveillance in the name of domestic and national security, but – and this has been even more controversial – the justices applied self-restraint when it came to their potential control over government surveillance. As Heidi Kitrosser argues, "insufficient checking breeds unnecessary, even counterproductive, secrecy"[301]. Furthermore, the lack of accountability leads to a deterioration of trust in government, through its use of non-verifiable arguments justifying excessive surveillance programs. According to intelligence community officials, the measures undertaken by the NSA in the 21st century led to the detection of several terrorist plots, but the real number of successful operations that were able to limit the number of terrorist threats, as well as the real character of these, remains classified. And even if the society at large

300 James R. Arnold, *Secrecy in the Sunshine Era…*, op. cit., p. 39.
301 Heidi Kitrosser, *Reclaiming Unaccountability…*, op. cit., p. 2.

understands the reason for keeping the statistics about NSA's successful operations secret, there is no way these statistics can be verified.[302]

Kate Doyle correctly observes that:

> "In a democracy, public tolerance of official secrecy tends to shift, obligingly, with the tides: in times of national emergency, such as war or civil unrest, the body politic is often willing to forgo open governance in exchange for safety; in peace, the citizenry becomes assertive once again, reclaiming its right to full and informed participation."[303]

There is no doubt that the American culture of secrecy is a product of a system in which the collection of data for security reasons leads to a vicious cycle. First, the government implements surveillance programs designed to collect information which may prevent any potential internal or external danger to the state and the society from being inflicted on them. These programs are founded on the mosaic theory, which in recent years has become in leading method of data collection, the implementation of which allows the executive agencies to secretly collect as much information as possible, thus expanding the scope and the area of surveillance. New pieces of data are collected, stored, and analyzed, raising questions about their relevance to the investigations being conducted, and leading to potential encroachments on the individual rights of American citizens. In order to maintain the operation of surveillance programs, as well as to limit public debate about possible limitations on freedom of speech or the right to privacy, the government strengthens the level of secrecy in the name of effectiveness. The effect is clear: existing secrecy is superseded by more secrecy.

As Edward Teller once noted, "secrecy, once accepted, becomes an addiction."[304] This addiction is partly possible as a consequence of the SCOTUS' involvement in sustaining and even deepening the impact

---

302 See: Paweł Laidler, *Secrecy Versus Transparency in the U.S. National Security Surveillance State* in: *Trust and Transparency in an Age of Surveillance*, Lora Anne Viola, Paweł Laidler (eds.), Routledge, London 2022, pp. 107–126.

303 Kate Doyle, *The End of Secrecy: U.S. National Security and the New Openness Movement* in: *National Insecurity: U.S. Intelligence After the Cold War*, Temple University Press, Philadelphia 2000, p. 92.

304 Michael J. Glennon, *National Security…*, op. cit., p. 22.

of secrecy on American politics, especially in the area of government surveillance; as we will see in the following this was possible due to the unification of the views of both conservative and liberal justices.

An Ideological Court

Several arguments can be raised in the discussion about the impact of the judicial branch on the operation of the executive, resulting in its legitimization of broader powers and secretive operations of presidents and their subordinate agencies. Some of these arguments strengthen the conviction that for political reasons the justices have a soft spot for particular presidents, treating them exceptionally well. Heidi Kitrosser has an interesting perspective on this issue, demonstrating the uniqueness of the relationship between the judicial and executive branches:

> "Despite the relative independence of federal courts from politics, courts' frequent willingness to defer to claims of executive prerogative without serious inquiry can be traced to at least three factors. First, federal judges are appointed by the president and confirmed by the Senate. Second, federal judges are not immune to the lure of the presidential mystique. The mystique is a cultural future of the imperial presidency, it amounts to a belief that the president alone has the knowledge, expertise, resources, and other tools to discern what is best for the nation. Third, courts have strong institutional incentives to avoid decisions that could undermine their legitimacy either by straying far beyond the bounds of public opinion or by risking the executive's branch refusal to cooperate. There is an institutional basis for judicial attraction to constitutional doctrines that foreclose serious probing of executive branch secrecy claims."[305]

The first argument raised by Kitrosser, in particular, encourages a brief discussion as it may bring an interesting perspective to the analysis of SCOTUS surveillance adjudication. She is definitely right in referring to institutional connections stemming from the checks and balances system, in which federal judges including Supreme Court justices are appointed by presidents with the advice and consent of Senate. Such a relationship may have serious consequences for the operation of the federal judiciary, and there have been numerous studies devoted to analyses of Court appointments and their effect on justices' adjudication. Many researchers have observed

305 Heidi Kitrosser, *Reclaiming Accountability...*, op. cit., pp. 7–8.

the politicization of the appointments process having an impact not only on individual justices' approach to constitutional interpretation but also on the general direction of the Court's adjudication.[306]

As was stressed in chapter one, the position of the SCOTUS evolved throughout history, making the institution politically active and thus attractive for the other branches of government, especially those having an impact on the Court's membership. In the 20th and 21st centuries particularly, presidents nominated candidates for judicial posts who either shared their ideology or were politically affiliated with their party, constituting a repetitive pattern of Republicans nominating conservatives and Democrats appointing liberals, with just a few exemptions. The Senate has also played an important role in the confirmation process, especially since 1930s, holding active debates on presidential nominees and conducting hearings during which Senators have sought to determine the approach of candidates towards constitutional issues, and, finally, voting to confirm or reject the candidate, usually along party lines.[307] The process called by Megan Shannon and Charles R. Shipan the "nomination game", played by the president and Senate[308], was especially visible over the last decade, when the legislative body blocked or pushed for some nominations of justices on the basis of political factors, thus influencing the current distribution of ideological votes in the Court. Examples of such tensions occurred in recent years when a Republican-led Senate prevented the nomination of Barack Obama's candidate to the Supreme Court, Merrick Garland, for a vacant seat following the death of Justice Antonin Scalia, but a few years later filled the seat left by Ruth Bader Ginsburg with Donald Trump's appointment of Amy Coney Barrett.[309]

Considering the politicization of the appointment process, it is easy to derive conclusions concerning the special relationship between the justices

---

306 See: Paweł Laidler, *The Supreme Court...*, op. cit.; Henry J. Abraham, *Justices, Presidents...*, op. cit.

307 *Ibid.*

308 See: Charles R. Shipan, Megan Shannon, "Delaying Justice(s): A Duration Analysis of Supreme Court Confirmations", *American Journal of Political Science* 47(4), 2003, pp. 654–668.

309 See: Paweł Laidler, *The Supreme Court...*, op. cit.

and presidents, although it has to be stressed that not every chief justice has been successful in nominating a specific candidate to the SCOTUS, due either to the lack of a Senate confirmation or other procedural issues. There have also been examples of presidents who believed they had "packed the Court" with proper candidates, but were disappointed by the adjudication and the direction of voting of their appointees, both in a concrete case or in the more general context, such as Dwight Eisenhower with the approach presented by Earl Warren and William Brennan, or Ronald Reagan with the performances of Sandra Day O'Connor and Anthony Kennedy.[310] Furthermore, there is a strong argument for judicial independence resulting from systemic solutions, in which the justices chosen by a president and confirmed by the Senate do not depend on the appointing institutions in the context of their later adjudication. The Founding Fathers aimed at the achievement of said independence by providing lifetime tenure for the justices, by depriving the executive of the power to remove them unless in an impeachment procedure, and by limiting the financial influence of Congress on justices' salaries.

The above-mentioned arguments, both theoretical and practical, suggest that assumptions about the results of direct connections between presidents and their appointees can be wide of the mark as such connections cannot be taken for granted. It would definitely be difficult to prove that the majority of justices have considered the views of the presidents who nominated them to the Court in their constitutional interpretation. However, the conduct of the appointment process reveals the ways in which both presidents and senators can anticipate candidates' voting choices in concrete disputes relating to important constitutional issues. If a SCOTUS candidate had served as a district or circuit court judge ruling in disputes concerning abortion, the right to bear arms, or the powers of federal government vis-à-vis states, it seems unrealistic to assume that as a justice that person would significantly change their approach to constitutional interpretation. Similarly, if a judge

310 See: Brett W. Curry, Richard L. Pacelle, jr., Bryan W. Marshall, "An Informal and Limited Alliance": The President and the Supreme Court", *Presidential Studies Quarterly* 38(2), 2008; Herman Schwartz, *Packing the Courts: The Conservative Campaign to Rewrite the Constitution*, Charles Scribner's Sons, New York 1998.

had read the Constitution in a way that adhered to the originalist mode of interpretation, there is only a slim chance that as a justice he or she would apply a functionalist approach, thereby becoming a proponent of living constitutionalism. Furthermore, the analysis of various issues adjudicated by the SCOTUS in the 20th and 21st centuries brings surprisingly unequivocal conclusions as to the impact of ideology on justices' judgments. In such areas as federal and state relations, the scope of congressional commerce clause prerogatives, the power of taxation, and the scope of most of the rights and freedoms of individuals, Republican-appointed justices have pursued a conservative way of reading the Constitution, while justices appointed by Democrats have provided a liberal approach towards constitutionalism.[311]

As a strong proponent of the arguments raised by the researchers who claim the dominance of the attitudinal voting in the Court, and the growing impact of ideology on justices' decisions, I have to admit that there have also been areas in which the determination of the direction of SCOTUS rulings was not so obvious, such as in cases concerning the scope of freedom of speech. In such disputes justices build coalitions regardless of their ideological attitude, voting to expand or limit the First Amendment's protection of different types of speech. For example, conservatives and liberals voted together to determine the appropriate degree of the constitutional protection of symbolic speech in a flag-burning case in 1989.[312] Similarly, I did not observe votes being cast along ideological lines with respect to the majority of the cases analyzed my research, in the spheres of domestic and foreign intelligence surveillance. Of course, in the disputes challenging government domestic surveillance and raising concerns as to the scope of the Fourth Amendment clauses, one can imagine that there are stronger inclinations of liberal justices to protect the individual right to privacy, contrary to conservatives paying a greater degree of attention to the effectiveness of law enforcement institutions. This is connected with the general support of Democrats for the Due Process Model (DPM), which prioritizes individual freedoms over the general notion of security, whereas Republicans have been the proponents of the Crime Control Model (CCM), first providing

311 Lawrence A. Baum, *The Supreme Court...*, op. cit.; Christopher Tomlins (ed.), *The United States...*, op. cit.

312 *Texas v. Johnson* 491 U.S. 397 (1989).

security and then taking care of the rights of the defendants. Proponents of DPM support limitations being placed on the powers of law enforcement officers, whereas CCM advocates believe that only equipping investigative units with broad competences can ensure their effective operation.[313]

The analysis of SCOTUS adjudication in the Fourth Amendment cases shows the efficacy of such a theoretical assumption, but to a limited extent, as there were not many disputes in which the ideological affiliation of justices had an impact on their voting. Such examples include *Mapp v. Ohio*, incorporating the exclusionary rule in the states, *Smith v. Maryland*, announcing the third party doctrine as the basis for the collection of phone records by the government, and *Carpenter v. United States*, in which, however, the liberal wing of the Court was joined by conservative Chief Justice John Roberts, Jr. On the other hand, there were surprisingly many disputes in which liberals and conservatives did not voting purely along ideological lines, such as in *Weeks v. United States*, where the Court unanimously recognized the exclusionary rule on the federal level, *Berger v. New York,* declaring the necessity of judicial supervision over eavesdropping procedures, *Katz v. United States*, introducing the reasonable expectation of privacy standard, and in *Terry v. Ohio*, when all-bar-one of the justices expanded the powers of law enforcement by applying the reasonable suspicion standard to stop and frisk procedures.

There were also narrow margin SCOTUS decisions concerning domestic electronic surveillance which were made in periods when ideological voting was a repetitive pattern in most of the cases, but in which the votes did not fall into an ideological pattern. In *Kyllo v. United States*, a dispute concerning the use of thermal devices to collect evidence against suspects, the majority decision was signed by Antonin Scalia and Ruth Bader Ginsburg, who represented contradictory approaches towards constitutional interpretation, whereas liberal John Paul Stevens dissented, joining three other conservative justices. This may suggest two things. First, that ideology was not the decisive factor in justices' voting, and second that even for Democratic-leaning justices, security has become an important

313 See: Abigail Hayes, Tamara Lynn, "Due Process vs Crime Control Models of Justice", *SACAD Entrants* 31, 2020, available at: https://scholars.fhsu.edu/cgi/viewcontent.cgi?article=1098&context=sacad.

value in the process of constitutional interpretation of law enforcement powers and their use of surveillance measures. In that context the legitimate end approach would prevail for justices over their adherence to ideological attitudes, especially at times when public expectations were consistent with temporary limitations being placed on their freedoms.

This leads to the next conclusion, that even if ideology played a limited role in the Supreme Court's domestic surveillance adjudication, it was less important still in foreign intelligence surveillance disputes and national security cases. Careful analysis of the distribution of the votes in such cases, as well as the substance of the justices' arguments presented in their individual opinions, confirms the fact that in times of emergency marked by references to the national security paradigm, the Court has been more likely to lean towards strengthening the powers of the government, including broad surveillance measures, rather than to the protection of individual rights and freedoms. The two World Wars, the Red Scare, the Cold War and the War on Terror created environments that were amenable to the judicial branch's expansion of government surveillance powers, and the majority of the justices legitimized such a direction of adjudication. There have been examples of unanimous rulings in which the Court confirmed the broad powers of the government in national security matters (*Schenck v. United States*, *United States v. Belmont*, *Pink v. United States*) and decisions which acknowledged the importance of the privileges strengthening the unique position of the executive in the separation of powers (*Totten v. United States*, *United States v. Nixon*, *Tenet v. Doe*, *F.B.I. v. Fazaga*). On the other hand, there have also been rulings in which individual justices issued dissenting opinions, being willing to limit the expansion of the powers of government during times of emergency and to strengthen the constitutional protection of individual rights, such as *American Communication Association v. Douds* and *Dennis v. United States*. However, in the vast majority of cases both conservative and liberal justices have acknowledged the necessity to effectively provide security to the American people, even at the expense of their rights and freedoms.

Two disputes have been adjudicated by SCOTUS in recent years in which ideology has played a more significant role in the distribution of the votes; these are *Trump v. Hawaii,* where conservative justices upheld a presidential executive order while their liberal counterparts dissented, and *Clapper v. Amnesty International* – the only NSA surveillance Court ruling – in which the liberal justices were outvoted by conservatives in rejecting the challenge due to its speculative and abstract character. Considering all the analyzed Supreme Court decisions in both domestic and foreign surveillance disputes, the above-mentioned examples cannot yet serve as proof that identifies a pattern of ideological voting in cases concerning government surveillance.

The Problematic Fourth Amendment

As was observed in the analysis in chapter two, the Fourth Amendment was designed to limit the intrusive power of government, which occurred during the colonial period when British officers used general warrants to search colonists and their premises and seize illegal goods. The real purpose of the Amendment with respect to the future functioning of the U.S. government was to prevent potentially arbitrary practices on the part of law enforcement and other investigative institutions in their activities aimed at fighting crime and capturing criminals. Security was at stake when the Founding Fathers were discussing the text of the Amendment, as they considered the general security of the society that had been achieved as a result of the government's protection of the people from internal and external threats, and the individual security of persons who were subject to investigative measures undertaken by the government. The Fourth Amendment became part of Bill of Rights in 1791 and its meaning and scope has changed throughout history thanks to its interpretation by the Supreme Court. The justices used several disputes relating to the operations of law enforcement and intelligence agencies affecting the privacy of individuals, thus determining the scope of the Search and Seizure and Warrant Clauses.

There is no doubt that, apart from clarifying the original intent and meaning of the amendment, the Court's role was to adapt the understanding of its provisions to the changing social and political reality, marked by the evolution of the leading paradigms of American domestic and international policies and the growth of technology that equipped the government with more enhanced investigative tools. Similarly to other important constitutional amendments introducing new judicial approaches to the scope of the rights of individuals, such as the types of speech protected by the First Amendment, or the procedures necessary to ensure the Fifth and Fourteenth Amendments' due process of law, the key phrases and concepts derived from the Fourth Amendment have been redefined by SCOTUS in its 20th and 21st century adjudication. This means that the justices faced the need to explain the constitutional meaning of the reasonableness of searches and seizures, the conditions that need to be met in obtaining warrants or conducting warrantless searches, the standards guiding the character of search and seizure, the types of institutions imposing search measures, the scope of the right to privacy of persons subject to searches and seizures, the types of institutions empowered to impose search measures, and the types of tools used by these institutions in exercising their search powers. The determination of most of these issues seemed obvious and necessary from the perspective of the nature of American constitutionalism and the needs of the changing political and social contexts, and the Court was able to keep up with the pace and character of these changes. Although not all of the justices accepted the direction of constitutional interpretation of the Fourth Amendment, there was no doubt as to the ability of the SCOTUS to adapt the Amendment's provisions to the domestic and international American realities.

However, problems arose in the second half of the 20th century, and especially the 21st, in disputes in which the justices had to face challenges regarding congressional legislation or actions undertaken by the executive branch which made it difficult to clearly determine their character from the perspective of the Fourth Amendment. The emergence of the new technologies used by the government to surveil its citizens and foreigners, and the enhancement of the procedures for collecting data derived from such surveillance, resulted in the authorities being able to access metadata pertaining to a variety of sensitive information about American citizens. In the name of domestic and national security, government agencies began to collect, store, process and analyze a near-unlimited amount of data and, via the gathering of seemingly unrelated small pieces of information from various sources, trying to connect them in order to obtain a broader picture of possible threats.[314] This process, based as we have seen on the

314 James R. Arnold, *Secrecy in the Sunshine Era…*, op. cit., p. 26.

mosaic theory, has brought serious challenges to the understanding of the Fourth Amendment's Search and Seizure Clause, raising questions about the adaptability of the Constitution to the changing surveillance reality.

Of course the application of the legitimate end approach via which the justices legitimized the expansion of executive powers allows us to assume that any, even the most significant change in the character of the means of the surveillance used by the government, does not prevent the Court from redefining the scope of Fourth Amendment's searches and seizures, provided their purposes are justified by the legitimate needs of the authorities. In that context, both the tools through which law enforcement and intelligence agencies collect evidence against people who threaten domestic and national security, as well as the scope of the surveillance measures, will be approved by the SCOTUS if the justices agree with the government's arguments. The problem with this expanding interpretation of the Constitution is that once the judicial branch allows a broader reading of a certain constitutional clause or provision it sets a precedent which can be both narrowed down or expanded in the future. This could lead to the conclusion that government powers can be unlimited, provided the Court adopts such an approach towards constitutional interpretation. In the context of government surveillance, it would mean that any type of interception of people's communications, both in terms of the tools used and the manner of their collection, could be declared constitutional, thereby leading to the placing of unacceptable limitations on the freedoms of individuals. That is not what was expected by the Founding Fathers, including Chief Justice John Marshall.

According to the legitimate end approach, the constitutionality of the means used by the government is dependent upon the purposes of the activities undertaken by the authorities, which have to be consistent with the supreme law of the land. Even if the institutions responsible for constitutional interpretation, including the SCOTUS, would read the concrete provisions of the Constitution in a way that referred not to its letter but to its spirit, the expansion of the powers of the government cannot be infinite. This was declared directly by Marshall in *McCulloch* in the words "we admit, as all must admit, that the powers of the government are limited, and that its limits are not to be transcended."[315] Although the analyzed part of 1819 precedent introduced the functionalist approach towards constitutional interpretation, as applied in several disputes concerning government surveillance, it is difficult to sustain the argument for the unlimited use of surveillance measures . Therefore, the problematic application of the Fourth Amendment to the reality of the massive collection of data on U.S. citizens resulting from government surveillance programs raises serious concerns as to the current interpretation of the Constitution.

The problem is even more significant if one realizes that the most recent important SCOTUS ruling which is invoked in the contemporary understanding of massive data surveillance was *Smith v. Maryland*, dating back to 1979. In *Smith*, which established the third party doctrine, the Court held that law enforcement's collection of telephone numbers called from a particular line did not require a warrant as there was no reasonable expectation of privacy in respect of information disclosed voluntarily to the telephone company. It remains unclear as to whether the position concerning the access to telecommunications metadata similarly lacks constitutional protection. An argument may be raised from the *United States v. Jones* rationale, the case related to a GPS tracker installed on a car, that the collection of metadata involves an unreasonable search given the privacy-invading nature of large-scale aggregations of data.[316] The question occurs of whether the third party doctrine should not be modified so as to address contemporary challenges presented by the government's collection of metadata derived from digital communications; it is definitely the role of the Supreme Court to address this question.

Observing the tensions stemming from the SCOTUS interpretation of the Fourth Amendment, Christopher Slobogin argues the following:

> "Under current law, most virtual searches are not Fourth Amendment searches or, if they, are, they can usually be carried out on little or no suspicion of they do not involve interception of communication content. Given the huge amount of information that virtual searches provide about everyone's activities and transactions, traditional physical searches are much less necessary than they used

315 *McCulloch v. Maryland* 17 U.S. 316 (1819), at 421.
316 565 U.S. 400 (2012).

> to be. Technological developments have exposed the fact that the Court's view of the Fourth Amendment threatens the entire edifice of search and seizure law."[317]

He continues by stressing that the lack of a distinct category in which to place virtual searches brings several negative consequences to the operation of government agencies and to the proper control of surveillance procedures:

> "None of this means that surveillance by the government should be prohibited. But it does suggest that it should be regulated under the Constitution, just as physical searches are. Furthermore, it suggests that back-end regulation of virtual searches, through provisions limiting information disclosure and use, will not be sufficient, because it will not prevent the subterranean abuse of information already collected, nor will it eradicate the feeling of being watched and the chilling effects occasioned by surveillance."[318]

Laura K. Donoghue lists four factors responsible for the fact that the law is not sufficient to protect citizens' privacy from the consequences of government surveillance: the dramatic expansion of technology resulting in the amount and type of information produced and stored; the government's broader authority to gain access to that information; the free flow of information across the Internet without users' approval; and the post-9/11 convergence between national security and domestic law enforcement. Donoghue argues that the multiplication and digitalization of interactions among people makes technology a driving factor in determining the networks to which people belong and the shaping of power relationships among social groups.[319]

Following this approach, it seems that law is not being created mainly to protect the rights and freedoms of the people, but, rather, to strengthen the effectiveness of the government's operations. All of this leads to a smaller degree of protection of the data and information concerning individuals who are subjects of interest to the authorities not only in the context of foreign intelligence but also law enforcement. In such a perspective an important role is to be played not only by the judicial branch, but mainly by Congress, which is responsible for implementing legislation which would serve the values of both security and freedom. One piece of legislation of

---

317 Christopher Slobogin, *Is the Fourth Amendment…*, op. cit., p. 19.
318 *Ibid.*, p. 23.
319 Laura K. Donoghue, *The Future of Foreign…*, op. cit., pp. 3–4.

this kind was the Freedom Act, which imposed restrictions on the collection of bulk metadata and required the government to obtain orders from judges granting them access to specific records from telecommunication providers. Despite playing an important role in the post-Snowden era of intensified transparency, the Act cannot serve as a remedy for the shortcomings of the Fourth Amendment.

The truth is, as Timothy Edgar observes, that "in an era of global mass surveillance ... the Fourth Amendment protects only a tiny fraction of the world's data"[320], leaving two possibilities for the future of government surveillance: either the gathering of data shall continuously expand, bringing further negative consequences to the scope of the right to privacy of individuals, or the SCOTUS will introduce a new interpretation of the Fourth Amendment that takes into account all of the challenges modern surveillance brings to the proper understanding of the Amendment itself. Looking at the problem from the perspective of the legitimate end approach, it seems that the justices will continue to justify the use of various means, even the most technologically advanced, if only the government will be able to make strong arguments for the need to protect domestic or national security. As Alexander Hamilton noticed in the initial phase of American statehood, "it is impossible to foresee or to define the extent and variety of national emergencies, and the correspondent extent and variety of the means which may be necessary to satisfy them."[321] It seems that the SCOTUS is on the right path to fulfilling Hamilton's vision of satisfying not only the challenges of national emergencies, but – above all – the executive branch by equipping it with broad and uncontrolled surveillance powers.

The National Security Surveillance State

The U.S. government's contemporary approach to the national security paradigm proves that the concept born out of the defense and military arguments included in the Truman doctrine has evolved and contains reference to various security-related issues, such as those pertaining to economy, politics, health, energy, the environment, cyberspace and even

320 Timothy J. Edgar, *Beyond Snowden...*, op. cit., p. 68.
321 See: Alexander Hamilton, *Federalist no. 23...*, op. cit.

culture. The diversity of the challenges and threats which the American government has been facing for the last 80 years forces each presidential administration to implement new national security strategies and policies which will meet the needs of a changing political and social reality marked by these challenges and threats. To effectively pursue national security goals, Congress has to introduce new legislation or modify the existing regulations, adapting them to the changing circumstances, including in the context of rapid technological development. The executive branch led by the president should operate within the scope of the powers delegated to it; however, as history has proved, from time to time the activities undertaken by the law enforcement or intelligence agencies go beyond this scope. As a consequence, to meet the requirements of security strategies new programs and policies are implemented, some of which are carried out in secret, beyond congressional and judicial control. At the same time the courts, with the Supreme Court as the most important institution within the judicial branch, are responsible for interpreting these laws, programs, and policies from the perspective of their constitutionality, by balancing the purposes of the government with the rights of the people. Usually, this means placing on scales of justice the need to achieve a level of security which allows the authorities and society to function safe from internal and external threats, on the one hand, and the need to protect the concrete freedoms of an individual or individuals, as guaranteed in the letter or spirit of the Constitution, on the other.

The effectiveness of national security strategies and policies depends on all three branches of government, which are, at least theoretically, equally responsible for the final result when it comes to the functioning of the government. As was mentioned earlier, the national security system established in the 20th century and further developed in the 21st is the result of a joint collaboration between the executive, legislative and judicial branches, although their respective involvement in strengthening the dominance of the national security paradigm in American politics was different in scope and character. There would of course be no fulfillment of the national security paradigm without Harry Truman's doctrine of containment, as well as such congressional legislation as the National Security Act, or the acts establishing the Central Intelligence Agency and the National Security Agency. However, without the indispensable role of the judicial branch the system would not have survived the Cold War era, when the SCOTUS either declared legislation and presidential acts constitutional or remained silent, allowing the political branches to operate. Still, if we can agree that all three branches contributed to the current state of affairs, regardless of whether Democrats or Republicans governed, there are no obstacles to recognizing the United States as a national security state. The fact is that national security is a central component of American foreign policy and public policy in general, as two-thirds of the employees of the national government and approximately 40 % of its budget are devoted to national security policy.[322]

One of the most crucial features determining the functioning of the United States as a national security state is the means by which the executive has decided to pursue its strategies and policies, in both the domestic and international arenas. According to the legitimate end approach, which is dominant in the way in which the role of government in providing security is understood, the choice of means and their effectiveness depends on the institutions responsible for enacting domestic and national security policies. Both the law enforcement units and intelligence agencies have been very active in employing various means which they assumed would become effective in providing security to American citizens. The choice of these tools, as well as the manner of their implementation, has depended on both the access of U.S. government to enhanced technology and the scope of their use as determined by political subjects coordinating certain policies. Surveillance became the most often used and effective means of ensuring security, understood from the perspective of preventing the impact of threats and dangers, as well as the reaction to negative consequences caused by their occurrence. Therefore, the imposition of surveillance measures co-evolved with both the advancement of technology and the growing needs of the national security state in which the government wanted to have access to information while seeking to prevent, at the same time, its having to disclose information concerning its own operations. As a result, the secretive system of surveillance programs was implemented, mostly beyond the control

322 George C. Edwards III, Wallace Earl Walker (eds.), *National Security…* op. cit. p. 1.

of the other branches of government, allowing the executive to grow in power proportionally to the expansion of the national security paradigm in U.S. domestic and foreign policy. Law enforcement and intelligence agencies launched programs which were aimed at collecting data and information on subjects hypothetically endangering the equilibrium of the American state. The collection and processing of data was done in order to prevent such threats as federal or state crimes, the spread of communism, terrorist attacks or any other threats which the government would define as dangerous for the national security of the country.

Although there were two types of surveillance put in place by the government as defined from the perspective of their scope, i.e. domestic or foreign intelligence, there seemed to be a clear theoretical line between them as they were determined by the subjects being surveilled – U.S. citizens were subject to the domestic interception of their communications, and foreigners of foreign intelligence surveillance. Despite this division it soon turned out that American citizens were also subject to foreign intelligence surveillance, especially in cases where national security arguments were raised by the government. Uncontrolled surveillance carried out by intelligence agencies such as the NSA directly or indirectly affected thousands of U.S. citizens, similarly to the interception program conducted by the FBI under J. Edgar Hoover, which covered people and organizations which were not the subjects of official criminal investigations. Everything happened under the label of national security. And even if these abuses were repaired in mid-1970's and new tools of oversight and control were introduced, another disaster for the functioning of the state and the society – the 9/11 terrorist attacks – reinforced the demand for greater security. With the development of increasingly sophisticated digital technology and the change in the mode of collecting data and information, the post-9/11 national security state expanded its surveillance powers and once again began to operate far beyond congressional or judicial control. Once again, secrecy became the core value in the process of implementing and carrying out surveillance programs, resulting in the collection of metadata and the application of the mosaic theory to its processing and analysis. In the aftermath of the Snowden Affair the society at large and civil rights organizations began again their quest for transparency; however, no serious changes appeared either in the operation of the executive or the means of controlling it used by Congress and the Supreme Court. All of this led to the establishment of a system which can be called the national security surveillance state. That is what the United States represents today.

I am convinced that such a situation would not be possible without the legitimate end approach of the Supreme Court justices to the process of the constitutional interpretation of the scope of government surveillance. The justices have legitimized all the issues responsible for the establishment and development of the national security surveillance state – they approved of the growth of executive power in the area of foreign policy, they accepted the national security paradigm as an argument justifying the application of broader investigative means, they established two different standards of privacy protection depending on the character of a government operation, they tipped the scales in favor of security at the expense of freedom and privacy, they strengthened the secretive character of the government's operations, and they did not prevent the executive's expansionist approach – and sometimes even the abuse of its powers – in the process of developing the national security surveillance state. The end, defined as the provision of security to the United States and its citizens, was legitimate and the means employed by the executive branch turned out intrusive and uncontrolled, but constitutional. The SCOTUS preferred to view things from the perspective of the functional interpretation of the Constitution, assuming that the main responsibility of the government is to provide security, at least in times of emergency.

There is no doubt that the executive branch has overused its powers by frequently invoking different doctrines and privileges which served as theoretical justifications for the expansion of government surveillance powers. Executive officers, including several presidents, have overused the paradigm of national security, building the network of executive and intelligence units that has been operating, exploited and, beyond the reach and control of the other branches of government. But mostly, they have overused the status of the emergency state. Whenever presidential administrations announced times of emergency, it meant an automatic change in the scope of the protection of basic civil rights, such as freedom of speech, assembly and association, due process of law, and the right to privacy.[323] This approach has usually been supported by the other branches of government, especially the courts, which followed the rule that in "times of emergency and peril" the scope of the constitutional protection of basic rights and freedoms may be limited (*Korematsu v. United States*, *Dennis v. United States*). There is no doubt that extended surveillance measures have played a significant role in the use of emergency powers by the U.S. government, and that national security arguments enabled the authorities to classify most of its operations in that respect. The paradox, however, is that periods of emergency have become a continuous reference point and justification for the executive in disputes in which citizens and civil rights organizations raise concerns about the violations of rights and freedoms of individuals.

Eric Posner and Adrian Vermeule list six periods of emergency which have occurred during U.S. history: the undeclared war with France in the late 18th century, which resulted in the Sedition Act; the Civil War of 1861–1865, which led to President Lincoln's suspension of habeas corpus; WWI and the Red Scare, which generated the Espionage Act, leading to prosecutions of critics of the war and the harassment of immigrants and aliens; WWII, which saw the internment of Japanese Americans, Cold War legislation and prosecutions of communists; and the post-9/11 emergency, resulting in aggressive security measures, including the detention without trial of suspected terrorists.[324] The analysis of the SCOTUS adjudication in national security case-law, including disputes around government surveillance, proves that since WWI there has been an ongoing period of emergency having different sources in historical events. Given this, I agree with Posner and Vermeule, who properly define these events and refer to the main consequences of the state of emergency for the management of the country, as well as for the scope of individual rights. The only modification which I would introduce concerns the division of modern American history into periods which I find unnecessary, as for more than a century the U.S. government has convinced its citizens of the existence of continuous

323 See: Susan N. Herman, *Taking Liberties…*, op. cit.; Anthony D. Romero, Dina Temple-Raston, *In Defense of Our America…*, op. cit.; Bruce Akerman, *Before the Next Attack…*, op. cit.

324 Eric E. Posner, Adrian Vermeule, *Terror in the Balance…*, op. cit., p. 3.

threats affecting their everyday lives. Such a change in understanding how emergency affects the interpretation of the Constitution may be significant for the operation of the government, but even more for the protection of the rights and freedoms of individuals.

As has been analyzed here, the justices who granted broader powers to the executive at the expense of freedom believed that the limitations imposed on the power of the people would be temporary, and that when an emergency would end the Court would restore the Constitution and provide the proper balance between security and freedom. But if there are no breaks in the state of emergency, it is difficult to imagine how and when SCOTUS could repair the damage caused by the activities of the overwhelming national security surveillance state. Of course, in official statements politicians agree that "even in times of emergency, government must respect Americans' rights"[325], but this seems impossible considering the vast executive machinery that invests time, energy, and resources in the collection of data and information about potential threats to the country and its citizens.

Sidney W. Souers, the first director of national intelligence, wrote that "national security can perhaps best be understood as a point of view rather than a distinct area of governmental responsibility".[326] National security rhetoric plays an important role in building the conviction that there exist internal or external threats which present dangers to the American people, but it also serves as an argument raised by the government in surveillance cases decided by the Supreme Court. While explaining the meaning of national security in different contexts, James E. Baker observes the way politicians use this rhetoric:

> "National security is also a compelling source of political motivation. However, overuse of the term can debase its value. If overplayed, the broader audience may discount real and legitimate assertions of security necessity as political slogans. They may be both. Such a perception may appeal to the political base, but degrade popular support for essential actions, with damaging results when facing an indefinite threat requiring generational commitment and continuity in response."[327]

---

325 Mary Graham, *Presidents' Secrets...*, op. cit., p. 180.
326 Robert M. Pallitto, William G. Weaver, *Presidential Secrecy...*, op. cit., p. 69.
327 James E. Baker, *In the Common Defense. National Security Law for Perilous Times*, Cambridge University Press, New York 2007, p. 15–16.

Without discussing the accuracy of Baker's assumptions about the overuse of national security rhetoric by politicians, it is clear that the potential consequences of such activities may have serious consequences for the results of SCOTUS adjudication in government surveillance disputes. In the majority of cases in which the authorities used the national security argument to justify the expansion of their powers at the expense of the rights and freedoms of individuals, the justices almost always approved such argumentation. There are no grounds for believing that the current Supreme Court consisting of politically appointed justices will have the strength and courage to stop the continuous evolution of the national security surveillance state.

Epilogue: The Illusion of Transparency

The legitimate end approach presented by the Supreme Court justices in their surveillance adjudication affects not only the powers of the government, the scope of the separation of powers and system of checks and balances, as well as constitutional limitations of the rights and freedoms of individuals, but it also has an impact on the level of government transparency. The importance of the confidentiality and secrecy of the operations undertaken by domestic law enforcement and intelligence agencies seems obvious and is understood by the vast majority of the subjects of these operations. Furthermore, the effectiveness of surveillance depends upon the secretive character of the programs that equip government agencies with eavesdropping and dataveillance powers; therefore, it is difficult to provide full access to information on crucial investigative measures. Full secrecy, on the other hand, doubled with the reluctance of government institutions to impose oversight and self-control measures raises doubts as to the fairness and honesty of the surveilling institutions, and the extent to which they should be allowed in the name of providing security. Such tensions are similar to the challenges concerning the assessment of the scope of individual rights and freedoms – the determination of the level of government transparency has become today one of the main factors now influencing the character of American democracy and the rule of law. Some U.S. presidents have understood their role as being keepers of the democratic values, including openness and transparency; this was the case, for example, with Barack Obama, who issued on the day after his inauguration, the Memorandum on Transparency and Open Government. He assured the American public during his State of the Union that "[t]ransparency and rule of law will be the touchstones of this presidency… This administration stands on the side not of those who seek to withhold information, but those who seek to make it known."[328] However, even President Obama acknowledged the need to maintain secrecy in many areas of his administration's functioning.

---

328 Martin E. Halstuk, Benjamin W. Cramer, Michael D. Todd, *Tipping the*

At the same time, researchers have noted that the times in which we live can be called an age of transparency, as the majority of countries are democracies and their citizens benefit from access to various types of information concerning their governance. Kristin Lord claims, that the recent rise of transparency is a result of at least five factors: "the spread of democratic governments, the rise of global media, the spread of NGOs, the proliferation of international regimes requiring the governments to disclose information, and the widespread availability of information technologies".[329] Without neglecting the impact of the factors mentioned by Lord, it seems important to note that in the context of U.S. government surveillance, the quest for transparency has always been a consequence of the public disclosure of the abuses of power on the part of the surveilling institutions resulting from press leaks, whistleblowing or legal challenges. In such a perspective Obama's rhetoric of transparency was provoked by the exposure of his predecessor's Terrorist Surveillance Program, and, later, by Snowden's revelations concerning the scope of the National Security Agency's foreign intelligence surveillance as it affected U.S. citizens. In fact, there is a parallel process in play in these matters: during periods in which the U.S. has faced serious national security threats the society has recognized the need to strengthen security measures at the expense of individual rights and freedoms; analogously, during the periods of intensified social concern over government surveillance programs the anti-secrecy and pro-transparency rhetoric becomes dominant. Usually, however, after a few years of increased public debate in which the arguments raised by the proponents of disclosure and open government prevail over the defenders of the secrecy and confidentiality of the government's operations, the situation goes "back to normal" and new surveillance measures are imposed in the name of safety and security.

Scales: How the U.S. Supreme Court Eviscerated Freedom of Information in Favor of Privacy in Davis, Charles N., Cuillier, David (eds.), *Transparency 2.0. Digital Data and Privacy in a Wired World*, Peter Lang, New York 2014, pp. 16.

329 Kristin M. Lord, *The Perils and Promise of Global Transparency. Why the Information Revolution may not lead to Security, Democracy, or Peace*, New York: State University of New York Press, 2006, p. 5.

This back-and-forth proves that there is a continuous process underway of seeking to determine the proper relation between freedom and security in general, and that the scope of government surveillance vis-à-vis the scope of the rights and freedoms of individuals is dependent on political and social circumstances, both national and international. In the post-Watergate and post-Snowden eras the authorities and the people shared similar expectations when it came to standards of governance, and references to such values as transparency, ethics, fairness, and the rule of law were repeated like mantras by all, regardless of their political affiliation or ideology. Contrarily, in the early years of the Cold War and the post-9/11 era Americans were united by a common enemy which threatened their security, and their allowed – and even demanded – the government's use of effective anti-communist or anti-terrorist policies which were deemed to require intensified surveillance. Clear differences between these periods are discernable only in the measures and instruments used, resulting from the growth of technology and the enhanced collaboration of intelligence agencies representing various countries sharing the same values in the latter case. As a result, the post-Snowden call for transparency seemed even more justified than the mid-1970s fight against systemic abuses of power by the leading law enforcement and intelligence agencies, as the scale of the NSA surveillance revealed by Snowden shocked not only American citizens, but also U.S. allies all over the world. The scale of the dataveillance revealed by Snowden initiated a discussion about the limits of government surveillance and legitimization of the powers of the surveilling agencies; however, it did not result in any significant legal or institutional changes based on a reevaluation of the meaning and importance of surveillance as an instrument of governance.

It is not the surveillance in general, but the excessive, continuous, and unreasonable use of it which raises concerns in the society at large, especially in periods which, according to many, should not be labelled by the authorities as "emergencies". According to Christian Parenti, "[s]urveillance instills discipline by forcing self-regulation. Constant surveillance brings forth loyal citizens, trained soldiers, obedient patients, productive workers, and docile, useful bodies".[330] In that context, it is understandable that the government aims to impose broad surveillance measures, even if they do not produce immediate benefits for the domestic

330 Christian Parenti, *Soft Cage...*, op. cit., p. 9.

or national security policies, because it wants to maximize its control over what is happening within its own jurisdiction. Still, the most significant outcome of this process is the growing culture of secrecy which can be seen developing in the rhetoric of national security and emergency. Regardless of the importance of transparency as a democratic value, it seems impossible to sustain the notions of government openness and disclosure, especially when the two other branches of government, the legislative and judicial, clearly support the arguments used by the leader of secrecy – the executive. Lack of effective oversight and control is not a result of institutional flaws in American democracy, but rather may be derived from the unified approach of all political actors towards the need to protect domestic and national security. The Supreme Court in particular, as a national policy maker, has played a significant role in legitimizing government surveillance, either by confirming an increase in the powers of law enforcement and intelligence agencies or by approving timely limitations to the constitutional protection of the rights and freedoms of individuals. In such a reality transparency appears as a dream which cannot be fulfilled, or an illusion that everyone sees but no one can catch.

Bibliography

Legal Sources

ACLU v. Clapper 959 F.Supp.2d 724 (2013); 14-42 2d.Cir (2015).

Alien Registration Act 54 U.S. 670 (1940).

American Communications Association v. Douds 339 U.S. 382 (1950).

Arar v. Ashcroft et.al. 585 F.3d 559 (2009).

Berger v. New York 338 U.S. 41 (1967).

Boumediene v. Bush 553 U.S. 723 (2008).

Boyd v. United States 116 U.S. 616 (1886).

Brown v. Board of Education 347 U.S. 483 (1954).

California v. Ciraolo 476 U.S. 207 (1986).

Carpenter v. United States 484 U.S. 19 (2018).

Chae Chan Ping v. United States 130 U.S. 581 (1889).

Champion v. Ames 188 U.S. 321 (1903).

Chicago & Southern Airlines, Inc. v. Waterman S.S. Corp. 333 U.S. 103 (1948).

Clapper v. Amnesty International USA 568 U.S. 398 (2013).

Clinton v. City of New York 524 U.S.417 (1998).

Communications Act, 48 Stat. 1064 (1934).

Communist Control Act 68 U.S. 775 (1954).

Dames & Moore v. Regan 453 U.S. 654 (1981).

Dennis v. United States 341 U.S. 494 (1951).

Dow Chemical Co. v. United States 476 U.S. 227 (1986).

El Masri v. United States 479 F.3d 296 (2007).

Executive Order 12333, December 4, 1981.

Executive Order 13769, January 27, 2017.

Executive Order 13780, March 6, 2017.

Ex parte Merryman 17 F. Cas. 144 (1861).

Ex parte Milligan 71 U.S. 2 (1866).

F.B.I. v. Fazaga 595 U.S. 20-828 (2022).

Fletcher v. Peck 10 U.S. 87 (1810).

Foreign Intelligence Surveillance Act 92 U.S. 1783 (1978).

General Dynamics Corp. v. United States 563 U.S. 478 (2011).

Gibbons v. Ogden 22 U.S. 1 (1824).

Goldwater v. Carter 444 U.S. 996 (1979).

Hammer v. Dagenhart 247 U.S. 251 (1918).

Hamdan v. Rumsfeld 548 U.S. 557 (2006).

Hamdi v. Rumsfeld 542 U.S. 507 (2004).

Hirabayashi v. United States 320 U.S. 81 (1943).

Internal Security Act 64 Stat. 987 (1950).

Katz v. United States 389 U.S. 347 (1967).

Klayman v. Obama 957 F. Supp 2d.1 (2013); 142 F. Supp. 3d.172 (2015).

Korematsu v. United States 323 U.S. 214 (1944).

Kyllo v. United States 533 U.S. 27 (2001).

Labor Management Relations Act 61 Stat. 136 (1947)

Lochner v. New York 198 U.S. 45 (1905).

Mapp v. Ohio 367 U.S. 643 (1961).

Marbury v. Madison 5 U.S. 137 (1803).

Martin v. Hunter's Lessee 14 U.S. 304 (1816).

McCulloch v. Maryland 17 U.S. 316 (1819).

McGrain v. Daugherty 273 U.S. 135 (1927).

Miranda v. Arizona 384 U.S. 436 (1966).

Morrison v. Olson 487 U.S. 654 (1988).

National Federation of Independent Business v. Sebelius 567 U.S. 519 (2012).

Nardone v. United States 308 U.S. 338 (1939).

New York Times Co. v. United States 403 U.S. 713 (1971).

Obergefell v. Hodges 576 U.S. 644 (2015).

Olmstead v. United States 277 U.S. 438 (1928).

Omnibus Crime Control and Safe Streets Act, 82 Stat. 197 (1968).

Palko v. Connecticut 302 U.S. 319 (1937).

Proclamation 9645, September 24, 2017.

Protect America Act 121 U.S. 552 (2007).
Rasul v. Bush 542 U.S. 466 (2004).
Riley v. California 573 U.S. 373 (2014).
Roe v. Wade 410 U.S. 113 (1973).
Schenck v. United States 249 U.S. 47 (1919)
Smith v. Maryland 442 U.S. 735 (1979).
Tenet v. Doe 544 U.S. 1 (2005).
Terry v. Ohio 392 U.S. 1 (1968).
Texas v. Johnson 491 U.S. 397 (1989).
Totten v. United States 92 U.S. 105 (1875).
Trump v. Hawaii 585 U.S. 17-965 (2018).
United States v. Belmont 301 U.S. 324 (1937).
United States v. Carolene Products Co. 304 U.S. 144 (1938).
United States v. Coplon 185 F.2d 629 (1950).
United States v. Curtiss Wright Export Corp. 299 U.S. 304 (1936).
United States v. Darby 312 U.S. 118 (1941).
United States ex rel. Knauff v. Shaughnessy 338 U.S. 537 (1950).
United States v. Jones 565 U.S. 400 (2012).
United States v. Lopez 514 U.S. 549 (1995).
United States v. Nixon 418 U.S. 683 (1974).
United States v. Pink 315 U.S. 203 (1942).
United States v. Reynolds 345 U.S. 1 (1953).
United States v. Robel 389 U.S. 258 (1967).
United States v. U.S. District Court 407 U.S. 297 (1972).
United States v. Zubaydah 595 U.S. 20-827 (2022).
USA Freedom Act, 129 Stat. 268 (2015).
USA Patriot Act, 115 Stat. 272 (2001).
Watkins v. United States 354 U.S. 178 (1957).
Weeks v. United States 232 U.S. 383 (1914).
Wickard v. Filburn 317 U.S. 111 (1942).
Wolf v. Colorado 338 U.S. 25 (1949).

Yates v. United States 354 U.S. 298 (1957).

Youngstown Sheet and Tube Company v. Sawyer 343 U.S. 579 (1952).

Zemel v. Rusk 381 U.S. 1 (1965).

Zivotofsky v. Kerry 576 U.S. 1 (2015).

Literature

Abraham, Henry J. *Justices, Presidents, and Senators: A History of the U.S. Supreme Court Appointments from Washington to Bush II*, Rowman & Littlefield, Boston 2007.

Acts of Congress Held Unconstitutional in Whole or in Part by the Supreme Court of the United States, available at: https://law.justia.com/constitution/us/acts-of-congress-held-unconstitutional.html.

Akerman, Bruce. *Before the Next Attack: Preserving Civil Liberties in an Age of Terrorism*, Yale University Press, New Haven 2006.

Amar, Akhil Reed, *America's Constitution. A Biography*, Random House, New York 2005.

A National Security Strategy for a New Century, available at: https://clintonwhitehouse3.archives.gov/WH/EOP/NSC/Strategy/.

A New National Security Strategy for a New Era, available at: https://trumpwhitehouse.archives.gov/articles/new-national-security-strategy-new-era/.

Angwin, Julia. *Dragnet Nation: A Quest for Privacy, Security, and Freedom in a World of Relentless Surveillance*, Henry Holt and Company, New York 2014.

Arnold, Jason R., *Secrecy in the Sunshine Era. The Promise and Failures of US Open Government Laws*, University Press of Kansas, Lawrence 2014.

Bailey, Michael A., Maltzman, Forrest. *The Constrained Court: Law, Politics, and the Decisions Justices Make*, Princeton University Press, Princeton 2011.

Baker, James E. *In the Common Defense. National Security Law for Perilous Times*, Cambridge University Press, New York 2007.

Ball, Kirstie. Snider, Laureen (eds.). *The Surveillance-Industrial Complex: A Political Economy of Surveillance*, Routledge, London 2013.

Bamford, James. *Body of Secrets: Anatomy of the Ultra Secret National Security Agency*, Anchor, New York 2002.

Banks, Christopher P., Blakeman, John C. *The U.S. Supreme Court and New Federalism: From the Rehnquist to the Roberts Court*, Rowman & Littlefield, Boston 2012.

Banks, Christopher P. (ed.), *Controversies in American Federalism and Public Policy*, Routledge, New York 2018.

Baum, Lawrence A. *The Supreme Court*, Congressional Quarterly Press, Washington D.C. 2021.

Bennett, Robert W., Solum, Lawrence B. *Constitutional Originalism. A Debate*, Cornell University Press, Ithaca 2011.

Berger, Raoul. *Government by Judiciary: The Transformation of the Fourteenth Amendment*, Liberty Fund, New York 1997

Bernstein, Carl. Woodward, Bob. *All the President's Men: The Greatest Reporting Story of All Time*, Simon & Schuster, New York 2014.

Bickel, Alexander M. *The Least Dangerous Branch: The Supreme Court at the Bar of Politics*, Bobbs-Merrill, New York 1962.

Biden Administration Announces $1.7 Billion Investment to Fight Covid-19 Variants, available at: https://www.whitehouse.gov/briefing-room/statements-releases/2021/04/16/fact-sheet-biden-administration-announces-1-7-billion-investment-to-fight-covid-19-variants/.

Biden Signs Reauthorization of Surveillance Program Into Law Despite Privacy Concerns, National Public Radio, April 24, 2024, available at: https://www.npr.org/2024/04/20/1246076114/senate-passes-reauthorization-surveillance-program-fisa.

Bloch, Susan L., Jackson, Vicky. *Federalism. A Reference Guide to the United States Constitution*. ABC-Clio, Santa Barbara 2013.

Brandeis, Louis D. *Other People's Money and How the Bankers Use It*, 1914, available at: https://archive.org/stream/otherpeoplesmone00bran/otherpeoplesmone00bran_djvu.txt.

Brenner, Saul, Whitmeyer, Joseph W. *Strategy on the U.S. Supreme Court*, New York: Cambridge University Press 2009.

Calabresi, Stephen G., Yoo, John R. *The Unitary Executive: Presidential Power from Washington to Bush*, Yale University Press, New Haven 2012.

Charles, Douglas M. *J. Edgar Hoover and the Anti-Interventionists: FBI Political Surveillance and the Rise of the Domestic Security State 1939–1945*, Ohio State University Press, Columbus 2007.

Cole, David. *Terrorism and the Constitution: Sacrificing Civil Liberties in the Name of National Security*, Norton & Norton Company, New York 2006.

Collier, Christopher. *Decision in Philadelphia: The Constitutional Convention of 1787*, Ballentine Books, New York 2007.

Coronavirus Resource Center, The Johns Hopkins University & Medicine, available at: https://coronavirus.jhu.edu/region/united-states.

Cowen, David J. *The Origins and Economic Impact of the First Bank of the United States, 1791–1797*, Garland Publishing, New York 2000.

Curry, Brett W., Pacelle, jr., Richard L., Marshall, Bryan W. "An Informal and Limited Alliance": The President and the Supreme Court", *Presidential Studies Quarterly* 38(2), 2008.

Dahl, Robert. "Decision-Making in a Democracy: The Supreme Court as a National Policy-Maker", *Journal of Public Law*, 6, 1957.

Davis, Charles N., Cuillier, David (eds.), *Transparency 2.0. Digital Data and Privacy in a Wired World*, Peter Lang, New York 2014.

Davis, Darren W., Silver, Brian D. "Civil Liberties v. Security: Public Opinion in the Context of the Terrorist Attacks on America", *American Journal of Political Science* 48(1), 2003, pp. 28–46.

Devins, Neal. Whittington, Keith E. (ed.), *Congress and the Constitution*, Duke University Press, Durham 2005.

Diffie, Whitfield. Landau, Susan. *Privacy on the Line. The Politics of Wiretapping and Encryption*, The MIT Press, Cambridge 2007.

van Dijck, Jose. „Datafication, Dataism and Dataveillance: Big Data between Scientific Paradigm and Ideology". *Surveillance & Society*, 1(2), 2014.

Dinh, Viet D. "Liberty and the Rule of Law After September 11", *Journal of Law and Policy* 19(1), 2005, pp. 31–38.

DiPaolo, Amanda. *Zones of Twilight. Wartime Presidential Powers and Federal Court Decision Making*. Lexington Books, Lanham 2010.

Donoghue, Laura K. "The Shadow of State Secrets", *University of Pennsylvania Law Reviews* 159, 2010.

Donoghue, Laura K. *The Future of Foreign Intelligence. Privacy and Surveillance in a Digital Age*, Oxford University Press, New York 2016.

Doyle, Kate. *The End of Secrecy: U.S. National Security and the New Openness Movement* in: *National Insecurity: U.S. Intelligence After the Cold War*, Temple University Press, Philadelphia 2000.

Dudziak, Mary L., *Cold War Civil Rights: Race and Image of American Democracy*, Princeton University Press, Princeton 2000.

Dylan, Huw. Gioe, David. Goodman, Michael S. *The C.I.A. and the Pursuit of Security: History, Documents, and Contexts*, Edinburgh University Press, Edinburgh 2020.

Ebben, Maurits A., Sicking Louis (eds.), *Beyond Ambassadors: Consuls, Missionaries, and Spies in Premodern Diplomacy*, Brill, Leiden 2020.

Edelson, Chris. *Power Without Constraint. The Post-9/11 Presidency and National Security*. The University of Wisconsin Press, Madison 2016.

Edgar, Timothy J. *Beyond Snowden, Privacy, Mass Surveillance, and the Struggle to Reform the NSA*, Brookings Institution Press, Washington DC 2017.

Edlin, Douglas E. *Common Law Theory*, Cambridge University Press, New York 2010.

Edwards III, George C., Walker, Wallace Earl (eds.), *National Security and the U.S. Constitution. The Impact of the Political System*, The Johns Hopkins University Press, Baltimore 1988.

Ellis, Richard E. *Aggressive Nationalism: McCulloch v. Maryland and the Foundation of Federal Authority in the Young Republic*, Oxford University Press, New Yok 2007.

Ellis, Richard J. (ed.), *Judging Executive Power. Sixteen Supreme Court Cases that Have Shaped the American Presidency*, Rowman & Littlefield, Lanham 2009.

Epstein, Edward Jay. *How America Lost Its Secrets. Edward Snowden, the Man and the Theft*. Alfred A. Knopf, New York, 2017.

Fallon, jr., Richard H. *Law and Legitimacy in the Supreme Court*. The Belknap Press of Harvard University Press, Cambridge 2018.

Farber, Daniel (ed.), *Security v. Liberty: Conflicts Between Civil Liberties and National Security in American History*, Russell Sage Foundation, New York 2008.

Farrand, Max (ed), *Records of the Federal Convention of 1787. Vol. I*, Yale University Press, New Haven 1966.

Finan, Christopher M. *From the Palmer Raids to the Patriot Act: A History for the Fight for Free Speech in America*, Beacon Press, Boston 2008.

Fisher, Louis. *The Supreme Court and Congress. Rival Interpretations*, CQ Press, Washington D.C. 2009.

Fisher, Louis. *Supreme Court Expansion of Presidential Power: Unconstitutional Leanings*, University Press of Kansas, Lawrence 2017.

Fisher, Louis. Harriger, Katy J. *American Constitutional Law*, Carolina Academic Press, Durham 2019.

Fletcher, Kimberley. *The Collision of Political and Legal Time: Foreign Affairs and the Court's Transformation of Executive Authority*, Temple University Press, Philadelphia 2018.

Foreign Intelligence Surveillance Act Court Orders 1979–2022, Electronic Privacy Information Center, available at: https://epic.org/foreign-intelligence-surveillance-court-fisc/fisa-stats/.

Frost, David B. *Classified. A History of Secrecy in the United States Government*, McFarland and Company, Jefferson 2017.

George Washington's Farewell Address available at https://www.educatingforamericandemocracy.org/primary-source/george-washingtons-farewell-address-1797/.

Gilbert, James L., Finnegan, John P. *U.S. Army Signals Intelligence in World War II: A Documentary History*, Center of Military History, Washington D.C. 1993.

Glennon, Michael J. *National Security and Double Government.* Oxford University Press, New York 2015.

Goldfarb, Edward (ed.), *After Snowden: Privacy, Secrecy, and Security in the Information Age*, Thomas Dunne Books, New York 2015.

Goldsmith, Jack. *Power and Constraint: The Accountable Presidency after 9/11*, W.W. Norton and Company, New York 2012.

Graham, Mary. *Presidents' Secrets. The Use and Abuse of Hidden Power*, Yale University Press, New Haven 2017.

Gray, David. *The Fourth Amendment in an Age of Surveillance*, Harvard University Press, New York 2017.

Greenberg, Ivan. *Surveillance in America: Critical Analysis of the F.B.I., 1920 to the Present*, Lexington Books, Lanham 2012.

Greenwald, Glenn. *No Place to Hide: Edward Snowden, the NSA, and the U.S. Surveillance State*, Henry Holt & Company, New York 2014.

Gruszczak, Artur. *Intelligence Security in the European Union. Building a Strategic Intelligence Community*, Palgrave Macmillan, London 2016.

Haggerty, Kevin D., Samatas, Minas (eds.), *Surveillance and Democracy*, Routledge, New York 2010.

Halperin, Morton H., Hoffman, Daniel. *Freedom v. National Security. Secrecy and Surveillance*, Chelsea House Publishers, New York 1977.

Madison, James. Hamilton, Alexander. Jay, John (eds.), *The Federalist Papers*, US Imports, New York 1999.

Hansen, Victor M., Friedman, Lawrence. *The Case for Congress. Separation of Powers and the War on Terror*, Routledge, New York 2016.

Hansford, Thomas G., Spriggs, James F. *The Politics of Precedent on the U.S. Supreme Court*, Princeton University Press, Princeton 2008.

Hayden, Michael V. *The Assault on Intelligence. American National Security in an Age of Lies*, Penguin Press, New York 2018.

Hayes, Abigail. Lynn, Tamara. "Due Process vs Crime Control Models of Justice", *SACAD Entrants* 31, 2020, available at: https://scholars.fhsu.edu/cgi/viewcontent.cgi?article=1098&context=sacad.

Herman, Susan N. *Taking Liberties. The War on Terror and the Erosion of American Democracy*, Oxford University Press, New York 2011.

Hirschl, Ron. *Towards Juristocracy: The Origins and Consequences of the New Constitutionalism*, Harvard University Press, Cambridge 2004.

Hubbart, Phillip A. *Making Sense of Search and Seizure Law: A Fourth Amendment Handbook*, Carolina Academic Press, Durham 2015.

Johnson, Loch K. *Spy Watching: Intelligence Accountability in the United States*, Oxford University Press, New York 2018.

Kaplan, Edward S. *The Bank of the United States and the American Economy*, Greenwood Press, Westport 1999.

Keller, William W. *Democracy Betrayed. The Rise of the Surveillance Security State*, Counterpoint, Berkeley 2017.

Kent Newmyer, R. "John Marshall, *McCulloch v. Maryland*, and the Southern States' Rights Tradition", *John Marshall Law Review* 33, 2000.

Kitrosser, Heidi. *Reclaiming Accountability. Transparency, Executive Power, and the U.S. Constitution*, University of Chicago Press, Chicago 2015.

Kuntze, Jan-Hendrik, *The Abolishment of the Right to Privacy? The USA, Mass Surveillance and the Spiral Model*, Tectum Verlag, Baden-Baden 2018.

Laidler, Paweł. *Sąd Najwyższy Stanów Zjednoczonych Ameryki: od prawa do polityki*, Wydawnictwo Uniwersytetu Jagiellońskiego, Kraków 2011.

Laidler, Paweł. *The Supreme Court of the United States: Legitimate Law maker and Constitutional Interpreter* in: *Constitutional Law and Precedent: International Perspectives on Case-Based Reasoning*, Monika Florczak-Wątor (ed.), Routledge, London 2022, pp. 9–31.

Laidler, Paweł. *Secrecy Versus Transparency in the U.S. National Security Surveillance State* in: *Trust and Transparency in an Age of Surveillance*, Lora Anne Viola, Paweł Laidler (eds.), Routledge, London 2022.

Laidler, Paweł. "To Divide and Rule: Political Impact of President Trump's U.S.-Mexico Border Wall Initiative", *Politeja* 6(81), 2022, pp. 253–278.

Laidler, Paweł. Stolicki, Dariusz. Jakubiak, Łukasz. Sokołowski, Jacek (eds.), *Constitutionalization of Politics in Comparative Perspective*, Routledge, London 2025.

Lester, Genvieve. *When Should State Secrets Stay Secret? Accountability, Democratic Governance, and Intelligence*, Cambridge University Press, New York 2015.

Lord, Kristin M., *The Perils and Promise of Global Transparency. Why the Information Revolution may not lead to Security, Democracy, or Peace*, New York: State University of New York Press, 2006.

Lyon, David. *Surveillance, Power, and Everyday Life* in: *Emerging Digital Spaces in Contemporary Society: Properties of Technology*, Phillip Kalantzis-Cope, Karim Gherab-Martin, (eds.), Palgrave Macmillan, London 2010.

Lyon, David. "Surveillance, Snowden, and Big Data: Capacities, Consequences, Critique", *Big Data & Society,* 1(2), 2014.

Lyon, David. *Culture of Surveillance: Watching as a Way of Life*, Polity, Oxford 2018.

Lund, Nelson. *The Destructive Legacy of McCulloch v. Maryland* in: *McCulloch v. Maryland at 200: Debating John Marshall's*

Jurisprudence, Gary Schmitt, Rebecca Burgess (eds.), American Enterprise Institute Press, Washington D.C. 2020.

Manheimer, Michael J.Z. *The Fourth Amendment: Original Understandings and Modern Policing*, University of Michigan Press, Ann Arbor 2023.

Markham, Jerry W. *From Christopher Columbus to the Robber Barons: A Financial History of the United States 1492–1900*, Routledge, New York 2002.

Marklund, Andreas, Skouvig, Laura (eds), *Histories of Surveillance from Antiquity to the Digital Era: The Eyes and Ears of Power*, Routledge, New York 2021.

Marx, Gary T. "What's New About the New Surveillance? Classifying for Change and Continuity", *Surveillance & Society*, 1(1), 2002.

McCabe, Andrew G. *The Threat: How the FBI Protects America in the Age of Terror and Trump*, St. Martin's Press, New York 2019.

Monk, Linda R. *The Words We Live By: The Annotated Guide to the Constitution*, Hyperion, New York 2003.

Moynihan, Daniel Patrick. *Secrecy: The American Experience*, Yale University Press, New Haven 1998.

Neal, Andrew W. *Security as Politics: Beyond the State of Exception*, Edinburgh University Press, Edinburgh 2020.

Nelson, Michael. *Trump: The First Two Years*, University of Virginia Press, Charlottesville 2018.

Northouse, Clayton (ed.), *Protecting What Matters: Technology, Security, and Liberty Since 9/11*, Brookings Institution Press, Washington D.C. 2006.

Olmsted, Kathryn. *Terror Tuesdays: How Obama Refined Bush's Counterterrorism Policies* in: *The Presidency of Barack Obama. A First Historical Assessment*, Julian E. Zelizer (ed.), Princeton University Press, Princeton 2018, pp. 212–226.

Order of the Centers for Disease Control and Prevention, Department of Health and Human Services, available at: https://www.cdc.gov/port-health/media/pdfs/CDC-Global-Contact-Tracing-Order-10-25-2021-p.pdf.

Pacelle, Richard. *The Role of the Supreme Court in American Politics: The Least Dangerous Branch?* Taylor and Francis, New York 2019.

Pacelle, Richard. *The Transformation of the Supreme Court's Agenda: From the New Deal to the Reagan Administration*, Routledge, New York 2019

Pallitto, Robert M., Weaver, William G. *Presidential Secrecy and the Law*, Johns Hopkins University Press, Baltimore 2007.

Parenti, Christian. *The Soft Cage: Surveillance in America. From Slavery to the War on Terror*, Basic Books, New York 2003.

Pew Research Center, *Terrorism: Public Opinion Polls 2018–2022*, available at https://www.pewresearch.org/topic/politics-policy/political-issues/defense-national-security/terrorism/.

Posner, Eric E., Vermeule, Adrian. *Terror in the Balance: Security, Liberty, and the Courts*, Oxford University Press, New York 2006.

Post, Robert C. *The Taft Court: Making Law for a Divided Nation, 1921–1930*, Cambridge University Press, New York 2023.

Prados, John. *The Family Jewels. The CIA, Secrecy, and Presidential Power*, University of Texas Press, Austin 2014.

Price, David S. *The American Surveillance State: How the U.S. Spies on Dissent*, Pluto Press, London 2022.

Raskin, Marcus G., LeVan, A. Carl. *The National Security State and the Tragedy of Empire* in: *In Democracy's Shadow. The Secret World of National Security*, Marcus G. Raskin, A. Carl LeVan (eds.), Nation Books, New York 2005.

Richman, Alvin. "Poll Trends: Changing American Attitudes Toward the Soviet Union", *The Public Opinion Quarterly* 55(1), 1991.

Risse, Matthias. *Political Theory of the Digital Age*, Cambridge University Press, New York 2023.

Romero, Anthony D., Temple-Raston, Dina. *In Defense of Our America: The Fight for Civil Liberties in the Age of Terror*, William Morrow, New York 2007.

Rourke, Francis E., *Secrecy and Publicity*, Johns Hopkins University Press, Baltimore 1961

Schulhofer, Stephen J. *The Enemy Within. Intelligence Gathering, Law Enforcement, and Civil Liberties in the Wake of September 11*, Century Foundation Press, New York 2002.

Schwartz, David S. *The Spirit of the Constitution: John Marshall and the 200-Year Odyssey of McCulloch v. Maryland*, Oxford University Press, New York 2019.

Schwartz, jr., Frederick A.O. *Democracy in the Dark: The Seduction of Government Secrecy*, The New Press, New York 2015.

Schwartz, Herman. *Packing the Courts: The Conservative Campaign to Rewrite the Constitution*, Charles Scribner's Sons, New York 1998.

Segal, Jeffrey A., Spaeth, Harold J., Benesh, Sara C. *The Supreme Court in American Legal System*, Cambridge University Press, New York 2005.

Shane, Peter M. *Madison's Nightmare. How Executive Power Threatens American Democracy*, Chicago University Press, Chicago 2009.

Shane, Peter M. *Democracy's Chief Executive. Interpreting the Constitution and Defining the Future of Presidency*. University of California Press, Durham 2022.

Shapiro, Martin M., Sweet, Alec Stone. *On Law, Politics, and Judicialization*, Oxford University Press, New York 2002.

Shevory, Thomas C. (ed.), *John Marshall's Law: Interpretation, Ideology, and Interest*, Greenwood Press, Westport 1994.

Shipan, Charles R., Shannon, Megan. "Delaying Justice(s): A Duration Analysis of Supreme Court Confirmations", *American Journal of Political Science* 47(4), 2003, pp. 654–668.

Slobogin, Christopher. *Privacy at Risk: The New Government Surveillance and the Fourth Amendment*, University of Chicago Press, Chicago 2008.

Slobogin, Christopher. *Is the Fourth Amendment Relevant in a Technological Age?* in *Constitution 3.0*, Jeffrey Rosen, Benjamin Wittes (eds.), Brookings Institution, Washington DC 2011.

Smith, jr., Charles W. *Roger B. Taney: Jacksonian Jurist*, University of North Carolina Press, Durham 2018.

Solove, Daniel J., *Nothing to Hide. The False Tradeoff between Privacy and Security*, Yale University Press, New Haven 2011.

State Laws Held Unconstitutional, available at: https://law.justia.com/constitution/us/state-laws-held-unconstitutional.html.

Stern, Nat. "Separation of Powers, Executive Authority, and Suspension of Disbelief", *Houston Law Review* 54, 2016.

Stone Sweet, Alec. "Judicialization and the Construction of Governance", *Comparative Political Studies* 32(2), 1999, pp. 147–184.

Stuntz, William J. "Secret Service: Against Privacy and Transparency", *New Republic*, Apr 7, 2006, pp. 12–15.

Taylor, Michael J.C. *The Constitution and the American Presidency*. Peter Lang, New York 2021.

Theoharis, Athan G. *Spying on Americans: Political Surveillance from Hoover to Huston Plan*, Temple University Press, Philadelphia 1978.

Theoharis, Athan G. *Abuse of Power: How Cold War Surveillance and Secrecy Policy Shaped the Response to 9/11*. Temple University Press, Philadelphia 2011.

Tomlins, Christopher (ed.), *The United States Supreme Court: The Pursuit of Justice*, Houghton Mifflin Company, Boston 2005.

Tushnet, Mark. "The Dillemas of Liberal Constitutionalism", *Ohio State Law Review* 42, 1981, pp. 411–426.

Tushnet, Mark (ed.), *I Dissent: Great Opposing Opinions in Landmark Supreme Court Cases*, Beacon Press, New York 2008.

Tushnet, Mark. *In the Balance: Law and Politics in the Roberts Court*, W.W. Norton and Company, New York 2013.

Viola, Lora Anne. Laidler, Paweł (eds.), *Trust and Transparency in an Age of Surveillance*, Routledge, London 2022.

Wells, Christina. "State Secrets and Executive Accountability", *Constitutional Commentary* 26, 2010.

Whittington, Keith E. *Political Foundations of Judicial Supremacy: The Presidency, the Supreme Court, and Constitutional Leadership in History*, Princeton University Press, Princeton 2007.

Yoo, John C. "The First Claim: The Burr Trial, United States v. Nixon, and Presidential Power", *Minnesota Law Review* 83, 1999, pp. 1435–1474.

Zuboff, Shoshana. *The Age of Surveillance Capitalism: The Fight for a Human Future at the New Frontier of Power*, Public Affairs, New York 2019.

Index

INTERNATIONAL RELATIONS IN ASIA, AFRICA AND THE AMERICAS

Edited by Andrzej Mania & Marcin Grabowski

Vol. 1 Olga Barbasiewicz (ed.): Postwar Reconciliation in Central Europe and East Asia. 2018.

Vol. 2 Adam Nobis: A Short Guide to the New Silk Road. 2018.

Vol. 3 Radka Havlová (ed.): Untangling the Mayhem: Crises and Prospects of the Middle East. 2018.

Vol. 4 Marcin Grabowski / Paweł Laidler (eds.): Global Development Policy in the 21st Century. New Challenges. 2018.

Vol. 5 Andrzej Mania / Marcin Grabowski / Tomasz Pugacewicz (eds.): Global Politics in the 21st Century. Between Regional Cooperation and Conflict. 2019.

Vol. 6 Marcin Grabowski / Tomasz Pugacewicz (eds.): Application of International Relations Theories in Asia and Africa. 2019.

Vol. 7 Адам Нобис. Краткий путеводитель по Новому Шелковому Пути. 2019.

Vol. 8 Olga Barbasiewicz / Marcin Grabowski / Ewa Trojnar (eds.): Security Dilemmas and Challenges in 21st Century Asia. 2020.

Vol. 9 Marcin Gabryś / Magdalena Marczuk-Karbownik / Magdalena Paluszkiewicz-Misiaczek (eds.): Canadian Political, Social and Historical (Re)visions in the 20th and 21st Centuries. 2020.

Vol. 10 Agata Wiktoria Ziętek / Grzegorz Gil (eds.): ASEAN in a Changing World. 2021.

Vol. 11 Maciej Kurcz: Urban Now. A Human in the Face of Borderliness and Urbanisation in Juba, South Sudan. 2021.

Vol. 12 Olga Barbasiewicz / Maciej Pletnia (eds.): Internal and External Aspects of Japanese Security. 2021.

Vol. 13 Olga Barbasiewicz / Michał Lipa / Karolina Rak (eds.): Historical and Collective Memory in the Middle and Far East. 2021.

Vol. 14 Tomasz Pugacewicz / Marcin Grabowski (eds.): Great and Small Games in Central Asia and the South Caucasus. 2022.

Vol. 15 Anna Pruska: Swiss Banking Secrecy and the US-Swiss Conflict Over Holocaust Claims. 2022.

Vol. 16 Łukasz Gacek / Rafał Kwieciński / Ewa Trojnar: Taiwan under Tsai Ing-wen. Democracy Diplomacy. 2023.

Vol. 17 Magdalena Musiał-Karg / Natasza Lubik-Reczek (eds.): The War in Ukraine. (Dis)information – Perception – Attitudes. 2023.

Vol. 18 Bogdan Góralczyk: China in the Xi Jiping's Era. 2024.

Vol. 19 Paulina Napierała (ed.): Religion and American Politics. Domestic and International Contexts. 2024.

Vol. 20 Kłosowicz Robert / Mormul Joanna : The Problem of *De Facto States* in International Relations in Africa. 2024.

Vol. 21 Paweł Laidler: The U.S. Supreme Court and the Legitimization of Surveillance. 2024.

www.peterlang.com

www.ingramcontent.com/pod-product-compliance
Ingram Content Group UK Ltd.
Pitfield, Milton Keynes, MK11 3LW, UK
UKHW041825031026
15587UKWH00002B/578

9 783631 863916